THE UPLIFT GENERATION

THE AMERICAN SOUTH SERIES

Elizabeth R. Varon and Orville Vernon Burton

EDITORS

THE UPLIFT GENERATION

Cooperation across the Color Line in Early Twentieth-Century Virginia

Clayton McClure Brooks

UNIVERSITY OF VIRGINIA PRESS

CHARLOTTESVILLE & LONDON

University of Virginia Press
© 2017 by the Rector and Visitors of the University of Virginia
Printed in the United States of America on acid-free paper

First published 2017
1 3 5 7 9 8 6 4 2

Library of Congress Cataloging-in-Publication Data

Names: Brooks, Clayton McClure, author.
Title: The uplift generation : cooperation across the color line in early twentieth-century Virginia / Clayton McClure Brooks.
Other titles: American South series.
Description: Charlottesville ; London : University of Virginia Press, 2017 |
Series: American South series | Includes bibliographical references and index.
Identifiers: LCCN 2016032563 | ISBN 9780813939490 (cloth : alk. paper) |
ISBN 9780813939506 (e-book)
Subjects: LCSH: Virginia—Race relations—History—20th century. | Virginia—
History—20th century. | Virginia—Social conditions—20th century.
Classification: LCC F231 .B85 2017 | DDC 975.5/043—dc23
LC record available at https://lccn.loc.gov/2016032563

Cover art: Children playing in a sandbox at Janie Barrett's Locust Street
Settlement in Hampton, Virginia, in 1903. (Courtesy of Harvard
Art Museums/Fogg Museum, Transfer from the Carpenter Center
for the Visual Arts, Social Museum Collection, 3.2002.232.3)

For Thomas, William, Nora, and Olivia.

You are my world—an often loud, messy, and crazy world, but *my* world.

CONTENTS

ILLUSTRATIONS

ACKNOWLEDGMENTS

THIS PROJECT HAS been one that has grown, changed, and expanded over many years, dating back to my graduate school days at the University of Virginia. The road to finishing and publication has been slow, through research, teaching, pursuing alternative research projects, and family, especially raising three fantastic and rambunctious children. However, I do not think the end product could have been possible without these diversions, as all helped to inspire new insights.

I have so many people to thank for their help over the years. My undergraduate years at Roanoke College and the wonderful faculty there helped instill in me a love of history. In graduate school, I was encouraged by a number of wonderful professors, especially Ed Ayers, Cindy Aron, and Grace Hale. Grace Hale, in particular, was a wonderfully dedicated adviser who helped push me in my research and learning, and whose example continues to shape how I work with my own students today.

During my postdoctoral fellowship at the Woodrow Wilson Presidential Library, I had the opportunity to revisit some my old research, in addition to a book I was working on for the National Governors Association. It was then that my ideas for the current volume took shape. I want to thank Ethan Sribnick for his advice in rethinking my project.

Since the fall of 2012, I have been teaching at Mary Baldwin University, and I am grateful to both my colleagues and students there for their support. I love teaching because it encourages a constant process of learning, and every day I learn from my students. Although research is the key to any new project, I found that through teaching I gained the perspective to rethink my earlier conclusions.

Throughout the research phase of my project, I relied on a number of libraries and archives whose staffs were all welcoming and supportive. I particularly want to thank those at the Library of Virginia, the Albert and Shirley Small Special Collections Library at the University of Virginia, the Virginia Historical Society, and the Perkins Library at Duke University. For their assistance in preparing illustrations for my manuscript, I am also very appreciative of the Hampton Museum, the Maggie Lena Walker Historical Site, the Special Collections Library at Virginia Tech, and Harvard University.

One of my earliest ventures in this line of research came through an article

I wrote for *Women Shaping the South: Creating and Confronting Change*, published by the University of Missouri Press in 2006. My thanks to the editors of that book, Judith McArthur and Angela Boswell, for their help in pushing me to refine my argument and writing. I also thank Graham Dozier for his help with an article about Mary Johnston I published in the *Virginia Magazine of History and Biography* in December 2014.

This book would not have been possible without the support that I received from the University of Virginia Press. In particular, Richard Holway has been supportive of my research for a number of years and has been of tremendous help in refining and shaping my project. I am also grateful to Anna Kariel and Morgan Myers for their invaluable help in seeing this book to publication.

I want to thank my sisters, my friends, and all my family for their support. My mother, Lois McClure, has always been my biggest supporter and willing to read any draft I send her way. Although I lost my father far too early to lung cancer, his memory continues to influence me every day, especially in his exuberance for life and drive to work hard for what you love. This project could not have been possible without the support of my husband, Thomas Brooks, who has encouraged me through thick and thin. And, finally, I want to thank my three spirited children, William, Nora, and Olivia, who tried to be patient during the many hours I spent writing and who, always, kept me entertained.

THE UPLIFT GENERATION

INTRODUCTION

The Uplift Generation

Efforts to better race relations make more palatable the various species of injustice dealt out to the Negro in America, and particularly in the South, by the dominant white race.
—John Mitchell Jr., 1932

WHEN THE ARTIST and lifelong activist Adele Clark sat down for an interview in 1964 at the age of eighty-two, she reminisced about the high and low points of her activism, especially for woman's suffrage. Clark was born in Montgomery, Alabama, on September 27, 1882, and moved around the South in her childhood, yet she spent most of her life in Richmond, Virginia. Although not from the wealthiest or most well-connected family, Clark enjoyed the advantages of an upper-class white Virginian. Her true love was art, and she devoted her life to not only her own art but promoting the arts in Richmond.[1] Reflecting back on her life, Clark viewed her suffrage activism with the hindsight afforded by many years. Perhaps as a result of the civil rights movement unfolding around her, she expressed regret that she and her white peers had not worked to more fully include black women in their suffrage crusade. Yet, her memories also revealed true moments of interracial activism now nearly forgotten by history.

After the Nineteenth Amendment was finally ratified in the summer of 1920, a number of white Virginians feared that a potential surge of black female voters would rock the balance of white supremacy in the state. Registrars attempted all sorts of creative roundabout tactics to keep black women from registering, and some white newspapers resorted to fear-mongering editorials. Rather than ignore or feed into these tactics, a number of white members of the Equal Suffrage League worked together to protest these actions and demand fairer registering procedures.[2]

Adele Clark, however, and her longtime friend and companion, Nora Houston, decided further action was needed to ensure the polls would not erupt into violence on Election Day. Thus, these women arranged a meeting one evening

a few days before the election at their art studio with several black female leaders in Richmond—Ora Stokes and Lillian Payne, among unnamed others. The
interracial group agreed that the best course of action would be for groups of
white women to visit all the African American polling places in the city on Election Day, hoping their presence would discourage any violence. And, so they did.
Clark, Houston, and other white suffragists borrowed and rented several cars and
organized a patrolling of the polls. Looking back from 1964, Clark recalled with
satisfaction that "everything went quite quietly, in spite of the fact that there had
been threats of bloodshed and riot and everything else, there wasn't any rioting.
The Negro women went up quietly and voted, but I think they were very much
heartened by the fact that there were four or five white women that went to the
polls to give them their backing."[3]

Although this story seems somewhat unusual and out of place in the history of
the segregated South, it was, in fact, entirely in line with a long tradition of interracial activism in Virginia that was well in place before the fall of 1920. It is also
tempting to see this event as a sign of liberalism and an early push toward civil
rights, yet it was not. Interracial activism in early twentieth-century Virginia was
common—a product of lingering paternalism rather than any latent visions of
racial equality. Instead of threatening segregation, these cross-racial efforts helped
build and reinforce the segregation of Virginia. This book focuses on that moment
in time, approximately 1900 to 1930, when paternalistic interracialism prevailed
in Virginia. This interracial activism arose in response to several major trends:
the increasing segregation of the state in the early 1900s, the growing strength of a
Progressivism movement aimed to encourage greater governmental participation
in welfare concerns, and a fervent focus on uplift and paternalism among some
Virginians. This form of interracialism began to fade out of style and influence by
the late 1920s, pushed out both by the decline in paternalism and ironically by a
loss of influence with the Progressives' success in pushing for greater governmental
control of welfare programs. It faded as well because its leaders aged and retired,
leaving the reins of their activism to be picked up by a new generation. Gradually,
this former version of interracial cooperation would be supplanted by a new more
latently liberal activism on both sides of the color line.

Yet, the generation that dominated interracial social activism in Virginia from
1900 to 1930 deserves to be remembered in their own right, not simply as a precursor of greater racial reformers to come. Both the black and white reformers in this
study were quite comfortable working together in cross-racial activism, seeing it as
in keeping with so-called Virginia tradition rather challenging any racial decorum.
Their efforts toward better "race relations" were not considered taboo in the least.
Other historians have focused on cross-racial activism before the civil rights move-

ment as well. One of the best examples of these studies was John Egerton's *Speak Now against the Day*, which uncovered signs of latent liberalism among white southerners from the 1920s to 1950s. Glenda Gilmore as well traced early civil rights activism in the South beginning in 1919 with her *Defying Dixie: The Radical Roots of Civil Rights*. Historians have also analyzed the Commission on Interracial Cooperation (CIC), founded in 1919, including Mark Ellis in his work on Jack Woofter in Georgia, and Wilma Dykeman and James Stokely's biography of the CIC organizer Will Alexander.[4] In addition, historians have considered the role of some southern whites in leading antilynching crusades. For example, Jacquelyn Dowd Hall's biography of Jessie Daniel Ames detailed Ames's groundbreaking work in founding the Association of Southern Women for the Prevention of Lynching in 1930.[5] Nor was the interracial activism unique to Virginia. In *Gender and Jim Crow*, Glenda Gilmore uncovered the story of similar activism between white and black women in North Carolina. She found black women, in particular, at the forefront of black political activism. Despite dedicated efforts of the women, they could not stop the worsening tide of racism. *The Uplift Generation* continues in this area of study, primarily considering the tradition of cross-racial activism already in place to be built upon when the CIC grew in the 1920s. It illustrates how this earlier group was a unique generation in itself, not simply a precursor of things to come.

In Virginia, interracial cooperation before the late 1920s was a means to create and mold rather than to oppose Jim Crow. However, historians have tended to focus on interracial cooperation as an intended or unintended threat to segregated racial order. Gilmore in her study argued that white women joined the interracial reform efforts "out of a desire for self-preservation," hoping to achieve through cooperation what they could not gain through political venues.[6] She demonstrated how these women strove to refine segregation rather than promote integration. Yet, Gilmore concluded, "however sporadic and confusing women's interracial contacts were, they represented a crack in the mortar of the foundation of white supremacy."[7] Janette Greenwood, as well, argued that interracial cooperation in Charlotte in the 1880s represented a moment where "race relations" could have been different and perhaps could have avoided the onslaught of disfranchisement and segregation. Dykeman and Stokely also emphasized the potentially subversive nature of interracial cooperation in their biography of Alexander, by highlighting his latent liberalism and questioning of southern society rather than his continuing support of segregation.[8] In her groundbreaking history of the "southern lady," Anne Firor Scott described white women's forays into cross-racial reforms as evidence of some women's questioning of the legitimacy of Jim Crow. Moreover, Hall interpreted the white women's antilynching crusade, headed by the southerner Ames, as a revolt against the white South's social order.[9] These historians have generally agreed that cross-racial cooperative work in the early twentieth century was a challenge, usually either covert or unintentional, to the culture of segregation. This study questions that assumption.

Activism on the African American side of the color line can perhaps be easily explained. These individuals made every possible effort to preserve their rights and opportunities in an atmosphere of increasing racism and the strictures of segregation. At times, this led some of the African American activists to embrace the philosophy of Booker T. Washington, seeing accommodation as the best avenue to try to convince whites that if segregation was inevitable, then at least separate should be indeed equal. African American uplift, especially in the early twentieth century, has been well covered by historians, particularly Darlene Clark Hine, Stephanie Shaw, Kevin Gaines, Deborah Gray White, and Evelyn Brooks Higginbotham.[10] Both Gaines and White, in particular, have demonstrated how uplift efforts in black communities in the early twentieth century embraced middle-class values, at times creating a disconnect between the self-proclaimed "better classes" and the African American community at large. White takes this further, analyzing how uplift concerns were often led by black women who appointed themselves as the moral leaders of the race who needed to direct both the "lower classes" and black men as well. Often these self-improvement or uplift efforts have been placed against the dichotomy of Washington versus W. E. B. Du Bois. Jacqueline M. Moore illustrated this perspective in her book *Booker T. Washington, W. E. B. Du Bois, and the Struggle for Racial Uplift.*

The Uplift Generation builds upon these works, particularly in trying to understand the motivations of the many activists who negotiated their way between the supposed extreme positions of Washington and Du Bois. Everyday negotiations were guided by a mixture of both practicality and racial pride. In correlation with the arguments of these historians, the African Americans reformers of this study tried to assert class connections with their white counterparts, but, over time, the strengthening of segregation weakened any attempted class bonds in favor of racial ones. Within this interracial activism, however, African Americans exhibited agency by initiating various efforts toward uplift within the black neighborhoods. Whites followed guidelines set by black activists as long as they conformed to the general strictures of segregation. Ultimately, black and white reformers alike played central roles in directing interracial cooperation work, which, in turn, helped determine the scope of segregation in Virginia.

It is more difficult for historians to pinpoint motivations on the white side of the color line. Some individuals acted out of a humanitarian impulse often spurred by the Social Gospel, but the work also fulfilled multiple purposes — humanitarian, moral, paternalist, as well as a Progressive fervor for "bettering" society that often, in practice, really meant social control. In *Gender and Jim Crow,* Glenda Gilmore observed that although some white suffragists "worked for black disfranchisement; others began to foster interracial cooperation in the years before woman suffrage." Yet, Gilmore found that "occasionally, the same woman did both. White women were overwhelmingly complicitous in shoring up white supremacy in 1898, yet they were at the vanguard of the movement for interracial cooperation by 1920."[11] Gilmore was speaking of North Carolina, yet this same pattern can be seen in Virginia. Some of the female and male leaders who were the most vocal supporters of the Lost Cause and the white racial order were the very same individuals involved in this early interracial activism. This study investigates not only what this activism was but how it had such seemingly contradictory aims. The answer lies in the fact that paternalism made these positions seem naturally compatible.

Paternalism, in this study, refers to the prevailing sense of racial noblesse oblige that was claimed during the antebellum era but also resurged in late nineteenth- and early twentieth-century Virginia with the Lost Cause. The Lost Cause not only worked to memorialize the Confederate efforts during the Civil War but did so, in part, by rewriting slavery as a benevolent institution. Thus, in the late nineteenth century, the Lost Cause redefined paternalism to apply to the modern era, arguing that whites still had a responsibility for aiding African Americans. The white paternalists in this study were concerned with overseeing and aiding the progress of African Americans, particularly under the new modern form of Jim Crow. Whites' obsession with the Lost Cause fed this lingering commitment to paternalism. In his study of race, Joel Williamson documented a revolt in the early 1880s of liberals who feared blacks were "losing sight of the ideals whites cherished" and, in turn, initiated a resurgence of antebellum ideals of paternalism. In most southern states, paternalism then faltered in the 1890s with the onslaught of economic depression and increase in racial strife and lynchings. White Virginians responded as did other white southerners in the 1890s to heightened tensions and began to segregate and disfranchise the black citizenry, but the rise in outright violence was minimal in Virginia in part because of a more diversified economy and lesser need to force blacks into situations like sharecropping as was more common farther south. Thus, paternalism survived in the Old Dominion well into the twentieth century because it continued to prove an effective means to impose racial order.

In J. Douglas Smith's *Managing White Supremacy,* he traced how white Virginians used paternalism to build segregation and enforce the color line in the first half of the century. He found, as does this study, that paternalism began to seriously wane in the state beginning in the 1920s. While Smith focused primarily on politicians and efforts within the political system, *The Uplift Generation* looks instead at paternalistic cross-racial activism, particularly in terms of social welfare, that happened outside of government. The activists of this study were governmental outsiders, although ones with social influence. By the late 1920s, these outside government social welfare reform efforts increasingly converged with the state government's assumption of some public welfare concerns. In both cases, paternalism functioned, in large part, to justify inequity and gloss over any personal disquiet or guilt. Yet, more important than this imprecise notion of making whites feel better, paternalism served a practical purpose of social control. While whites across the South (and at times in Virginia as well) resorted to violence and vigilante lynchings to enforce racial order, some twentieth-century white Virginians believed paternalism to be a much more effective alternative. These whites argued that the preservation of white supremacy depended on a recommitment to the ideals of paternalism updated for a new century. Paternalism in twentieth-century Virginia entailed an organized effort by some whites to redefine private benevolence into public Progressive reforms that both aided African American uplift and ensured compliance with the culture of segregation.[12]

Paternalism and Progressivism became interconnected in Virginia. Disagreements continue among historians over the definition of "Progressivism" as well as the difference between progressivism and Progressivism. This study uses the term "Progressivism" broadly to refer to the general national fervor for political, municipal, and social reform. This definition includes a wide range of activities from clean milk campaigns, child labor initiatives, and election procedure reform to woman suffrage. The commonality of all these concerns was a demand for greater governmental participation, and the interracial activists central to this study supported that demand. Obviously, differences existed among states as well as local arenas as far as positions on certain issues and reforms prioritized. The problem or paradox, to use the term of the historian William Link, of southern progressivism is that these divisions of both locality as well as concerns with maintaining the racial order diluted the effectiveness of the Progressive movement in the South.[13] While this may be true in looking at the region as a whole, the activists of this study were largely successful in their efforts to encourage greater government funding of their uplift causes as well as pushing for the inclusion (albeit on a segregated basis) of African Americans in new governmental programs. However, the governmentalizing of many of these reform efforts in the Progressive Era would eventually push many of these paternalist and uplift reformers out of the process. In cases like Janie Porter Barrett's Virginia Industrial School for Colored Girls and others causes, these activists found that over time they lost personal control and were pushed out of decision-making positions. As reformist Progressives working as outsiders of the governmental system, success ironically meant a decline in their own influence.

This is a study not just of activism but of individuals. Although this work began as research into the interactions of black and white women, this focus soon changed as the scope widened and many men across the color line became active players in the story. The piecemeal nature of this early interracial work does not lend itself to neat lists as to who was involved and who was not. Instead, this work loosely encompassed a number of organizations each working on different causes. Thus, there is no single membership list to define who was an interracial activist. Yet, this study does see a community of activists emerge who appear again and again: Mary Munford, Ora Stokes, Annie Schmelz, Joseph Mastin, Maggie Lena Walker, Martha McNeill, John Mitchell Jr., T. C. Walker, and Janie Porter Barrett.[14] At different points, we meet these individuals, and others, as they worked over decades in these interracial conversations. Each has their own unique and distinct story to tell.

Janie Porter Barrett, for example, was perhaps the most skilled of all these at interracial activism and used this skill to advocate for the social reforms she believed to be most needed — particularly helping troubled young African American girls. Barrett was born in Athens, Georgia, in August 1865, only months after the end of the Civil War. Although the daughter of former slaves, she had unusual advantages as a child. She grew up in the home of a white family, the Skinners, who employed Janie's mother as a housekeeper and a seamstress. Atypically, the Skinner family raised her with their own children, educating her in mathematics and literature as well as other classical subjects. When Barrett's mother remarried and moved away, Janie continued to live with the Skinners. The break, however, came when it was time for Janie to go away to school. Since she was light-skinned, Mrs. Skinner attempted to convince Janie's mother to allow the Skinners to send Janie away up North where she could pass as white. At this, Janie's mother refused and instead sent Janie to Hampton Institute in Virginia to be trained as a teacher. This background made Janie Porter Barrett uniquely able to communicate and influence whites, helping to aid her own reformist zeal. The result of her interracial project, the Virginia Industrial School for Colored Girls, brought national praise and attention to the cross-racial activism happening in the state, and particularly the work spearheaded by women.[15]

Although one of the most influential, Barrett is just one of the many activists whose stories are woven throughout this book. Defining and characterizing this diverse group is not an easy task. Generally, the whites were upper-class and well connected in family relations to the Virginia aristocracy — the First Families of Virginia. Their actual wealth varied, but in terms of family connections they typically moved in upper-class circles. And, in early twentieth-century Virginia, family ties were often the most important determining factor in social status. Thus, these paternalists were at least listened to because of their social clout. The black leaders are also challenging to define. Not surprisingly, few, if any, had the financial resources of their white counterparts, and their family names were not social currency in Virginia society. However, they were prominent members of the African American community and labeled themselves as among the "better classes." These individuals were typically professionals—lawyers, editors, ministers (or spouses of ministers), or entrepreneurs of some type. The most nationally well-known among the African Americans was certainly Maggie Lena Walker, famous for being the first African American female bank founder and president in the United States. Among whites, Mary Munford was prominent among national Progressive circles, and Mary Johnston was a household name as well, although more for her historical fiction than her activism. At points, this study uses the term "elites" in discussing both black and whites. This should be interpreted not in terms of financial assets but of social standing. Although the African Americans in this study were better off materially than most of their African American neighbors, their wealth was not comparable to the typical white reformer presented in this study. Yet, the term "elite" is used in referring to these African American leaders because that is how they perceived themselves. They felt they had many commonalities with their white reformer counterparts despite the differences in their actual wealth and skin color. As a result of the social composition of these leaders, this study is one primarily of the upper and middle classes who controlled these reforms rather than the working classes and poor whom they hoped to aid.

To understand these individuals, we must first consider the world in which they lived. Segregation never created mutually exclusive black and white worlds. Even during the height of Jim Crow, there always existed overlap, interference, economic commonalities, and strategic exceptions. White segregationists claimed to desire separation, but from the beginning this was always a story of social control. Whites hoped to create safe spaces to contain, carefully encourage, and restrict blacks while never forgetting the foremost goal of securing white supremacy. At heart, segregation was built on fear and an obsession with bringing order to a rapidly changing world. As such, Jim Crow harbored a number of contradictions. Foremost was the fact that separation was never whites' true goal.

Segregation was not conceived as a polished plan but a piecemeal project that evolved over the years. It was not a reimagination of the antebellum slave culture but was proffered as a modern solution to the changing demands of the twentieth century. In Virginia, this was a decades-long process. The first segregation law pertaining to public transportation was passed in 1900, but the most stringent and defining Jim Crow law addressing public assemblages was not passed until the mid-1920s. No Virginians, black or white, could foresee the future. As the new century dawned, few predicted the eventual damaging course of this form of racial discrimination. Many African Americans believed it was not a matter of immediate concern, and many whites saw the so-called reforms as unnecessary and even a betrayal of their claimed paternalistic tradition.

The Uplift Generation considers how a group of Virginia elites, black and white, dealt with the contradictions of segregation. It follows the interaction between these reformers throughout the early twentieth century from 1900 to 1930, adjusting to the evolving concerns facing Virginians and the tide of segregation. In a society that rhetorically promoted separation but economically and even socially depended on the ties between the races, interracial cooperation and communication became necessary to maintaining lines of understanding and promoting public peace. Through these efforts, whites could claim support for separate black communities but also direct and oversee what they determined to be proper reforms and proper avenues of racial uplift. This work not only fit perfectly into their paternalistic outlook but also gave these white elites influence within the white power structure as the go-to spokesmen for black Virginians. African Americans fully understood the patronizing mind-sets of the whites with whom they worked, but they played into these whites' sense of goodwill out of practicality, trying to make the best situation out of increasingly limited options. This was a racial dialogue in the midst of which many had grown up, and they were well versed in its rules. Over the years, these activists developed a rapport and familiarity. Their relationships typically did not challenge racial decorum but did result in considerable openness. These interracial efforts were most important not in their results (although the low level of vigilante violence in Virginia was a significant achievement) but in their frank discussions of race. These discussions shaped the course of segregation, positively and negatively; at times they were a product of and at other times a reaction to this work.

These early efforts differed radically from later incarnations of "interracial cooperation." The whites of this generation focused on attempting to make segregation work by keeping open the lines of interracial communication and helping to ensure racial order and peace. In this manner, interracial cooperation helped build segregation. Cross-racial activism evolved, however, by the late 1920s. The attitudes of whites involved in these efforts remained rather consistent, but the black leaders with whom they worked became increasingly pessimistic that paternalism had any practical benefits. African American elites had tried to build class alliances across racial lines with their white counterparts but found their attempts rejected. Despite a mutual respect that developed from years of working together, most of these whites could not entirely look past their counterparts' skin tone. Segregation itself also killed this attempted alliance. Elite African Americans could avoid the indignity of Jim Crow in public transportation, but residential segregation and, later, segregation of public assemblages offered no class exemptions. As black leaders began to focus more on racial rather than class alliances, their patience with paternalism and paternalistic interracial cooperation waned. They continued to join this work and became involved in new organizations like the Commission on Interracial Cooperation; however, they became more strident in their demands and public denouncements of Jim Crow. At the same time, the older generation that had pioneered these interracial efforts began to age, retire, and generally lose their influence to effect political and social change. And, a new generation, on both sides of the color line, rejected the outdated ideas of paternalism. This change coincided as well with greater governmental involvement with many of the social welfare concerns that had been the center of older interracial activism. Although decades would pass before interracial cooperation organizations began to criticize segregation, perceptions of the work changed in the 1920s, making it suspect in the eyes of some Virginians when it had previously been applauded.

By focusing on Virginia, this study makes no claims that Virginia was the only state that witnessed this early form of interracial cooperation. Variations of this work could be found across the South. Yet, Virginia was unique in several important ways. Virginians cared deeply about their state's self-image as the aristocratic mother of all states, priding themselves on its supposed racial harmony and few instances of vigilante violence. As a part of this mind-set, white elites clung to the philosophy of paternalism long after it had been discarded as outdated in other states. African American elites, who also prided themselves on being Virginians, encouraged this commitment to paternalism and played into whites' professions of goodwill for their own practical purposes. In this context, Virginia made considerable efforts to extend Progressive reforms (although not equally) to its black population. But it also, ultimately, led the nation in testing the bounds of segregation and pushing the limits of racial discrimination.

Virginia history, like that of the South as a whole, cannot be divided neatly along racial lines. Southern history has too often been segmented and segregated. This book instead attempts to integrate the history of the Jim Crow by examining the interaction across the racial line that helped define life in twentieth-century Virginia. Although segregation prevails, this is not a one-sided story of white dominance. White elites attempted to dictate the lives of African Americans. Yet, black elites fought back by both defying white control and also playing into white expectations for their own benefit. More than an account of managing white supremacy or defying white control, this is a tale of activism, persistence, agency, and also compromise. Their conversations across the color line made unlikely allies in this unique generation of bold black and white elites who worked doggedly to manage one another.

1

Paternalism and Cooperation in the Old Dominion

The liberal minded white men of the Southland must be encouraged in their efforts to aid us in our march forward. The actions of the Negro hating white elements should not cause us to lose our discretion and self-control to the extent of using language and acting in a way to drive this element from us and there by causing us to lose their support. *God is on our side, but these kinds of white folks can do much to better our condition* before He gets to work punishing these agents of the Devil who are so active in this world of sin and sorrow.
—John Mitchell Jr., 1906

THIS STORY OF attempted cooperation and uplift in the Progressive Era is, like all of southern history, deeply rooted in place. The activism was rooted, in part, in a belief in Virginia's superiority that resulted in an uncomfortable mixture of virulent racism and civility characterizing segregation in the Old Dominion. Although its rampant repression and inequity found parallels throughout the United States and particularly in the South, the tale of race in twentieth-century Virginia is unique. Virginians depended on and promoted interracial cooperation and communication to institute order and minimize overt racial violence. To achieve this end, Virginians, across the color line, did what came naturally by seeking answers in their own braggadocian history. White leaders revitalized the language of paternalism while African American elites appealed in hope to whites' professed goodwill. These conversations across the color line, over time, molded the boundaries of a new segregated order.

Like their slaveholding ancestors, many white Virginians at the turn of the twentieth century obsessed over maintaining white supremacy and patrolling the boundaries of racial identity. To impose greater control on the interracial world in which they lived, they turned to segregation—a modern, Progressive reform that they hoped would solve their perceived "race problem."[1] Although opting for a repressive Jim Crow system like the rest of their southern neighbors, white Virginians cultivated a distinctive form of "polite racism" that, although as destructive and inequitable as elsewhere, was concerned with a pretense of civility and reaffirming their state's imagined but beloved glory days. Image, these men and women believed, was everything.

Virginians loved nothing more than to sing the praises of Virginian supremacy, taking pride in their state's self-proclaimed aristocracy and acclaim as the birthplace of seven of the first twelve United States presidents.[2] Although Virginia was the largest and most influential state in the era of the New Republic, the commonwealth's power had seeped away, and no resident of Virginia had been elected president since James Monroe won his second term in 1820.[3] By the early twentieth century, the Old Dominion was no longer the dominant national power it had once been. Burdened by debt and a tarnished reputation from its Confederate secession, Virginians struggled to rebuild the image of the "mother of all states" that many felt had slipped away. Seeking to change the perception of their state as one left behind by modernity, whites promoted their state as an idyllic haven of racial harmony, where segregation brought peace and interracial goodwill and vigilante violence was viewed with distaste as unseemly. Toward this end, a number of elite white Virginians reacclaimed their faith in paternalism, arguing that benevolence was more suitable than hostility for handling their "white man's burden."

African American leaders, on the other hand, acutely aware of the dangers of the interracial world in which they lived, hoped to alleviate their situation and stop the gradual ebbing of their civil and political rights by encouraging whites' paternalism. Earl Lewis in his book *In Their Own Interests*, a study of race in Norfolk, Virginia, in the twentieth century, argued that African Americans "never abided racism, 'polite' or otherwise." While this may be true on an internal level, the black reformers in this study were not opposed to using racist paternalism to their advantage whenever possible.[4] Initiated by both races, interracial cooperation functioned to extend segregation while offering black communities needed material concessions.[5] These efforts served to reinforce many Virginians' conviction of their state's superiority. While outwardly promoting the state as a lingering sanctuary of American aristocracy, white and black leaders engaged in cooperative initiatives that, despite white claims of amity and blacks' struggles against racial discrimination, helped to build in Virginia one of the most restrictive segregated societies in America.

Many black leaders (Maggie Lena Walker, Janie Porter Barrett, Ora B. Stokes, Giles Jackson, John Mitchell Jr., and Thomas Walker, among others) decided to work with white paternalists who asserted that it was their "moral duty" to assist in the uplift of their believed racial inferiors. Recognizing the deterioration of African

American neighborhoods while often ignoring the role of segregation in creating these conditions, white paternalists inspired by the fervor of the Progressive Era (Mary Munford, Elizabeth Cocke, Jackson Davis, James Dillard, Annie Schmelz, and Joseph Mastin, among others) sought out the black middle class to "instruct" them on needed reforms.[6] Black leaders encouraged these whites, hoping to gain the same material concessions and municipal services that white communities received. These individuals worked together to address a wide range of modern societal problems, including overcrowded and insufficient housing, disease epidemics, poor sanitation, and abandoned or delinquent children. They concentrated their work on solving primarily urban problems because cities, like Richmond and Norfolk, represented potentially dangerous sites of racial interaction. This "interracial cooperation" was not based on equality or equitable bargaining power but rather was a means for whites to justify their interference in a world they had worked to define as separate from their own. Black and white leaders alike spoke on the importance of "cooperating" and making friends with the opposite race.

At the turn of the twentieth century, interracial reformers in Virginia were neither silent nor secretive about their work. Instead, the whites involved proudly acclaimed what they believed to be exemplary paternalism. Perhaps the most well-known of this generation of paternalists at that time was a white woman—Mary Cooke Branch Munford. Munford accumulated an impressive résumé of work throughout her life yet was significant as well for simply what she represented—the epitome of Virginia paternalism. Although she never held political office, historians should not overlook Munford and her significant role in shaping Progressive social welfare and education in the state. Munford, like her counterparts across the color line, believed fervently in working to better the lives of all Virginians and, despite its limitations, saw interracial cooperation to be essential.

Before becoming involved in cross-racial reforms in the early 1910s, Munford was already recognized across the state as a prominent supporter of woman suffrage, increased educational opportunities for women, and various other Progressive social causes. Like many of her fellow white activists, including Lucy Randolph Mason and Elizabeth Cocke, Munford's Virginia roots ran deep. Born in 1865 as the Civil War ended, she grew up in Richmond and not only belonged to one of the most prominent families in the state but was related to numerous other First Families of Virginia. Although Munford's family never experienced poverty, she became interested at a young age in social welfare issues. This passion intensified after her 1893 marriage to Beverley Munford.[7] Beverley was also interested in social issues and dedicated his 1909 *Virginia's Attitude toward Slavery and Secession* to his wife. This book claimed, in very much the Lost Cause tradition, that the Civil War, or War of Secession (in his view), resulted from northern aggression against

Mary Munford. (Courtesy of the Virginia Historical Society)

the South's sovereignty; it also asserted, somewhat contradictorily, that white Virginians were largely against slavery but also that slavery was more "humane" in the state. In a featured article commemorating his life at the time of his death in 1910, the *Richmond Times-Dispatch* declared the work to be an "unanswerable defense of Virginia's attitude toward an institution in connection with which she has been misrepresented."[8] Although of questionable historical accuracy, the book was well received and widely read at the time by white Virginians because it so clearly fit the prevailing view of white paternalism, a philosophy that shaped Mary Munford's activism as well.

In the 1890s, Munford organized and headed the Saturday Afternoon Club, a weekly study and social club of elite white Richmond women. Her involvement declined over time, however, when she could not convince the group to study "unfeminine" issues such as child labor and municipal sewage systems rather than just topics like Homer and Goethe. She also became involved with the Richmond Education Association, which promoted public education (still a hotly debated issue in Virginia at the time, following its mandated implementation by Reconstruction), including a focus on African American educational opportunities. Connected with a national organization, the group held or attended national conferences every year that usually included a tour of some of the South's African American educational institutions. Although membership in the Richmond Education Association was restricted to whites, the organization had both male and female members, and Mary Munford (as well as Lila Meade Valentine) served as president for a number of years. Munford also joined and frequently held offices in many other organizations, including the National Consumers League, the Equal Suffrage League of Virginia, the National Municipal League, and the YWCA. She led a fervent, although ultimately unsuccessful, campaign to found a coordinate college for (white) women at the University of Virginia because she felt her sex had kept her from having a true education.[9] By the second decade of the twentieth century, Munford had established herself as a dedicated advocate of education, health, and labor reforms, as well as woman suffrage.

Beginning around 1910, Munford focused increasingly on the plight of African Americans out of a sense of responsibility to her family's and state's history. According to her biographer, Walter Russell Bowie (her nephew and a social activist himself), Mary Munford took great pride in her family's heritage and the aristocracy it implied. She believed this status gave her the right and duty to speak on behalf of African Americans. The Richmond black newspaper, the *St. Luke Herald*, run by Maggie Lena Walker, praised Munford by highlighting her lineage: "She [Mary Munford] belongs to that distinctive group that the colored people in the South call 'real' white people or 'bloods,' and sometimes, the entire descriptive phrase 'the blue bloods of Virginia.' We say this not with a bragging boast, but by way of explanation, that there are only a precious few white people in the South who gain such an estimate from the colored people."[10] Munford became an advocate of African American concerns from an ingrained sense of noblesse oblige, believing like her slaveholding ancestors that it was her responsibility as a white aristocrat to care for the black race. Rather than rejecting white-supremacist ideologies like the Lost Cause, she drew inspiration from Confederate commemoration, often citing the love and loyalty of her family's ex-slave servants as the reason for her activism in African American uplift causes.[11]

The unusual circumstances of her father's death also shaped Munford's commitment to racial paternalism. After the Civil War, Thomas Branch, a Confederate veteran, joined the Conservatives, a group of white politicians who hoped to regain their former power within the state and rebuild postwar Virginia by winning the votes of newly enfranchised blacks, believing naively that freedmen would turn to their former masters for guidance. As part of their campaign, on July 2, 1869, the Conservatives held a picnic designed especially to attract black voters on Vauxhall Island in the James River in support of their gubernatorial candidate, Gilbert C. Walker. Two hundred and fifty white and African American men gathered under a banner of "United we stand; divided we fall."[12] In bitter irony, the pedestrian bridge out to the island collapsed under the weight of the crowd, and several individuals died; Munford's father was one of the victims. According to Bowie, Branch "was flung into the river, with a beam from the bridge pinning him down upon its rocks. Many men tried to save him, among them a Negro who himself was badly hurt, but they could not get him free in time."[13] Throughout her life, Munford frequently referred to this act of attempted heroism on the part of the black man as the impetus for her activism. In the words of Douglas Southall Freeman, the white editor of the *Richmond News Leader* and member of the Board of Charities and Corrections: "It was because of the circumstances of his [Thomas Branch's] death that her work for justice to the Negroes had a vigor and a positive persistence that could not be balked. . . . One of her ideals . . . was to follow the same kindly road of amity and helpfulness to the Negroes."[14] The dramatic story of her father's demise in literal "sacrifice" to the "protection" of the African American race and the unnamed black man's effort to save her father influenced Munford to become one of Virginia's most vocal white advocates of paternalistic interracial cooperation.

Through her work with the Richmond Education Association, Munford expressed her concern about the problems and limitations of African American educational opportunities, and in the 1910s, she broadened her approach to include a full-scale critique of the difficulties facing Virginia's African Americans, particularly those living in urban areas such as Richmond. She never publicly spoke against segregation as the root cause, but Munford recognized the growing problems in communities like Jackson Ward, the primarily African American district in Richmond, which never received the same sanitation, modernization, and maintenance as white sections. She deplored the inadequate, overcrowded housing. In the words of her fellow reformer Elizabeth Cocke: "The most extensive of these conditions exist among the negroes. These appear to be the most squalid and least progressive, but this I believe to be largely due to the demoralizing effects of bad housing and surroundings which do not tend to any uplift."[15] Motivated by Progressive ideals of increasing government activism, Munford frequently attended city council meetings to petition for improved services for black residential and business districts.

In February 1912, Munford and Cocke encouraged the council to organize an "inspection tour" of Jackson Ward, in order for members to see for themselves the overcrowded and unsanitary conditions. Abandoning statistical lectures that had failed to persuade, Munford argued that action was desperately needed and that the "work would shine forth as a beacon light for movements of a similar character."[16] Although several African American residents also spoke out on the need for such an inspection, Munford's and Cocke's presence convinced the council to agree to the visit. Munford, in particular, continued lobbying efforts at city hall as well as helped to found organizations such as the Community House for Negro People, which trained black social workers, among other programs and services.[17] Munford hoped that her actions and her position among the social elite would remind whites across the state of their neglected paternalistic duty to encourage African American uplift.

Although younger than Munford, Elizabeth Preston Cocke was also a vocal advocate and particularly dedicated to public health reforms. Born to one of the most prominent Virginia families in 1891, Elizabeth set upon her career path of nursing early in life when attending Sweet Briar College from 1909 to 1912. In 1917, during World War I, she joined the army yet was forced to serve stateside in a training and organizing capacity due to poor health. After the war, she returned to Richmond, where she served in numerous health-care and training capacities until her death in 1981. Her career was indeed long, and this campaign with Mary Munford marked one of her first public efforts. Elizabeth, like Mary, was the product of one of the families in Virginia whose name was a social currency that demanded respect. And Elizabeth, like Mary, used that to her advantage to push for the Progressive health and sanitation reforms that were her zealous crusade throughout her life.[18]

Despite a sincere desire to help, Mary Munford and Elizabeth Cocke and their fellow white reformers sometimes had a limited understanding of the needs of black Virginians. They dealt with immediate issues such as poor street mainte-nance without acknowledging that residential segregation laws were the real cause of the problem. Acting from a white-centric viewpoint, they often misunderstood African American concerns. Interracial interaction, however, helped to clarify some of these misconceptions. In a speech before a meeting of the National Mu-nicipal League held in Richmond in 1912, Elizabeth Cocke revealed that she now understood that it was "a fallacy that the poor do not want good housing."[19] She had learned this fact after hearing a black woman proclaim a year before during a child welfare conference: "We would use the bath tub as frequently and enjoy it as much as our white brother and sister, if we could afford to rent houses which have the bath tub in them. We do not prefer dilapidation and discomfort, nor being forced to live in districts where there is only depravity and low surroundings."[20]

Although at times naïve and perhaps condescending, white women like Cocke and Munford sincerely sought to bring African Americans the same Progressive reforms they desired for whites, arguing that this was not only their Christian duty but the only way to bring racial harmony (and racial order) to the state. Speaking before a group of black women at the Richmond Hospital in 1911, Mary Johnston, a prominent white novelist and social activist, encouraged the women to become involved in municipal, child-care, and health reforms and to "think about the good of your people, of your State, *our* State . . . every woman with every other woman, every small group or societies with other groups or societies, cooperation means working together, organization means drawing things [needing] help by themselves into a whole that is anythnig [*sic*] but helpless. It means united we stand: divided we fall."[21] Johnston identified a common need that united women across racial lines. She argued that they must work together in order to create the Progressive society they desired. Ever-mindful of cultivating these bonds of coop-eration, Mary Burrell, the African American organizer of the event, wrote soon after to "personally thank" Johnston "for the great service rendered to the women of the Richmond Hospital, particularly and the race in general for your inspiring talk" and praised Johnston for her "kindly interest in my people."[22] Although the majority of white women in Virginia remained indifferent to any requests for assis-tance from the African American populace, Johnston, Munford, Cocke, and oth-ers were liberal-minded idealists who believed in the Social Gospel, Progressivism, paternalistic noblesse oblige, and striving to make separate more equal.

Despite the obsession with paternalism and image, interracial activism was not exclusive to Virginia. The historians Glenda Gilmore and Jeanette Greenwood have detailed similar work in North Carolina, and, in fact, interracial efforts could be found throughout the segregated South.[23] However, Virginia offers a unique perspective on this interracial activism. Although located in the Upper South and one of the last states to secede from the Union and join the Confederacy in 1861, the Old Dominion was quintessentially one of the most "southern" states. The first recorded slave ship to land in what would later become the United States arrived in 1619 at the Jamestown settlement.[24] And the state led the nation in terms of total numbers of enslaved people until Emancipation. During the Civil War, Richmond served as the capital of the Confederacy despite its precariously close proximity to Washington, D.C., and many of the men that white southerners later revered as heroes of the war hailed from Virginia, including Robert E. Lee, Thomas "Stonewall" Jackson, and J. E. B. Stuart. Although the state was stereotypically "southern," early twentieth-century white Virginians, as well as many African Americans, believed their state to be superior to the rest of the region. They wanted Virginia to be a state that led rather than followed.

White residents prided themselves on their state's supposed racial harmony at the same time they were implementing segregation. They pointed to Virginia's relatively low occurrence of lynchings and vigilante violence without regard to the state's common legal executions as evidence of a strong bond of friendship between blacks and whites.[25] Whites frequently congratulated themselves on peaceful relations, ignoring evidence of racial discord and injustice. Governor Henry C. Stuart, speaking in support of the 1915 national Negro Exposition in Richmond, declared that the "friendly relations" between whites and African Americans in Virginia were "a source of gratification to both races" and traced this goodwill to "enduring bonds of friendship" resulting from the "fidelity displayed by slaves during four years of [Civil] War."[26] On another occasion, the Honorable William T. Dabney of the Richmond Chamber of Commerce argued that the "relationship between the white and the colored people here was most friendly" and rosily concluded that, despite evidence to the contrary, "there were less handicaps to colored people in this community than anywhere else."[27] Annie Schmelz, a white Progressive activist from Hampton and a leader of the interracial movement, encouraged "the Negro" to remember "his best friend—the best Southern white people."[28] White Virginians devoted an enormous amount of time perfecting, in the words of the historian Ann Field Alexander, a "veneer of civility" to advertise their success in dealing with their "race problem."[29]

Virginian leaders across racial lines believed frequent professions of racial harmony were beneficial to either maintaining racial control (whites) or promoting the advancement of African Americans (blacks). Rhetoric of this type was commonly found in newspapers throughout the state. The white-owned and -operated *Richmond Times-Dispatch*, for example, argued that "the oft-repeated statement that colored folk are best off at home in Dixie [was true]. . . . Our colored people live in peace and friendship with the white race, receive the protection of good laws and continue to thrive and multiply." The *Richmond Times-Dispatch* editorialized that blacks were not hampered by the region's system of segregation; on the contrary, "their growing prosperity would be the best answer to the critics of Virginia's political policy if there were any critics of consequence left."[30] Most white leaders were confident of the success of segregation and convinced that it was universally accepted among Virginians. Although African American leaders were opposed to the discriminations of segregation, their efforts to remain in the good graces of paternalistic whites often quieted their protests or at least confined them to within black communities. Their support of the influential Booker T. Washington varied, yet nevertheless they co-opted some of his accommodationist strategies. This practice of downplaying criticism only fueled whites' optimism about Jim Crow.

Apart from occasional denunciations of racial discrimination, African American newspapers did little to contradict whites' assumptions. The *Richmond Planet*, for example, worked to foster greater racial understanding by counseling readers that "we have many true friends in the Southland. Let us do nothing that will estrange them or rob us of their support."[31] Black newspapers also frequently included accounts of African Americans bravely coming to the aid of whites in order to combat the negative image of blacks solely as criminals that pervaded even the friendliest of white newspapers. One May 1912 story lauded the heroism of a black man who dove in front of a train to save a white child. The reporter concluded that "colored men are constantly doing favors for white men and their families and will continue so to do. They are not thinking about a reward but only desire the heartfelt approval of the better class of white people, whom they love so well."[32] The African American community's emphasis on their friendly feeling toward and concern about whites was not an act of subservience but rather an attempt to call attention to their similarities with whites, shared experiences, and common humanity.

Many black and white Virginians alike stressed the importance of these nebulous ties that bound the races as necessary to maintaining open communication. Trying to make the best of their rather precarious position in the state, black Virginians cultivated good relations with white public officials. White leaders as well worked to promote interracial goodwill. To this end, governors of Virginia frequently made appearances within black neighborhoods. On May 11, 1912, for example, Governor William Hodges Mann "delivered an able address" exclusively for African American citizens at the Richmond city auditorium.[33] The local black newspaper, the *Richmond Planet*, stressed Mann's "popularity among the colored people" and that "the mention of his name causes the multitudes to stop and listen and voice words of commendation."[34] At another public appearance in August 1912, Mann spoke before the Fifth Street Baptist Church, one of the largest and most prominent African American congregations in Richmond. In this speech, he sought to educate his listeners on "national pride, state pride, Christian pride, and church pride." He pled for the "purity of the home" and encouraged mothers to keep a tighter rein on their children.[35] Mann used his influence to preach a white code of ethics to black Virginians, unaware that the black middle class shared similar ideals of family and religion. Mann desired to subdue protest and encourage acquiescence to the status quo, but his policies did help maintain racial peace throughout the state and prevent vigilante violence. At the time of Mann's retirement in 1914, the *Richmond Planet* concluded that "his many visits among the humble and lowly, his intention to go where he could 'do some good' will be remembered long after he has gone to his final reward."[36]

The *Richmond Planet* and its editor, John Mitchell Jr., were not alone in their respect of Mann. On February 22, 1914, the *Richmond Times-Dispatch* printed a letter from James T. Phillips, an African American professor at the Virginia Normal and Industrial Institute. Phillips believed that the governor had "been able to show the colored people of Virginia that he has been their Governor too." Answering his own question of, "And how?," Phillips outlined how the governor treated them as true citizens, even if not always equal: "By calling upon them in their public meetings, addressing them on questions of vital interest, and thus constantly assuring them of his friendship and concern in their welfare; and, further, by evidencing his sincerity at these points through generous recommendations of legislation in their favor."[37] Although Mann did little real good to improve the lots of black Virginians, his paternalistic approach offered African Americans opportunities to at least express their concerns, even if they were only then politely ignored.

Mann's successor, Governor Henry C. Stuart, took a slightly different approach in his relations with black Virginians. At an open meeting of the African American branch of the YMCA in 1914, Stuart detailed the rules and boundaries to which he expected black Virginians to adhere during his administration. First, in an unapologetically patronizing tone, the governor lauded the loyal and trustworthy qualities of blacks. He recalled with "tears welled up in his eyes" his own loving mammy and also a childhood friend and servant "who had played with him and over whose grave he had erected a monument as a testimonial to his sterling qualities." Praising the individuals now dead, he conveniently forgot the inequitable conditions his mammy and servant faced while alive. Instead, he believed affectionate bonds between master and slave had been a keystone of the slave South and still survived in twentieth-century Virginia. Stuart hoped to use this perceived connection to speak openly to his African American constituency. "I came here," Stuart professed, "to give you assurance of the friendliness of my administration for the colored people. I wish though to speak plainly to you. I am in favor of your people having all of your rights, with the understanding that you have no part in the government of this country." He conceded his support for black advancement (with the exception of political rights) but only as long as "you do not jostle us on our side of the line." Stuart recognized the expediency of promoting black autonomy and promised blacks a "square deal" but insisted that they acquiesce to the "decree of the Ages" that "the two races must live apart." Yet, he concluded that, despite separation, interracial cooperation was necessary to progress. "You need us," Stuart preached to his black audience, "and we need you in accordance with the plans that I have outlined."[38]

African Americans were both offended and appreciative of the governor's blunt assertions. John Mitchell Jr. commented in the *Richmond Planet* that Mann largely "won the confidence" of his audience through his honesty and goodwill, despite their disagreement with several of the politician's key positions.[39] While Mitchell and the other audience members accepted the sincerity of Stuart's tears prompted by memories of his black mammy, they viewed him as out of touch and understood that they "were listening to the fatherly advice of an ex-slave owner, who had in mind the 'Old Ante-bellum Negro'" rather than his twentieth-century descendants.[40] Stuart, like many whites, feared the progress made by African Americans following the end of the Civil War. Although he continued to express individualized love of his family's "Negroes," Stuart was weary of the black race as a whole. He viewed African American involvement in politics as a threat to white supremacy, and though he supported African American uplift, he believed whites needed to remain vigilant that blacks did not threaten whites economically, politically, or socially. Mitchell accepted Stuart's affection for his long-dead mammy but understood that "when it came to anyone else, unless distantly or intimately related, he [Stuart] looked the person over with the cynical eye of a Southerner, who had his doubts about trusting the average Negro."[41]

Mitchell found Stuart's position to be refreshing in its honesty but still condemned the governor for allowing social and party pressure to justify his refusal to uphold his "sworn obligation to recognize the civil and political equality of all men before the law."[42] Mitchell chided Stuart for allowing "the scum of Europe . . . to participate in the affairs of this government, while the worthy offspring of his black mammy and his faithful body servant, both of whom believed in him, would be denied that privilege."[43] Stuart argued that separation was the only way to achieve racial harmony, yet he believed it was in the best interests of both races for whites to keep a careful watch over black communities. Legislated Jim Crow was not an old tradition but a largely twentieth-century innovation, based not primarily on separation but on whites' fear of change and loss of control.

Despite the sometimes contentious nature of these meetings, the interplay between white public officials and their African American constituents was frequent and encouraged. Although blacks in Virginia were largely shut out of the political process and absent from governing bodies and offices, white leaders, concerned with their Christian duties and presumed national reputation of benevolence, still sought to keep up a facade of good relations with blacks. In October 1906, Richmond mayor Carlton McCarthy spoke before a gathering of the African American organization of the Grand United Order of Odd Fellows. According to the *Richmond Planet*, McCarthy "expressed his desire to see a meeting called for the purpose on the part of the colored people of this state to express their confidence in the white people of the commonwealth."[44] Blacks shied away from the suggestion, in the view of the reporter, because of "designing politicians who would take it to mean a tacit approval of all of the mischievous legislation that mischievous politicians have inflicted upon us," but the reporter also asserted that "there are white men, who regret the racial rancor that is everywhere apparent" and who want to give "the colored people a 'square deal.'"[45] Despite their intimate understanding of ever-increasing discrimination, many African American leaders believed that "when the better class of white people and the better class of colored ones decide to combine for the common good, the day of jubilee will be at hand."[46] African American elites, at least before 1920, argued that class bonds should trump race.[47] They hoped that if "better class" whites recognized their shared similarities, then perhaps the leaders of both races could meet on more common ground and enable more equal negotiations. Although white Virginian elites never accepted class alliances as necessary to the maintenance of "racial harmony," white and black leaders alike believed cultivating a friendly dialogue across the color line was necessary to navigating the interracial world in which they lived.

White Virginians' adoration of aristocracy and idealization of noblesse oblige resulted from Lost Cause romanticization of the antebellum era, an imagined past in which whites and their slaves had lived together as one large happy family in the "glorious" era of the pre–Civil War South.[48] Lost Cause remembrance along with the agenda of proving Virginia's supremacy revived this lore in the early twentieth century, leading whites to profess the values of paternalism rhetorically central to the long-past slaveholding culture. Frequently, whites "reminisced" about their families' experiences and relationships with loyal slaves. During a speech at Hampton Institute where Booker T. Washington himself was educated, Walter Bowie, a white Virginian activist and minister, spoke of the time his grandfather was wounded at Gettysburg and praised the black man who carried him from the field and "went with him in the ambulance . . . [then] took him out and stayed with him by the road, when he [Bowie's grandfather] could endure the agony of that

jolting transit no longer."[49] Appealing to the sentimentality of whites in the audience as well as the goodwill of the African Americans present, Bowie concluded
dramatically: "Such devotion only an ingrate could forget. . . .We, the white race,
are bound to the Negro people by ties too deep and sacred to be severed. . . . By
the growing instinct of co-operation the Negro can be assured of that fairness of
opportunity which will best build up the self-respect and the creative social values
of the race."[50] Bowie and his fellow reformers believed that taking a paternalistic
interest in the care of African Americans was not simply an act of charity for their
social inferiors but a responsibility and burden to be carried in order to honor
their heritage and ancestors. Their strong sense of duty ironically was rooted in
prevalent beliefs in white supremacy. While many whites, southern and northern,
understood white supremacy as a reason for lynching and the rebirth of the Ku
Klux Klan, some white activists interpreted white supremacy as a justification for
benevolence, not violence. They believed that the color of their skin obligated
them to be responsible for those they considered subordinate.

White and black Virginians alike appealed to a tenuous bond of affection between the races that was deemed the product of long years of interaction. Whites
argued that the supposedly wholesome relationship between the races within the
state was the product of paternalistic slavery and benevolent masters in the antebellum era. One white Richmonder informed a *Richmond Planet* reporter that
since "your average Virginia planter was a gentleman of the highest type," he
took better care of "his Negroes" and, unlike his neighbors farther South, was
rarely an absentee landlord, taking care of his slave men and women, who were
"accustomed to improving contact with white gentlefolk."[51] The source claimed
that Virginians rarely sold their slaves, only resorting to the inhumane practice
to get rid of "bad" individuals.[52] "Thus," the white man claimed, "the tendency
was to keep well-behaved Negroes in Virginia and to supply other States with the
unruly ones. Naturally, then, the Virginia Negro of today, being descended from
'selected stock' . . . may be expected to average somewhat higher in human virtues
than the offspring of slaves of the black belt."[53] This argument ignored the central
role that Virginia played in the domestic slave trade while twisting these historical
inaccuracies to fit popular ideas of scientific racism inspired by Darwinist theory.
This mind-set held that black Virginians were of a superior nature and more capable of progress (with whites' help) than the lesser "stock" of African Americans
found throughout the rest of the nation.

Romanticized Lost Cause ideals, particularly that of the loyal slave, became
common points of discussion. Whites (including Governor Stuart, among others)
often attempted to establish their "mammy" credentials before addressing black
audiences.[54] While few blacks believed in this cheery revision of antebellum South,

African American leaders viewed "mammy" rhetoric as a useful way to cultivate the goodwill of whites. Black newspapers as well as white carried stories of heartfelt mammy and master reunions.[55] When John Mitchell Jr.'s mother died in a horrific house fire in January 1914, Mitchell chose not to be insulted by white papers eulogizing her as an "old 'mammy.'"[56] He understood, as one anonymous white southerner once quoted to him, "the difference between the Northern point of view and the Southern point of view is this: In the North you love the Negro race but hate the individual; in the South we hate the race but love the individual."[57] Southern whites often feared African Americans as a race but loved individuals, particularly their remembered mammies or other favorite family servants. Some even believed this connection obligated them to aid African American uplift causes. In the words of the northern reporter Ray Stannard Baker, who traveled the South in 1908 trying to understand the complex color line, "Southern people possess a real liking, wholly unknown in the North, for individual Negroes whom they know."[58] Black leaders, in turn, tried to manipulate whites' declared love of individuals when they had no other effective tools for stemming whites' hatred of the black race. They reminded white activists that the descendants of their beloved mammies deserved better treatment.

While twentieth-century whites never called for or wanted a return to slavery, they still took solace in their romanticization of antebellum doctrines of paternalism. As part of Lost Cause remembrance, many white Virginians reminisced about an imagined past of racial harmony where loyal black slaves loved their benevolent masters who provided them with not only material comforts but also moral guidance to overcome their "savage" natures. Some slave owners were more humane than others, but this twisted historical memory of contentment existed only in the minds of whites. In the twentieth century, whites continued to argue that this idyllic racial Eden had been destroyed by an "unnecessary" Civil War. They claimed that their race's loving care of blacks had been rebuffed and betrayed during the "dark" days of Reconstruction and that many whites had been forced to abandon their racial obligations. Now, they argued, was the time for white southerners to reestablish themselves as the benefactors of the black race. Like their forefathers, they believed that African Americans could advance successfully only through white guidance. Furthermore, these professions of "benevolence" as a means of social control aligned nicely with Progressive reform ideals that took hold. White reformers used cross-racial activism to practice an updated modern conception of white paternalism.[59]

Twentieth-century paternalism built on antebellum beliefs but applied them to a new Progressive era and racial order. Many whites no longer considered the household to be the center of paternalist care of individual blacks but instead now regarded the African American race as a whole as the responsibility of the "master race." While nineteenth-century paternalists cared primarily about the personalized relationships under slavery, these later whites were more concerned about abstract notions of race. These Virginians had a vested psychological interest in proving the supposed bond between the races was real. Benevolence not only gave these individuals a sense of moral superiority but also, in a state so obsessed with heritage, justified the righteousness of their forefathers and relieved any lingering burden of slavery.

White Virginians' obsession with their paternalistic self-image shaped discussions of race; they prided themselves on their civility and practiced what is best labeled as "polite racism." White extremists denying the possibility of any future for African Americans within the United States occasionally spouted their beliefs in newspapers and other public forums, but the majority of white Virginians accepted the presence and recognized the benefits (often in the form of labor exploitation) of blacks as long as they remained in their social "place" as defined by the culture of segregation. Few individuals acted upon noblesse oblige and joined cross-racial activism initiatives, but those who did tended to be influential leaders and members of prominent southern families.[60] These men and women were not called to action for any one shared reason, but rather they were moved by personal and often unspoken reasons. Some felt religiously compelled by the Social Gospel to help those they saw in need. Some were concerned with making sure segregation was done "right." And a few likely had deep yet silent concerns about the inequity of the world they witnessed. As with their African American counterparts, they generally self-identified as members of the "better classes" and thus felt called to action. In Virginia, these paternalists became social and political leaders whose ideology ultimately helped determine the way the state was segregated. Virginia paternalists were not unique regionally in terms of their views or reforms, yet they gained a particularly strong voice in the state.

Although similar trends could be found across Virginia, Richmond became the epicenter of much of this resurgence of paternalism.[61] This fervor, in part, resulted from the city's long history. Founded in 1725, Richmond succeeded Williamsburg as the state capital in 1779 and was incorporated as a city three years later in 1782.[62] As the capital of the largest slaveholding state, racial division shaped the city from its onset. In the years preceding the Civil War, slave traders were prosperous, establishing the city as a central market to cater not only to Virginians but large slaveholding plantations in the Lower South. Yet, a large permanent population of African Americans also lived in Richmond, both enslaved peoples employed in a variety of uses from domestic to industrial as well as a substantial number of free blacks.[63] In the late nineteenth century following the 1865 armistice, Richmond rebuilt in the midst of ashes, and the population boomed as displaced individuals across the state and region flocked to the city seeking employment and hoping to improve their lives. In 1880, Richmond was home to 63,600 people, but by 1890, the population had ballooned to more than 81,388 (32,330 blacks and 49,058 whites).[64]

As Richmonders worked to bring their city into the twentieth century, whites held on to their antebellum traditions of racial order through an idealization of their past. As the capital of the former Confederate States of America, Richmond became the center of Lost Cause remembrance. Memorials to Confederate war heroes (Robert E. Lee, Thomas "Stonewall" Jackson, and Jefferson Davis, among others) were erected on Monument Avenue, creating unavoidable, visible reminders of the state's slaveholding past. Individuals from across the South flocked to the city for massive Confederate veteran reunions, celebrating a common commitment to white supremacy. Organizations like the Daughters of the Confederacy and the Sons of the Confederacy attracted large memberships and held frequent meetings, parades, and other events. White residents turned to a celebration of an imagined past of a harmonious slaveholding society to justify segregation and the necessity of clinging to the ideals of paternalism to solve problems of modernity. The Lost Cause became the justification of both liberal activists and conservatives.

In the midst of this celebration of white supremacy, African Americans, living primarily in Jackson Ward, built vibrant black neighborhoods that were home to a prosperous middle class.[65] In the early years of the twentieth century, the city boomed and became one of the centers of African American population within the state, along with the broader Tidewater and Southside regions. From 1910 to 1920, Richmond's population increased by 20 percent.[66] In 1916, 156,687 individuals lived in the city, of whom 62,676 were black.[67] Expansion brought problems common to all modern cities — overcrowding, disease epidemics, poverty, economic competition, and difficulty providing needed municipal services. In a divided city with African Americans emancipated only a few decades before and many whites facing economic hardship after their family's fortunes (if there ever were any) were lost in the war, urban problems took on a racial dimension. Whites worried that the relatively new freedom of black Virginians combined with widespread destitution among blacks and whites would confuse racial identities. African Americans, in particular, suffered poverty in greater numbers than other city residents. Despite the reassurances of paternalists, many white Virginians feared racial strife would be the natural outcome of this uncomfortably interracial environment.

Interracial welfare initiatives were unique negotiations across the color line, but they were never based on equality. Although segregationists claimed to be creating separate but equal black and white worlds, black and white communities in Virginia were never really separate or equal. Some historians have argued that segregationists achieved (and desired) complete separation. Raymond Gavins, for example, has asserted: "In Richmond, Negroes knew a lot about biracialism. For the capital city contained two societies, one black, one white—separate and unequal."[68] Yet, life was not so neatly divided across the color line. Instead, segregation was messy and required constant vigilance to regulate and manage the enforced social status quo. Whites had no real interest in allotting black space and were hesitant in allowing black autonomy. All space was ultimately under the domain of white supremacy. Whites viewed the black community as a subset of the larger white world, and all reform efforts were set within this matrix. White activists conveniently drew upon their professed history of paternalism as an excuse to oversee and dictate the terms of African Americans' lives. Black Virginians exhibited agency in courting whites' aid in building and supporting reformatory schools, medical facilities, and organizing community uplift efforts, but they were always constrained by segregation. In order to receive needed material and monetary aid from Progressive white reformers and gain access to political leaders, they were forced to play the inequitable role expected of them by segregation.

This pattern of interracial communication extended into various project initiatives and causes across the state. In 1913, a group of African American prohibitionists in Norfolk worked with Captain Taylor, a well-respected white lawyer, to close twenty saloons within the city, including several in black neighborhoods.[69] When education activists brought a compulsory education law before the General Assembly in an effort to compel children in Virginia to attend school until they were are least fourteen years old, they explicitly included black and white children alike. The Richmond School Teachers' League supported the bill despite the controversial racial inclusion.[70] Furthermore, prominent whites, apart from elected public officials, frequently addressed African American audiences. In April 1914, Dr. Douglas S. Freeman, introduced by the prominent African American activist Ora B. Stokes, lectured before the YMCA on the "Corner Stone to Manhood."[71] Even Jessie Woodrow Wilson, daughter of the president of the United States, traveled to Richmond to speak to a large group of African American women at the First Baptist Church, an event organized through the YWCA. Although, according to the *Richmond Planet*, "her voice was faint and but few of those present heard all that she said," the women "all were highly gratified over the visit."[72] Her message meant little in comparison with the fact of her presence. Whites across the state and beyond believed they had a responsibility to demonstrate their paternalistic interest in their black neighbors.

Whites also occasionally took active roles in African American organizations, such as the Negro Organization Society (NOS). Founded in 1912, the NOS was an outgrowth of the annual interracial Hampton Negro Conference, which met from 1896 to 1912 and brought together African American leaders, particularly throughout the South, for the purpose of promoting and advertising the progress of black Americans. Although the NOS's membership was entirely African American, the group made interracial support one of its primary goals.[73]

At the first annual meeting of the NOS, held in early November 1913, Mayor George Ainslie and the white activist Mary Munford spoke before the largely African American crowd. Organized by Robert Mussa Moton at Hampton Institute the previous year, the NOS worked to advocate for African American concerns across Virginia. According to the newspaper coverage, Ainslie "explained in detail his efforts to improve the living conditions of the colored people" in Richmond while Munford delivered a prepared lecture entitled "How White People Can Aid This Movement" to demonstrate her support of the NOS's policy goals concerning educational, health, and housing improvements.[74] Apart from these appearances, the conference featured Friday-evening addresses by Governor William Mann and Dr. Booker T. Washington.[75] Fostering these demonstrations of goodwill, Washington praised Mann for his interest "in the education and uplift of all the people in Virginia" and concluded that it was "because of the leadership and guidance of such state officials as you have that the Negro in Virginia has gone forward as fast as he has."[76] In keeping with his accommodationist approach in working with white leaders, Washington supported his argument by naming in some detail a variety of interracial cooperation efforts within the state, while ignoring the fact that in spite of this work, Virginia had a skyrocketing death rate among African Americans as well as deteriorating housing conditions within black neighborhoods.

Public demonstrations of interracial goodwill such as those given at the NOS meeting were primarily viewed as opportunities to praise the harmonious nature of black/white relations in Virginia rather than as efforts to bring about any meaningful change. Yet, the very need for these demonstrations was proof of the existing inequality. The ambivalent nature of these interchanges, well-meaning but lacking in substance or extractions of concrete promises, worked to the advantage of whites who saw these interracial initiatives as forums to monitor black autonomy through "genteel" white supervision.

Although this study focuses on interracial efforts in Virginia, this work was not exclusive to the state and could be found across the South. While many initiatives were private endeavors kept out of the public eye, several regional associations espoused the importance of cross-racial communication. The Commission on Interracial Cooperation (CIC) founded in 1919 by Will Alexander would be the most famous, yet it had predecessors. One of the first was the Southern Society for the

Promotion of the Study of Race Conditions and Problems in the South. Edgar
Gardner Murphy organized the group and staged the Montgomery Conference
in 1900. Although the conference ultimately endorsed the disfranchisement movement, its members supported African American uplift (with white guidance) and
invited a wide range of speakers including Booker T. Washington to address the
meeting. Nearly a decade later, the University Commission on Southern Race
Questions (1912) built upon this tradition. Composed of white professors from
universities across the South, the group encouraged interracial meetings with community leaders and conducted studies of black life and methods of best relating
with the opposite race. Yet, notably the group included no African American
professors among their ranks. The Southern Publicity Committee (1917) sought
to extend this concern of some elites for the welfare of African Americans to the
general public. This association, headed in part by Lily H. Hammond of Georgia,
believed an "enlightened" press was needed to better inform the general white
populace and improve race understanding. They released complimentary articles
on African American uplift to newspapers and discouraged the overdramatization
of the so-called "black criminal element."[77]

Another regional example of white interest in interracial cooperation was the
Southern Sociological Conference founded in 1912. Led by Willis Duke Weath-
erford, this biracial group dealt with urbanization and industrialization issues including public education, child labor, penal reform, factory regulation, and prohibition, among other concerns. While these Progressives had no desire to promote
the political rights of blacks or challenge segregation, they hoped to employ Progressive reforms to improve conditions in African American neighborhoods. The
National Association for the Advancement of Colored People (NAACP) and its
journal, the *Crisis*, praised the Southern Sociological Conference for its efforts in
promoting greater interracial understanding. "For the first time in history," the
Crisis declared, "Southern white men and Southern black men have met under
Southern white auspices and frankly discussed the race problems of the South
before an audience of both races."[78] Although the NAACP editorialist was correct
in recognizing the significance of the scale of the conference and the remarkable
attendance of approximately three hundred to four hundred individuals at each
of the four sessions, interracial work was not uncommon or even new in 1913,
particularly in Virginia.

The NAACP kept a careful eye on the status of interracial cooperation in
Virginia and across the South.[79] Accordingly, the NAACP decided to highlight
southern interracial work at their 1913 convention with a "New Southern Attitude
Panel" to "bring out the spirit of the New South toward the race problem."[80] Professor Joel Spingarn, a northern white man and longtime activist with the NAACP,

James Dillard at his home. This photograph was taken by
Jackson Davis. (Jackson Davis Papers, Albert and Shirley Small
Special Collections Library, University of Virginia)

promoted the session as "an opportunity for our Association to allow the Southerners to answer the Bleases and Vardamans," yet noted cautiously that "if they
should play us false . . . we could answer them the following session."[81] A number
of white southerners were invited to participate, including Mary Munford, but
only three accepted the offer, Dr. James H. Dillard, Dr. Howard Odum, and Lily
Hammond. Dillard was the only Virginian.[82] Spingarn's concern with potential
damage control proved unwarranted. Although none of the three denounced or
even acknowledged the inequities of segregation, they did support educational
advances, strengthening African American property rights, and reducing mob violence and lynching. The white southerners spoke from an unapologetically white

paternalist stance, and the NAACP attendees largely appreciated their efforts. "We are training the people to see white and colored side by side," Hammond of Georgia explained, "and to see the relation of the one to the other. . . . We are children in this respect, and perhaps you are not quite grown up; but we will call you the big brother, and big brothers, you know, are apt to be impatient with the younger ones of the household."[83]

That same year, a series of lectures were held at the University of Virginia professing to offer a detached academic analysis of the issue. Not surprisingly, the organizers included only southern white male speakers and addressed a white audience. They brought in a variety of acknowledged experts on race, including James H. Dillard.[84] Dillard was born in July 1882 to an old Virginia family who had been slaveholders. He had the advantage of not only his race but an advanced education, attending Washington and Lee University and later becoming a professor himself. He served as a Latin professor at Tulane University in New Orleans until returning to Virginia in 1907 to work with the Jeanes Fund and later Slater Fund, both organizations aimed at improving the educational opportunities of African Americans.[85]

Dillard typified liberal-minded southern whites' understanding of their black neighbors.[86] First, he argued that most Virginians, blacks and whites, were "going on quite peacefully about their business," yet this harmony was forgotten by the public's obsessive focus on the troublemakers.[87] Setting himself apart from radicals who saw no future or place for African Americans in white America, he placed blame for the racial tension not solely on "deviant" blacks but on whites, from the Radical Republican Thaddeus Stevens, who "forced" too many rights on newly freed slaves following the Civil War, to the rabid racist Governor Coleman Livingston Blease of South Carolina. Dillard concluded that the best way to deal with racial strife was to promote goodwill between the races, a project he suggested should be worked "first along the lines of education and religion." While he predicted that "there will always be race problems, for races are different and the differences will persist," he saw "no reason why the white people and the colored people may not continue to live in the South with a natural segregation and yet in mutual co-operation and good will."[88] Dillard, like many white Virginians, concluded that the best way to control the unpredictable segments of society was by the formalized separation of the races sanctioned by laws along with an altruistic, yet profitable policy of cooperation. To Dillard, segregation was the "natural" choice of the races and under ideal circumstance would be implemented simply by social mores rather than tedious laws. Rather than seeing cooperation and segregation as contradictory, he viewed them as interdependent.

Interracial cooperation in early twentieth-century Virginia was not a potential threat to the culture of segregation as it was later during the civil rights movement but rather an effective policy to manage racial interaction. Many white paternalists believed their work to be essential to the continuance of white, as well as Virginian, supremacy. Accordingly, most white Virginians accepted the work as beneficial as long as it avoided any embarrassing questions of political or social equality. Rather than challenging racial discrimination, "efforts to better race relations," in the words of John Mitchell Jr., were employed only to "make more palatable the various species of injustice dealt out to the Negro in America, and particularly in the South, by the dominant white race."[89] Segregation was not simply legislated but actively molded on a daily basis through ongoing conversations across the color line.

2

Encroaching Segregation

We want our white friends who are so anxious to erect every possible barrier they can to keep Negroes from touching or rubbing against white people to make full and complete success of the job. We would like to see the streets and stores Jim Crowed. We want a real sure-enough separation.
— Maggie Lena Walker, 1904

THE GENERATION OF interracial activists prominent in Progressive reforms in the first decades of twentieth-century Virginia were not raised in a strictly segregated world. Most of these individuals were born around the time of the end of the Civil War and into a society that was in flux. Among the African American activists, John Mitchell Jr., Maggie Lena Walker, Ora B. Stokes, T. C. Walker, Giles Jackson, and Gordon Hancock had all long experienced racial discrimination and were accustomed to the inferior treatment they received at the hands of whites.[1] These individuals grew up in the shadow of the war, either as children of slaves or having known slavery themselves at a very young age. Signs of former servitude surrounded them and shaped their lives. Some reminders were visible, such as a nearby honey-pod tree that marked the location of antebellum slave auctions for T. C. Walker, but others were internalized lessons. These men and women were comfortable in their cross-racial interactions because they had grown up in close proximity to whites and unaware of the eventual extent of segregation.

For example, John Mitchell Jr. born July 11, 1863, in the midst of the Civil War, grew up in the white household of his one-time owner, James Lyons, a well-to-do and influential Richmond attorney.[2] Although a servant, Mitchell lived in one of the wealthiest Richmond homes and never knew hunger or deprivation as a child. His relationship with his employer, however, was not the idyllic one depicted by paternalistic whites of former masters and slaves. Lyons had little interest in Mitchell as an individual and no motivation to encourage his employees to better their lots in life. Against Lyons's wishes, Mitchell, with the help of his mother, received an education. In 1881, seventeen-year-old Mitchell graduated as valedictorian of the Richmond Normal and High School.[3] He worked several years as a teacher until, in 1884, he lost his job as a result of a mass firing of African American teachers following the collapse of the interracial experiments of the Readjuster movement.[4] That year, he assumed the debts of a floundering new newspaper, the *Richmond Planet,* and became both owner and editor.[5] He then built the paper into a well-known forum for protesting racial discrimination and segregation as well as the promoting of racial pride, running the *Richmond Planet* successfully for forty-five years until his death in 1929. In addition, Mitchell became the founder and president in 1902 of the Richmond Mechanics Saving Bank, an institution affiliated with the Knights of Pythias, which he headed until the bank's demise in 1922. In 1921, he ran for governor under the "lily-black" Republican ticket to protest whites' efforts to expunge blacks from Virginia's Republican Party.

John Mitchell Jr. became well known among white Virginians as a formidable leader of African Americans in the state. Growing up in the Lyons' home, Mitchell had been schooled in the rules of white society and proper etiquette. From his immaculate dress to impeccable manners, he used these lessons of youth not to play a role of subservience but to live as a Virginian gentleman. Although at times put off by his assertive attitude and sometimes arrogance, whites generally responded favorably and were willing to cooperate with Mitchell in various interracial initiatives because nothing in his manner could be specifically faulted. Personally aware of the limitations of paternalism and importance of self-improvement and autonomy, Mitchell was one of the most vocal supporters in the state for building a harmonious working relationship with "better class" whites.[6]

Mitchell was not alone in his experience. Maggie Lena Walker, T. C. Walker, and Janie Porter Barrett also grew up in white homes. Throughout their lives they drew upon this sense of familiarity to help manage their relations with whites. They understood the intricate rules of racial etiquette and, thus, could work and communicate with white paternalists without fear of committing some potentially dangerous racial offense. In turn, white activists were more comfortable working with these individuals because, in whites' eyes, these black leaders were success stories of the ability of paternalism to uplift African Americans through the benevolent guidance of whites. Accustomed to white interference in their lives, these African American reformers realized that good behavior was of the utmost importance. Mitchell, for example, instructed his readers to remember that it was "absolutely essential that we be more polite and more obliging to the better class of white people. Strive to win their friendship and merit their approval. They will then do much to defend us against the unjust imputation of their own people."[7] Walker, Mitchell, and the others were experts at "handling" whites, knowing when

John Mitchell Jr. (From Caldwell, *History of the American Negro and His Institutions*)

to compliment, when to beseech, and how to appeal to whites' sentimentality for "their Negroes." They were able to influence and prod whites. Most importantly, they were able to do this without the knowledge of white paternalists. Although these African American leaders never believed in racial inferiority, they enacted the roles prescribed for them by segregation when it suited their purposes. "We know that segregation is a bad thing," exclaimed Gordon Hancock, "but . . . the consequences of not accepting it may be worse. . . . Herein lies the pity!"[8]

African Americans' willingness to join interracial cooperation efforts with whites was not (as many whites interpreted) a signaled acquiescence to segregation but rather a strategic ploy to fight ever-increasing discrimination. They had no illusions about the supposed benevolence of Jim Crow laws. In the words of one anonymous letter writer, "No matter what other reasons may be assigned, the real, true and chief object is to impede the Negro's progress and as far as possible degrade and discourage him in his efforts to rise to the highest degree of manhood, civilization and citizenship."[9] Black Virginians chose to fight this imposition of discrimination rather than dwell on injustice. They could not know the eventual extent of these laws. "We have no time to grieve and repine over existing conditions," the *Richmond Planet* reminded its readers; "we must scheme, plan and work along all legitimate lines with a view of increasing our usefulness to the community and adding to our own coffers."[10] Black leaders hoped that encouraging white benevolence and interest in African American causes would result in stronger, healthier, and more financially independent black neighborhoods. They turned to interracial cooperation, hoping this strategy would succeed by acquiescing to white racial control in exchange for limited black autonomy.

John Mitchell Jr. not only preached this course of action to his readers as well as black Virginians across the state but attempted to lead by example. In his interactions with whites, he acted in accordance with whites' assurances of goodwill and racial harmony, attempting to avoid conflict through his impeccable behavior and by reminding whites of their presumed manners. As president of the Richmond-based Mechanics Savings Bank, Mitchell was one of the few African American members of the American Bankers' Association (ABA). Despite his minority status, he attended the national annual meetings held in various locations across the country, expecting and usually finding that he was treated as simply another banker rather than a racial oddity. In October 1914, however, he encountered some embarrassing difficulties when the conference was held in his home city of Richmond.

Entering the prestigious Jefferson Hotel where the meeting was held, Mitchell was stopped first by a stenographer registering ABA members. He patiently handed over his engraved business card, which a manager took and shortly re-

turned with instructions for the young woman to proceed with the registration. Re-
counting the event, Mitchell emphasized the woman's embarrassment as she apol-
ogized that she "stated only what she had been instructed to state."[11] At the next
station, where he needed to pick up his ABA badge, Mitchell again encountered
a worker who refused to help him. This time the Mechanics Bank president was
forced to wait for Mr. Fitzwilson, the assistant secretary of the American Bankers'
Association, who was at lunch. Mitchell politely sat aside until the assistant secretary returned and then, upon his arrival, appealed to him to "straighten these
young gentlemen out. They are doing a good service, but they don't understand
my case."[12] Mr. Fitzwilson promptly corrected the issue. To ensure he would not
face further complications at future sessions, Mitchell then spoke to an unnamed
local white banker about his concerns and "asked him to take the matter up with
the committee and thus avoid further annoyance."[13] The banker did so, and the
situation was quietly resolved.

Mitchell recounted this experience to his readers with pride at his successful
handling of the uncomfortable situation rather than with any sense of embarrassment for being singled out. In many ways, the editor and banker was an unre-
pentant elitist who believed on a certain level that racial discrimination would be
solved once whites recognized that what they determined to be a "racial problem"
was actually a "class problem" that cut across racial lines. Regardless, he believed
his adventure held lessons for all African Americans in dealing with whites. He
asserted that the best way to get along with whites was simply to play by their
rules, to the letter, holding whites to the same level of genteel courtesy that they
expected. He stressed that problems could usually be solved quickly and quietly
without resorting to open denunciation. Mitchell's attitude reflected that of many
leading black Virginians during the early twentieth century who believed that
the worst aspects of segregation could be stymied through interracial cooperation
with well-meaning whites. They believed their own material success as prosperous
members of the black middle class qualified them to work together with the "better
class" whites. "Colored people," Mitchell preached, "should cultivate the friendship of the white people in all parts of the country and especially in the Southland.
This should not be done by a sacrifice of principle or by supine submission for both
of these methods breed contempt."[14]

Although informal segregation was common at the turn of the twentieth century,
legalized segregation (apart from the new public school system formed in the
1870s) was rare. In 1900, legislators passed Virginia's first segregation ordinance
by a majority of one vote.[15] De facto division had long occurred, but this law separating races on railroad cars along with the adoption of a new state constitution

the following year initiated a new era in the racial history of the state. Although based on antebellum traditions, legally enforced Jim Crow was a distinctive product of the late nineteenth century. In 1955, C. Vann Woodward concluded in his famous work *The Strange Career of Jim Crow* that segregation broke from past practice by replacing an informal and fluid color line with formal and inflexible statutes.[16] Woodward argued that whites considered Jim Crow laws to be Progressive reforms to help maintain order and racial peace (that is, white control) in interracial communities. In 1971, Charles Wynes tested Woodward's thesis in his study of race in Virginia in the late nineteenth century. He concluded that Woodward was basically correct that the racial situation dramatically worsened around the turn of the twentieth century. Wynes, however, stressed that a golden age of "race relations" did not really occur during the 1870s and 1880s but merely a brief period of flexibility. In 1992, Edward L. Ayers argued the modernity of segregation, illustrating how modern technological innovations such as electric streetcars and expanded railway travel became sites where the color line was often tested.[17] These places of interracial contact were the impetus and excuse for many of the initial segregation statutes. In Virginia, racial mixing in public transportation became the first problem addressed by segregationists. These whites feared that interracial seating might fuel African Americans' hopes of equality. Moreover, they worried that the presence of well-dressed African Americans (particularly in Richmond with its prosperous black middle class) in first-class cars while working-class whites, unable to afford such luxury, rode in second-class accommodations might blur racial identities.[18]

The segregation of Virginia was an ongoing process that took decades to develop.[19] The initial 1900 law was only the first stage in building what the historian Grace Hale has called the "culture of segregation."[20] Some historians, however, have claimed that Jim Crow was "settled" by 1920. For example, Elsa Barkley Brown has argued that "in Richmond, as elsewhere, a system of race and class oppression including segregation, disfranchisement . . . and enforcement of racial subordination through intimidation was fully in place by the early twentieth century."[21] Joel Williamson has also stated that "after 1915 the era of legal segregation expired."[22] Yet, the practice of segregation was in flux in Virginia throughout this era. J. Douglas Smith has demonstrated that the harshest laws were not passed until the mid-1920s.[23] After lobbying by the state's Anglo-Saxon Clubs (Virginia's more "civilized" alternative to the Ku Klux Klan), the General Assembly passed the Racial Integrity Act of 1924, narrowing the definition of white, as well as the Massenburg Law in 1926 requiring segregation in all public assemblages. With the latter, Virginia went further than any other state at that time to extend segregation to pervade all aspects of African Americans' lives. In the words of Smith, the

Massenburg Law became "the broadest and most restrictive measure of its kind in
the United States," defining segregation until the passage of the Civil Rights Act of
1964.[24] Despite protestations of Virginia's supremacy and the civility of the state's
racial order, white Virginians created one of the most inequitable segregated societies to be found in the United States.

Despite white Virginians' insistence that racial harmony prevailed, black Virginians in the early twentieth century were beginning to feel the debilitating effects
of legalized discrimination. Living conditions worsened, particularly in urban areas, and death rates skyrocketed. Fueling these problems along with disfranchisement and the onslaught of Jim Crow laws, white Richmond city leaders in 1903
abolished Jackson Ward as a political entity.[25] This decision left the poorest section of Richmond and its heavy concentration of African American residents with
little political means to address the increasing racial discrimination. Left with few
other options, African American leaders decided that interracial cooperation was
their best recourse for solving some of the worst social welfare problems facing
black neighborhoods. Although they had attempted interracial cooperation in the
past, they placed a new emphasis on appealing to whites' claimed paternalism,
especially since this work aligned with their Progressive interests. Some white Progressives, in turn, reached out to these black leaders, hoping to mask examples of
existing inequity that via the media were becoming an embarrassment to the state.
Out of these motivations, the theory of interracial cooperation took hold.

Interracial cooperation efforts attempted to reconcile a central contradiction of
segregation: black autonomy and white control. Although created as a means to
protect white supremacy, Jim Crow, by definition, supposedly created a separate
black world. White Virginians never actually wanted separate racial existences but
rather only to protect "whiteness" through absolute, legally defined racial identities. Yet, by espousing the doctrine of "separate but equal," white segregationists
paradoxically committed themselves to at least a limited degree of black independence. To resolve this inherent discrepancy, white Virginians evoked policies
of paternalism and interracial cooperation. White paternalists offered the "gift"
of black independence to justify the righteousness of segregation but insisted on
maintaining a diligent and supposedly benevolent watch over black Virginians
to ensure they did not challenge or threaten the color line. They encouraged the
growth of black communities but believed this could only be achieved through
whites' guidance and kindly interest in African American uplift. African American
leaders, in turn, exploited this loophole of segregation by manipulating whites'
concern with separation to fight for greater social, economic, and cultural independence. In doing so, they sought to protect their race from an unjust white so-

ciety that increasingly denied them their basic civil rights as Virginian citizens. In his study of Norfolk, Earl Lewis drew a similar conclusion: "One of the hidden ironies of segregation was the power it unwittingly bequeathed to blacks."[26] Lewis argued that African Americans in Norfolk emphasized the importance of congregation over segregation. Black leaders in Richmond used similar rhetoric. Cross-racial initiatives gave black reformers some room to maneuver within the growing confines of Jim Crow, enabling them to push their own reform agendas while accessing, however indirectly, the white power centers of the state. Simply put, African Americans sought autonomy, and whites desired control. Activists, black and white, turned to interracial cooperation to coordinate and justify these dual goals.

In 1904, black Richmonders staged their first major protest against segregation. After a law enacted by the General Assembly allowing (but not requiring) Jim Crow seating in streetcars, the Virginia Passenger and Power Company began to enforce segregation.[27] In response, on April 19, John Mitchell Jr. called for a boycott of the city's streetcars when addressing a large audience at the True Reformers Hall. Thousands of black Virginians joined the effort and began to walk rather than submit to the inequity of segregated public transportation. They continued the boycott for more than a year, but the movement eventually lost momentum when the Virginia Passenger and Power Company refused to acquiesce. Many black Richmonders, unable to afford any other means of conveyance, had little choice but to again patronize the public transportation system. African Americans returned to the cars out of necessity rather than convenience. Although it brought black Richmonders together, the boycott did little to stop the proliferation of Jim Crow. In 1906, the General Assembly passed an ordinance requiring segregation in streetcars.[28] African Americans resented the suggestions made by whites that their eventual patronage implied a tacit acceptance of Jim Crow. "The Richmond Negroes," John Mitchell Jr. reiterated, "fought the 'Jim Crow' law in every way conceivable and there are many here still fighting it. . . . They accept all of these discriminations under protest."[29]

Even after the passage of the 1906 law and the collapse of the boycott, many African Americans refused to accept that segregation was inevitable. They decried the inequitable manner in which segregation was enacted. The *Richmond Planet*, for example, resented the abuse of power by conductors who frequently pushed hardworking blacks out of neutral seats: "It is indeed unfortunate that so much power should have been given to so many of these incompetent white men. They are in many instances drawn from the lowly walks of life, with but little experience and no judgment."[30] Early on, blacks saw through the empty promise of separate but equal as Jim Crow seating was always enforced to the benefit of whites, placing the comfort of white passengers over the needs of black passengers.

Ironically, however, whites were also confused by the new rules and felt perse-
cuted when they inadvertently sat in the wrong seats. "Strange as it may seem,"
a reporter for the white daily *Richmond Times-Dispatch* complained, "the practical
working of the Jim Crow law has been more annoying to the white people than to
the colored."[31] These incidences of supposed white discrimination highly amused
John Mitchell Jr., leading him to comment that the reporter's whining was apro-
pos of the "Shakespearean declaration 'hoist on his own petard.'"[32] Blacks hoped
the inconveniences of segregation would convince white leaders of its impractical
nature. The *Richmond Planet* optimistically prophesized that "race prejudice has
always proved a boomerang and it always will."[33] Yet, despite the minor difficulties encountered by a few white Virginians, segregation was always enacted
to ensure preferential treatment for whites rather than any supposed creed of
separate but equal.[34] Regardless, black leaders continued to insist to any whites
willing to listen that the new laws would only bring trouble. They lamented that
while whites claimed the "Jim Crow street car arrangement would tend to produce
peace among the races, they "insisted that it would tend to produce strife"; and
they frequently reported little skirmishes and arguments that broke out between
the races.[35] Although this tactic was ultimately unsuccessful, black leaders hoped to
shame whites into facing how such blatant discrimination made a lie and mockery
out of whites' claims that Virginia was an Eden of racial harmony.

This facade of idyllic racial harmony was crumbling in the mid-1910s. Despite
the existence of a prosperous black middle class in Richmond, health and housing
conditions among the city's African American residents were among the worst
in the nation. Residential segregation choked black neighborhoods by physically
limiting expansion and forced black Richmonders to crowd several families into
dwellings not adequate to accommodate everyone. The city failed to provide
proper sanitation, such as sewer and trash pickup service. In 1914, Theodore Jones,
a black resident of Richmond, described the situation in vivid and shocking terms:
"Not alone must we live in houses built for us in blind alleys, but we must live in
houses built for us in the rear of other houses where there are no alleys, blind or
otherwise, and where entrance and egress for the family in the rear house are to be
gained only through the actual living rooms of the family in the front house. There
is located in Jackson Ward no public play grounds for children, no public parks
for adults, but in their stead is maintained a cemetery a public dump for the city's
refuse matter, a creamatory [*sic*] for the diseased, dead, and putrefying animals. In
this Ward we must live, move and have our being."[36] The situation, which became
a great concern especially to the city's Progressives, only became worse as the
city's population grew, resulting in widespread disease and death. Although many
whites tried to gloss over these conditions, the city received unwanted national

Dilapidated homes in Jackson Ward, Richmond. A city dump is seen
at the end of the street. (Jackson Davis Papers, Albert and Shirley
Small Special Collections Library, University of Virginia)

publicity. Embarrassed that Richmond's distinction of having one of the highest
black mortality rates in the United States might hurt claims of Virginian superiority, white and black leaders, hoping to encourage government involvement in
these issues, stressed the need for detailed studies on how to combat the myriad
problems and promoted tours of the primarily African American Jackson Ward
by white city officials.[37] In 1913, the NAACP's *Crisis* praised one such investigation
for "arousing public sentiment in favor of their betterment."[38]

In June 1913, Mayor George Ainslie of Richmond commissioned the study,
later recognized by the NAACP, to document, explain, and analyze the numerous
problems of African American neighborhoods. The report revealed the black race
to have a 68 percent higher death rate than whites. Although "comprising only
37 percent of the population," Ainslie summarized, "the race furnished 51.8 percent of all deaths."[39] The mayor criticized the Board of Health for failing to address the needs of African American residents apart from occasional clean-up days
and called for increased spending to combat the conditions causing the high mortality rate. In addition, Ainslie encouraged the city council to conduct a further
investigation that he believed would be "welcomed and assisted by all members
of the colored race who are genuinely interested in its preset [*sic*] condition and
future welfare."[40] Ainslie understood the devastating effect of municipal neglect
in African American neighborhoods, but he failed to identify the role of segre-

gation and disfranchisement in creating these conditions. The loss of the ballot compounded problems by ensuring that the needs of black Richmonders would be ignored. The city council had little motivation to aid the voteless. Although a positive step in terms of public recognition of conditions, the mayor's study failed to admit the root of the problem.

African Americans welcomed whites' concern with neighborhood improvements and were careful not to point out that the recommended reforms were no more than the minimal needed services that they had a right to expect as citizens. But black leaders also encouraged their race to first help themselves. John Mitchell Jr. chastised the members of black burial societies for their willingness to "contribute eighty-eight cents for a seat in a carriage to follow a dead member to the graveyard" but not be willing to give "eight cents to keep this same member from the poorhouse."[41] He urged black Richmonders to not merely study the problems but create a fund to help those in need. Mitchell and others questioned the commitment of white activists to follow through on their many reports and translate their studies into definitive action. African Americans, he argued, needed to take control of the situation and attack the problems head-on rather than waiting for assistance. While Mitchell acknowledged that "the white people can do much for us," he reminded his readers that "we can do much more for ourselves."[42] Despite this assertion of agency, black leaders saw the practicality of cultivating white favor. "There is a concerted movement . . . of the patriotic justice-loving white people of this city to better the living conditions of the colored people of this community," the *Richmond Planet* noted. "We should not do anything to 'chill' this movement or to create the impression that these efforts are not appreciated."[43] The editor of the white daily *Richmond Times-Dispatch* agreed that the problem "can only be solved by the unselfish cooperation of both races."[44] The white paper, failing to recognize white Richmonders' role in creating the problems of African American neighborhoods, reminded its readers that "economic necessity and every tender sentiment of a humane people demand that we give the Negro a square deal, put him in proper surroundings, and then help him to overcome his own weakness and realize his possibilities."[45] White activists saw health reforms as their Christian duty, and although the interracial initiatives were marked by condescension, African Americans had little choice but to welcome whites' support.

Black and white leaders sometimes disagreed over what Progressive actions were most practical in addressing the needs of black Virginians. The white editor of the *Richmond News Leader,* for example, praised the Virginia Hospital's efforts to care for the city's poor but concluded that the project could not be supported if no efforts were made to include ailing black residents. Believing the white press could "do more to facilitate and increase the friendly feeling between the white and colored people of this community than any other agency," the paper advocated the inclusion of African Americans in health care reforms and championed their worthiness: "Richmond negroes are among the best and most law-abiding in the world. They suffer from the misconduct of the disreputable element, but in the main, they are prosperous, self-respecting and thrifty. Moreover, they are being decimated by disease and are suffering from the lack of medical attention. . . . Heart disease, bronchial complaints, and other ailments without number afflict them. From a purely selfish viewpoint, we must protect ourselves by caring for our Negroes; from a broad standpoint of humanity, we must give them better sanitation and abundant hospital facilities."[46] Black Richmonders had access to small private hospitals operated by African American doctors, but the white editor regretted blacks' inability to receive "the attention of a competent white physician" without resorting to the "humiliation" of the almshouse or "a free bed in the colored ward of memorial hospital."[47] Although a segregationist, the editor felt health care could only be adequately administered under the supervision of whites and distrusted any separate African American institutions.

While John Mitchell Jr. hoped that white activists would listen to the *Richmond News Leader's* appeal, he believed that black Richmonders must first support their own institutions and raise money for the African American–run Richmond Hospital. "Self-help," Mitchell declared, "is the watch-word and progress our guiding start. With the white people helping us at the Virginia Hospital and we helping ourselves at the Richmond Hospital our health condition must necessarily be improved and our death rate curtailed."[48] Black leaders tried to gain any potential advantage, advocating improvements within and outside their domain of control. Although Mitchell and others desired the advanced medical facilities and treatments available only to whites, they advocated first and foremost improving the institutions under their power rather than relying solely on the "goodwill" of white Virginians.[49] Black Richmond leaders embraced Booker T. Washington's policy of self-help, then radicalized it to achieve greater autonomy.[50]

In spite of the ongoing segregation of Richmond and restriction of African American rights, the city gained renown nationwide for its flourishing African American communities. After Emancipation, black Richmonders established several large churches, primarily Baptist and Episcopal, which remained centers of African American life far into the twentieth century. In addition, the city had numerous beneficial societies, which provided not only life insurance but were also known for their many social and cultural events. Other organizations such as the Tuesday Club held May musical festivals annually and sponsored literary events, including poetry readings by African American poets.[51] Residents could choose from among four African American weekly newspapers (the *St. Luke Herald*, the *Richmond Planet*, the *Reformer*, and the *Progressive Citizen*) that spoke against the strictures of segregation as well as stressed racial pride, advertised social happenings, and encouraged support of African American businesses. The city also offered various educational opportunities apart from the underfunded primary public school system, including Virginia Union (a prominent African American college), Armstrong High School (founded in 1867), and Van de Vyver College (a Catholic school for blacks headed by the white priest Father Charles Hannigan).[52]

Black Richmonders successfully built neighborhoods with well-developed cultural centers by striving for as much economic independence as possible from white Richmonders. To encourage autonomy and economic growth, black Richmonders founded many businesses, including four banks. In 1903, Maggie Lena Walker became the first African American woman in the country to run a bank when she established the St. Luke Penny Savings Bank, an institution that she headed for many decades.[53] Walker believed thriftiness was central to African American uplift and saw her bank not only as a business venture but essential to the progress of the race. Moreover, she understood that for African Americans to

Interior of St. Luke Penny Savings Bank. (Courtesy Maggie L. Walker National Historic Site, National Park Service)

prosper, they needed to spend money within their own neighborhoods and not simply give their hard-earned money to white merchants. "If you don't remove the stumbling block of supporting white business and support black business," Walker preached in 1909, "we deserve the name of inferior and should be treated as such until we cease to fall over the block."[54] In order to create this infrastructure, black Richmonders often used their mutual benefit societies to finance and operate numerous African American–owned ventures, such as Walker's bank as well as the True Reformers Bank and the Mechanics Savings Bank (headed by the editor John Mitchell Jr. and associated with Knights of Pythias). By encouraging economic racial unity, women and men like Maggie Lena Walker and John Mitchell Jr. built thriving African American neighborhoods with a prosperous black middle class. In 1917, E. D. Caffee, writing for the National Association for the Advancement of Colored Peoples' (NAACP) *Crisis*, declared that there was "no city, probably, in the whole country that does as much Negro business as Richmond."[55]

Black community leaders stressed the importance of fostering black businesses because they believed that if segregation could not be stopped, then it could at least be exploited. African Americans understood that the true motive behind segregation was white control and not racial autonomy. Thus, they sought to exploit the discrepancy between the stated promise of "separate but equal" and the reality of white supremacy. In the words of the historian Darlene Clark Hine, "black professionals identified the Achilles' heel of white supremacy: Segregation provided blacks the chance, indeed, the imperative, to develop a range of distinct institutions that they controlled." Blacks "exploited that fundamental weakness in the 'separate but equal' system."[56] Black Richmonders acted upon this opportunity. Speaking through her newspaper the *St. Luke Herald* in April 1904, Maggie Lena Walker explained: "We want our white friends who are so anxious to erect every possible barrier they can to keep Negroes from touching or rubbing against white people to make full and complete success of the job. We would like to see the streets and stores Jim Crowed. We want a real sure-enough separation."[57] Walker decided that if boycotts against segregation failed, then maybe the situation could at least be potentially manipulated for the benefit of black businesses. She knew that despite the letter of the law, Jim Crow was never really about separation. But by calling for African American autonomy, she hoped to gain the opportunity to shape her own community and foster the growth of African American businesses and organizations. Although never acquiescing to the degradations of segregation, black Virginians took advantage of all available opportunities to make the best of a bad situation.

In the midst of this prosperity, however, African Americans living in Richmond faced numerous problems. Although a black middle class thrived, the average black resident had few employment options. Richmond had some factory work open to African Americans such as in tobacco processing, but the city did not offer the same number of new industrial job opportunities as nearby Norfolk. Most black Richmonders were stuck in domestic or other menial positions, usually working for whites who paid them poorly and treated them as inferiors. Poverty was common among African American families. Many people worked countless hours at backbreaking labor only to struggle to keep their families adequately housed, clothed, and fed. Under these conditions, overcrowded housing became a major concern, along with the accompanying issues of poor sanitation, rampant disease, and lack of proper health care. Black residential areas were in poor condition and became increasingly worse with the progression of segregation. Knowing that they did not need to care about the potential for angry African American voters, white city officials placed seven of the municipal dumps and crematories in these crowded neighborhoods, then neglected to provide these sections with basic services such as street cleaning or even needed water and sewage utilities.[58] Not surprisingly, black Richmonders faced one of the highest death rates in the country. While segregation did help foster the growth of African American businesses, Jim Crow ultimately was detrimental to black neighborhoods. African Americans, rural and urban alike, felt the degrading effects of discrimination, but black city residents experienced a particularly modern form of segregation. Like other cities nationwide, Richmond entered the twentieth century in an era of accelerated urbanization and technological innovation. The population boomed, but African Americans generally suffered rather than prospered.

In 1912, an anonymous man from New York wrote John Mitchell Jr. as editor of the *Richmond Planet* upon hearing a rumor that blacks were not able to walk or drive on certain city streets. In response, Mitchell crafted a detailed response explaining the conditions under which African Americans lived in Richmond. First, he debunked the claim that blacks were prohibited from walking on any public streets, but he clarified that they were restricted from living in certain sections due to the recent residential segregation law that had "caused untold annoyance and embarrassment." "We can go anywhere we please in Richmond," Mitchell explained, "provided we have the price and provided the people in charge want us and our money." Yet, many restrictions abounded. Some barrooms refused to sell liquor to blacks, and others would only accommodate black customers if they "bought it in a bottle . . . and carried outside the establishment." Hotels catering to white people were closed to African Americans except as servants entering through the back door. Thus, Mitchell noted wryly, "Colored men here accordingly are eating and sleeping in the finest hotels in this city—in the servant's apartments, of course." Blacks could travel in any section of the city, including through any parks, "without molestation." They could own cars, and it was "a fact that some of the most expensive cars in the city are operated by colored men — as chauffeurs." Yet, streetcars had racially segregated seating, meaning a white person wishing "to sit beside a colored one and converse about a job . . . is not permitted to do it."[59] Apart from these segregation statutes, Mitchell also denounced the city council for recently raising the pay of white elementary school teachers while barring their black counterparts from similar increases.

Despite these discriminations, however, Mitchell believed that "still colored people are progressing here and they are adding to their material and financial possessions." African Americans' property in the city, he noted, was valued at more than $2 million. He was optimistic about this material success as well as the relative lack of violence between white and black Richmonders. "While conditions are in some respects discouraging, in many others they are encouraging," Mitchell concluded; "We are here standing up as citizens of Richmond and of Virginia and we shall continue to contend for our rights as long as we have strength." Despite this assertion of rights, Mitchell, like white paternalists, continued to argue that "a friendly relationship exists between the better class of white people and the better class of colored people," and expressed hope that those ties would help bring about change.[60]

Some segregationists only paid lip service to the goal of black autonomy, strategizing how to best maintain racial dominance. One of the best examples exposing this contradiction is Richmond leaders' efforts to impose legalized residential segregation upon the city beginning in 1911. Although informal patterns of residential racial separation existed throughout Virginia dating back to the Reconstruction era, Richmond became one of the first cities in the United States to legislate what had formerly been custom. The laws constructed in this former capital of the Confederacy later became models for other cities throughout the region, most notably Louisville, Kentucky, and Baltimore, Maryland. Richmond was the first city in the state to enact such provisions, but State Senator J. M. Hart pushed a bill through the General Assembly of Virginia giving all localities the right to segregate, shortly after the passage of Richmond's Vonderlehr ordinance.[61] The complications and numerous interracial discussions surrounding this new form of discrimination highlight the complex interplay of race within the city as well as the difficult task of molding and managing a segregated society.

When City Councilman A. L. Vonderlehr's bill for codified residential segregation (popularly known as the Vonderlehr ordinance) was voted upon and put into effect in 1911, numerous Richmonders were far from convinced of its necessity. A number of African American citizens, including John Mitchell Jr., attempted to protest the proposed ordinance before city council when the bill was first offered

in February of that year, yet little became of these efforts apart from a temporary delay of its passage.[62] Although the white daily newspaper the *Richmond News
Leader* pronounced segregation to be "an unmixed blessing" that "has proved to be
[a] mitigation, if not a solution of the race problem," its publisher, John Stewart
Bryan, a leading white Richmond citizen active in various interracial initiatives,
had questions about the new Vonderlehr ordinance.[63] Before a national child welfare conference held in Richmond in early 1912, Bryan argued: "They [African
Americans] are segregated in Jackson ward, and under a new ordinance they are
being still further segregated. That is radically wrong, it is economically wrong,
and nothing in the world can change it but an awakening of public sentiment,
and it ought to be awakened and it will be."[64] Bryan and Mitchell were not alone
in their reservations, although their protests were rooted in dramatically different
motivations.

While black leaders sought to counteract the ebbing away of their civil rights,
Bryan feared that white segregationists were losing sight of their paternalistic
promises to African Americans. His concern was not with the efficacy of the system
itself but with how it was implemented. He believed, as did many black activists,
that racial problems could best be solved through quiet communication rather
than crass displays of prejudice. The Vonderlehr ordinance, more than streetcar or railway segregation statutes, made a mockery of the pretense of separate
but equal. Bryan saw little point in a measure that attempted to uncivilly dictate
what "tradition" had never opposed. To Bryan, the Vonderlehr ordinance was
an unnecessary measure that threatened to disrupt what he interpreted as racial
harmony within the city. Vonderlehr and others believed, by contrast, that the
integrity of the white race was threatened and that legalized residential Jim Crow
was necessary to maintain the purity of racial identities.

Earlier segregation ordinances had supposedly created equal facilities on public
transportation that could be willingly patronized or not by the consumer, but the
Vonderlehr ordinance struck at the heart of any American's rights, that of property. Under the statute, a man could be arrested for attempting to live in a home
that he had lawfully purchased if the color of his skin did not coordinate with that
of his neighbors. Some overzealous whites attempted to interpret the ordinance to
bar African American Richmonders from using the city auditorium, a public arena
frequently utilized by both races. Despite an effort on the part of the city attorney to
justify the new policy, the auditorium ban did not hold because it was without legal
justification. "The Negroes are taxpayers; they have as much right to assemble in
the auditorium as to meet in the Capital Square," protested Bryan's *Richmond News
Leader,* stating that "the sooner the Vonderlehr ordinance is amended the better for
Richmond, and the better for that ordinance. The colored people of this city have

rights that the white people cannot afford to withhold."[65] White segregationists realized that there were legal limits to the discriminations they attempted to legislate. Paternalists, in particular, were well aware of these boundaries and believed interracial cooperation was the best way to bestow what blacks deserved as citizens, yet to do so under an explanation of benevolence. Whites hoped to make guaranteed rights seem like privileges granted on grounds of "good behavior."

The major difficulty of the new residential segregation ordinance was its limitation of African American expansion. In the early twentieth century, nearly every major city nationwide faced overcrowding and house shortages, and Richmond was not an exception. This urban crisis was a major concern of Progressives throughout the nation, including Virginia. The Vonderlehr ordinance exacerbated this condition. Although the ordinance claimed to be racially blind by declaring that no family white or black could move onto a block in which their race was not in majority, African Americans, many of whom were residents of the lower-income inner city, were disproportionately affected. The new ordinance, though it seemed clear on paper, caused major confusion among city residents. Some city blocks were already so divided racially that residents found themselves legally stuck, unable to sell their homes and move into new neighborhoods. Others found themselves prevented from moving into residences they had legally purchased. In short, the Vonderlehr ordinance stymied Richmond's former growth pattern. The long-established process of African Americans moving into homes left vacant by whites moving out of the inner city was disrupted. While whites retained the option of pushing farther out into the suburbs, blacks, as the minority race, were corralled into small, primarily downtown pockets with practically no areas of expansion. African Americans were barred from entering many half-abandoned white blocks regardless of their financial ability to do so.[66]

As a result, black neighborhoods, most notoriously Jackson Ward, became dangerously overcrowded. Landlords, many of whom were white, exploited the situation by raising rent and neglecting upkeep because they knew black Richmonders had little choice but to pay the exorbitant rates and accept the squalid conditions. This deplorable situation concerned many different people: working-class black families with little hope of improving their situations, the black middle class and elite who had money for better housing but nowhere to move, white Progressives sickened by the degrading health conditions of black neighborhoods, and real estate agents across the color line whose businesses were handicapped by their inability to sell a myriad of properties. In response, various annexation proposals were brought before the city council, usually by paternalistic whites looking for a solution to the Jackson Ward dilemma.[67] Despite the desperate overcrowding, African Americans were skeptical of these "quick fix" schemes.

Turn-of-the-twentieth-century disfranchisement had limited black Virginians' access to the ballot and public office, but they were not entirely barred from the political process. Although their protests to prevent the passage of the Vonderlehr ordinance failed, blacks continued to petition the city council regularly, hoping to shape the interpretation of the ordinance to best protect their civil rights. While at face value the city's consideration of a proposal to annex land in order to offer new expansion areas to the middle-class blacks seemed a positive action to fight inner-city overcrowding, black Richmonders were wary of the offer. They protested, in what amounted to a public denunciation of the veracity of whites, that they had little reason to believe the annexed region would receive any better municipal services than those they currently had to endure. They argued that the old areas needed to be fixed before new ones were developed. "What was the use of making arrangements to build a utopia in Henrico county for colored people," the *Richmond Planet* decried, "and to leave the long lanes of streets in old Jackson Ward[,] unpaved alleys with their cess-pools of filth[?]"[68] The paper urged its readers to recognize the promises as false and only "part of the scheme of the political disturbers of the peace between the white and colored people of this community to enable them to win over the conservative white people to the support of this pernicious and trouble breeding ordinance."[69]

African American leaders balked at the annexation plan because they feared it would signal acquiescence to segregation. Indignant, John Mitchell Jr. declared: "We insist that we are not Indians, and cannot be lawfully segregated. We are not Chinese and we cannot be lawfully segregated. We are citizens and when we purchase property lawfully, we have the lawful right to occupy the property purchased, whether we select so to do or not."[70] This argument expressed his own prejudice, revealing that he was more opposed to discrimination against African Americans in particular than to segregation in theory. Mitchell believed in racial superiority. Only, unlike whites, he defined African Americans as one of the superior races. Thus, Mitchell argued that blacks, as a superior race, deserved the full rights of citizenship. African American leaders resented the fact that blacks, who over the centuries had proven themselves worthy Americans, were treated like new immigrants or American Indians. Seeking to demonstrate their capability as citizens, black Richmonders crowded city council meetings to express their concerns.

In January 1912, African American leaders from various backgrounds across the city appeared before a meeting of the Council's Domiciliary Committee to speak against land annexation.[71] These protestors, including S. B. Steward, D. Webster Davis, W. H. Hughes, Ben Jackson, and W. A. Jordan, argued that improvements to Jackson Ward should take precedence. Well-prepared with facts and statistics, they described to the council the poor conditions in that section with its deteriorated streets and housing, lack of curbing, and need for adequate water and sewage facilities. While the committee attempted to shift blame to property owners (ignoring the fact that many of these were white landlords concerned with little except profit), they had no defense when countered with facts that black neighborhoods failed to receive even the basic services that white areas took for granted. Chairman Vonderlehr, father of the notorious residential segregation ordinance, promised that water, gas, and sewage would all be available in any new annexed areas, but the African American citizens, revealing their limited faith in paternalism and politics, refused to trust him and "still insisted that the city should first guarantee more improvements in the section already occupied by them."[72] The protestors were not cowed by the chairman. Upon hearing complaints about the disproportionate number of barrooms allowed licenses within black residential neighborhoods, Chairman Vonderlehr hastily demanded, "If the saloons are a nuisance, why don't you protest against them?" "We have protested, but it did no good," W. A. Jordan retorted; "We have wearied of protesting."[73]

These black leaders were not alone; they were joined by Mary Munford and Elizabeth Cocke. Rather than quietly sitting on the sidelines, these white women pleaded that the council recognize the growing problems of Jackson Ward. Although neither spoke against the practice of segregation, they were deeply concerned with the conditions of black neighborhoods. Munford and Cocke challenged the council to accept their responsibility in terms of needed Progressive municipal improvements. Aided by the influence of the two respectable white women, W. A. Jordan and the other black leaders present convinced the committee to plan an inspection tour of Jackson Ward to see the conditions for themselves.[74]

Although these protests did bring some attention and minor, though mostly temporary, improvements to various black neighborhoods, the Richmond city government continued to treat blacks as second-class citizens. Whites candidly admitted this neglect. Following the late January meeting of the Domiciliary Committee, the city's dominant morning newspaper, the *Richmond Times-Dispatch*, reported "that the City Council has not dealt fairly with the Negro since his elimination from politics was tacitly admitted last night, when it began a general discussion of the housing problems of the Negro race."[75] Rather than offering excuses, the paper explained: "Members of the committee had no defense. One member, who is also a member of the Street Committee, admitted that improvements had gone where they would do the most good politically, and that since the Negro has been ousted from politics he had little chance in a body where appropriations are divided according to ward lines and expended by those fighting for re-election."[76]

While white city officials did occasionally seek to better the African American situation, they rarely relied on the frequent advice and requests they received from
the black Richmonders.

Segregationists were supposedly in favor of black autonomy, but they preferred
to keep tight control over black neighborhoods, in part because whites believed
their assumed racial superiority better suited them to judge what was best for black
Richmonders. Thus, by March 1913, white newspapers announced with pride the
planned development of a new subdivision for African Americans, Washington
Park, to be located in the suburbs. The *Journal* announced that "Richmond is to
be congratulated in being the first city in the South to solve the problem of the
congestion of its Negro population by opening up a suburban section which is to
be entirely devoted to the erection of colored homes."[77] The following year, the
Richmond News Leader praised the progress of the new neighborhood, offering the
highest compliment they could imagine. "The suburb," the *Richmond News Leader*
declared, "has advantages that would make it attractive to white people."[78] The
black middle class, desperate for new housing, took advantage of these opportunities and purchased real estate lots in Washington Park.

One of the more heated debates wrought by the ever-increasing strictures of
segregation was sparked by a seemingly benign topic, a public park. In 1913, when
white city officials first proposed a new park to be built in one of Richmond's
black neighborhoods, they expected to be praised by African Americans for their
benevolence. Yet, instead of hearing protests from any white residents upset about
municipal funds being spent on their black neighbors, Mayor Ainslie and the city
council faced, to their surprise, bitter denunciations of the proposal by several
prominent black leaders. The controversy first began when Rev. William Stokes,
pastor of Ebenezer Baptist Church, one of the largest African American congregations in Richmond, wrote Mayor George Ainslie a letter expressing his objections
to the new park: "While I am sure that the gentlemen of the Council feel that this
will be of real benefit to the colored people, and their purpose is for good; yet, Mr.
Mayor, representing as I do the very best people in our city, I beg leave to say
that the establishing of a public park will do a great deal of harm and will retard
the efforts greatly of those of us who are trying to lead our people to a higher and
more desirable plane of citizenship."[79] Shocked that his black constituents were
not grateful for the proposed measure, Ainslie promptly responded that while
he imagined it was "*possible that you know much better than I do* the sentiment among
your people in this regard . . . I sincerely hope that you have misinterpreted it,
for I cannot understand how parks can be good things for white people and bad
things for colored people."[80] He requested Stokes bring a delegation including
John Mitchell Jr., Webster Davis, and Giles Jackson—African Americans whom

Ainslie found acceptable and had worked with in the past — to visit him to discuss the issue in person. Stokes arrived several days later but brought black leaders of his own choosing: J. J. Carter, John T. Taylor, N. B. Brown, and E. Payne. To the mayor's disappointment, Stokes had not changed his mind on the issue and continued to argue that "attempts to solve the open-air problem by providing separate parks for the colored people . . . would end in failure because they would become the meeting grounds of the rougher elements," causing "the parks to become new recruiting grounds for already well-established evils" and forcing "better class" blacks to stay away.[81] In an ironic twist of fate, this reasoning left Ainslie and the white advocates to argue that the African American park could be "as decent and law-abiding as those provided for the exclusive use of the white population."[82]

As days passed, however, the park controversy became not a white-versus-black debate but a very public and bitter struggle among African American leaders. After hearing the objections of Stokes and his supporters, Mayor Ainslie called John Mitchell Jr. directly, hoping to court a second opinion from black Richmonders, and requested that Mitchell, along with a selected few, meet with him to discuss the issue. Responding to the negative publicity against their race, Mitchell assembled a delegation recommended by Ainslie (lawyer J. Thomas Hewin, lawyer J. R. Pollard, real estate agent George W. Bragg, lawyer Giles B. Jackson, Rev. Thomas H. Briggs, and general contractor William A. Jordan, among others) and visited the mayor at his offices.[83] Received in the formal reception room, Mitchell presented a resolution in support of the park. Speaking for the group, he stated that a park was needed not simply "upon the grounds of public policy" but "upon the grounds of public health." Furthermore, he reassured the mayor that "the question of disorder should not enter into the discussion of this matter. From the time when the first slave landed in this country and the multiplication of the colored people began, our race has been noted for order and not disorder."[84] The quintessential diplomat hoping to encourage the benevolent interest of whites without appearing to cow to their wishes, Mitchell concluded by praising white Virginians of Ainslie's "type and standing" and pointedly reminded the mayor of his assurance that "humiliating conditions and compromising methods will not follow as a result of the confidence which we now in you repose."[85] The white newspapers, such as the *Richmond News Leader*, encouraged the cooperative sentiment expressed by Mitchell and his delegation, pronouncing, "We have in this city the best colored people on earth, and we feel that some of their leading citizens do the race a great wrong when they declare that the colored parks would reflect discredit upon the race by the disorder they would permit."[86] Siding with the pro-park faction that more closely correlated with their own racial assumptions, whites were surprised by the struggle among African American leaders over the park issue.

White Virginians, despite their assertions that they understood blacks better than anyone, failed to comprehend the real issues behind the public park debate. Reverend Stokes's major concern was not that the proposal would lead to higher crime rates. Instead, he chose this vein of argument because he believed it would be readily accepted by whites, particularly the white media that reveled in dramatizing the dastardly deeds of the black "criminal element." Instead, J. Thomas Hewin, a pro-park attorney who accompanied Mitchell, tried to enlighten Mayor Ainslie that although "these people may tell you one thing, Your honor[,] . . . the real reason some of the colored people oppose the park is because they believe that if you have a public park in the colored section, you will segregate them . . . and exclude them from the other parks of the city."[87] Mayor Ainslie vehemently denied that any of the promoters intended to ban blacks from other city parks but suggested that one could assume "a natural segregation" may lead people to patronize the facilities nearest to their homes.[88]

Hewin and his colleagues believed this claim and saw more benefits than drawbacks in supporting this rare city-supported effort to improve African American residential areas. Mitchell as well had faith in the promises of whites, arguing that "liberal minded, public-spirited white citizens are interesting themselves in the improvement of our civic conditions and this action is not taken from a mercenary or selfish standpoint" and that those, namely Stokes, who worked against these efforts were in fact hurting black Richmonders.[89] He asserted that there was no basis to believe a public park would be segregated because it was "virtually a public street" and, furthermore, that "there is no need of any 'Jim-Crow' park or any park exclusively for us. The very fact that the park is established will bring colored people to it and relieve the congestion in the other parks of the city. Colored people of this city do not force themselves upon the white people."[90]

The white media's reaction to the debate hinted that the pro-park African American leaders were too quick to dismiss the probability of further segregation. Although the *Richmond News Leader* in early August 1913 still denied that a new park would result in the extension of Jim Crow laws, an editorial on the issue threatened that the infighting among black factions would "likely result in no park whatever for the colored people of this city and the exclusion of Negroes from the present parks of the city," berating the race for not appreciating the "wondrous spirit of cooperation with the white people, who are their friends and earnestly wish to help them by giving them a park all their own."[91] Although it enthusiastically supported a "separate" park for African Americans, the *Richmond News Leader* reiterated that "the allegation that this park project is for the purpose of further segregating the Negro" was "baseless."[92]

By the fall of 1913, the discord between the two African American factions meant little. White activists continued to insist on the necessity of bestowing through their benevolence a park upon black Richmonders, yet their concern only amounted to endless talk and never resulted in any actual parks being built. Two years later, in July 1915, the white Business Men's Club again revitalized the idea of building a park within Jackson Ward, between Duval and Baker Streets, for "the exclusive use of Negroes."[93] This time African Americans offered little protest, realizing that their input would only be dismissed and that promises of a park, even if desired by blacks, were unlikely to be fulfilled. By that time, police had begun to enforce segregation in the city's public parks even though no official statue had been passed by the city council. In the fall of 1915, city police arrested Mr. E. B. Wallace, a young black Virginia Union University student, for sitting in a park located in one of Richmond's white residential sections. Wallace was informed that "niggers were not allowed in the park" and fined eleven dollars.[94]

As the case of the park demonstrated, whites were unsure of the eventual extent of segregation and, instead, molded the system in a rather ad hoc manner. In Virginia, white paternalists used benevolence as a justification for reworking and redefining Jim Crow. These whites believed a lack of adequate recreational facilities in Richmond was contributing to the supposed immorality of the black race by leading blacks to seek refuge in bars and dance halls rather than the healthy, fresh air of a public park. Indeed, the city had several parks, but the underlying, though usually unspoken, concern of white reformers was their desire to remove African Americans from their own recreational areas and ensure the sanctity of white space. Thus, they became obsessed with the idea of an African American park, seeing it as an ideal opportunity to prove their benevolence while also extending Jim Crow. Some black leaders, like Stokes, saw through the paternalistic rhetoric to the true intent of the plan. The ensuing controversy did not stop the expansion of segregation but only further restricted African American rights. Although the black parks were not built, the intentions of whites were well served. Debates over issues such as the park and also the Immanuel Church helped to set the eventual boundaries of Jim Crow in Virginia. While the park fiasco demonstrated the gradual process of molding and justifying segregation, the church case illustrated the bureaucratic red tape and confusion whites faced in implementing their new racial order.

The trouble began in 1913 when the white congregation of the Immanuel Baptist Church, located on the corner of Fifth and Leigh Streets, decided to sell its building to an African American congregation (the highest bidder). The white church members wanted to rid themselves of the property in what they feared was becoming an increasingly black neighborhood and relocate out to the suburbs. The sale appeared to be proceeding smoothly to the benefit of both white and black congregations when nearby white residents attempted to halt the transfer with petitions and legal action.[95] The controversy stemmed from confusion as to how to interpret the Vonderlehr ordinance. Leigh Street, where the entrance was located, was unquestionably white. Yet, Fifth Street was less easy to define. If individual family residences on Fifth Street, including apartments, were counted rather than dwellings, then the block would be labeled black, and, if not, then the block was white. Also, few agreed on the exact boundaries of the block in question, because a side street, Jackson, entered but did not intersect Fifth Street. If Jackson Street was determined to mark a separation, then the block was white. If not, then the block was legally black.[96]

In response to the controversy, City Councilman Jones pushed through an amendment defining blocks as demarcated by partial side streets, yet confusion still prevailed.[97] The technicalities and mechanics of separating blacks and whites were overwhelming to homeowners, real estate agents, and city officials. What had seemed a relatively easy task became extremely difficult, with endless red tape and unclear guidelines for color classification. Richmond, for years, had been deeply interracial, with whites and blacks occupying different areas of the same neighborhoods. Few knew where, literally, to draw the color line.

Black Richmonders were bitter over the irony that their self-professed Christian white neighbors were barring them from a house of worship. "Is it possible," the *Richmond Planet* queried, "that the well-meaning white people of this community who profess to be interested in the progress and success of our people, have no influence to stop this constant agitation . . . against one of the kindliest races of people on the face of the globe?"[98] While black Richmonders protested that the holdup of the sale would hurt whites as well as blacks, their efforts did little to influence white public opinion against the residential segregation ordinances.[99] In the late fall of 1914, after numerous legal appeals and decisions, the sale was permitted, and the white Immanuel Baptist Church minister, William Thomas Hall, congratulated his congregation's generosity in recognizing that "the condition of the Negro in this city is as bad as that of the immigrants in New York, and . . . they should have a proper place in which to live and grow.[100] A few other whites agreed with Hall, including Rev. Walter Bowie, Mary Munford's nephew and a frequent participant in interracial reforms, who pronounced that "the negro race should be permitted to expand out of its present crowded and, in many instance unsanitary surroundings."[101]

The black congregation of what then became the Leigh St. Memorial M.E. Church bought the property and changed the entrance at considerable expense from Leigh Street to Fifth Street to comply with segregation ordinances. But upon officially taking possession of the church in the early spring of 1915, Rev. E. M.

Mitchell and several trustees were promptly arrested in violation of the Vonder-lehr ordinance.[102] Although the courts wavered over whether Reverend Mitchell and the others were guilty and liable for the one-hundred-dollar fine, the congre-gation was barred from using the church that it had purchased for twenty-one thousand dollars, not including the cost of moving the entrance.[103] Three years later, in November 1917, the building remained vacant.[104]

News of the injustice of the church controversy spread outside Richmond's city limits and was commented upon by national publications. In addition to the NAACP's *Crisis,* the *Nation* mocked the city's stance on the Immanuel Church case: "This reaction in Richmond, when it desires to be known as a progressive, up-to-date city, recalls . . . these words of a distinguished native [of England] as a reason for the marked loyalty to Great Britain in its present distress: 'When I think of the large Negro populations in the United States, as the republican Americans treat and govern them, I thank God that I am a British subject.'"[105] The negative press embarrassed white Virginians who were so concerned with their self-image. Rather than relenting on residential segregation, however, they instead dismissed much of the criticism as the ill-informed views of radical extremists. White poli-ticians in Richmond convinced themselves of the righteousness of their new leg-islation, justifying that these statutes only fostered African American autonomy and uplift.

Although white Richmonders still sought to promote the city as a haven for ra-cial harmony, the poor conditions of black neighborhoods, exacerbated by the res-idential segregation ordinance, became difficult to ignore. "When a citizen cannot control his own property when he pays taxes and is denied the protection of the government," John Mitchell Jr. protested bitterly, "then the line between freedom and slavery is only imaginary, for serfdom and tyranny are the twin evils which we suffer."[106] Mitchell believed that whites had finally pushed the boundaries of con-stitutionality too far, reluctant to concede that discrimination against blacks had reached an unprecedented and unimagined level. The situation was not as bad as some writing letters to the *Richmond Planet* from northern cities feared, with African Americans barred from even walking on certain city streets. However, residential segregation did desperately hurt black neighborhoods by forcing overcrowding and enabling rent gouging.[107]

With these difficulties, the already momentous health and sanitary problems worsened. In August 1915, Theodore W. Jones, a black resident of the besieged Fifth Street, sent a brutally honest critique of the situation to local newspapers. "While I lay claim to having no authority to speak for other than myself," Jones began, "I do feel that I bespeak the sentiment of the overwhelming majority of my race in Virginia . . . that our civic pride in Richmond is as great and as staunch as is the civic pride of any race."[108] Jones, however, was deeply bitter about African American living conditions within his beloved city:

> Here we are cooped up like fowl in a crate, packed together like sardines in a box, piled upon each other like rats in a trap. . . . In this Ward our children must be born, eke out a miserable existence and finally die. For this congested unsanitary and unhealthy manner of housing we must pay fifty percent more rent than other people pay. . . . It is obvious that God in his goodness has bounteously supplied Richmond with air, space and land, available for every human need, so that none may suffer or die because there is not enough for all and to spare. Hence on the one hand these natural resources are infinitely greater than is the demand of the white people for them. On the other hand there is a great unsatisfied need, a crying want due to a neglect of the council to widen the segregated district for our people.[109]

Jones resented the impediments that segregation forced upon his race and demanded that whites recognize the basic human rights of African Americans to health and the opportunity to prosper.

White Virginians were not entirely deaf to these pleas. Paternalist reformers were concerned (and embarrassed) about the squalid conditions. Many of these whites had been against residential segregation, at its onset, as a supercilious insult to tradition. Yet, despite their qualms with the "rudeness" of unnecessarily extending de jure segregation, they did not speak openly against Jim Crow. Rather than seeing segregation at the root of these Progressive problems, they often blamed the deplorable situation on the failure of African American autonomy without proper white supervision. Apart from any sense of paternalistic benevolence, they were quick to understand the practical benefits of improving black neighborhoods. "Richmond [white] people," the *Richmond News Leader* appealed to its readers, "do not need to be reminded that a city which employs thousands of colored people as domestics, as operatives and as laborers cannot get the maximum return for wages paid unless these workers live decently."[110] Editor Bryan argued that a high death rate among blacks would not only decrease the labor pool but would lead to higher death rates among whites. "The cook or nurse who contracts tuberculosis," he explained "is not kept by any special Providence from infecting the mistress she serves or the infant she attends."[111] Many white activists, such as Munford and Cocke, strove to better these conditions and, in line with Progressive strategy, to force the city to increase its maintenance services in Jackson Ward and other black neighborhoods. Small improvements came through interracial cooperative projects. For example, the biracially founded Community House for Negro People helped to train black social workers by arranging affordable and convenient extension classes in social work for African Americans. This organization was fairly small in scope, and much of its work was usurped by the larger Richmond branch of the National Urban League. Many of the same individuals were officers in both organizations, like Mary Munford and Maggie Lena Walker. Primarily, the Community House for Colored People functioned as a central locale to hold community lectures, meetings, etc. as well as offered courses in reform work for African Americans, sometimes in conjunction with Virginia Union.[112]

Unwilling to wait solely on this interracial work to improve conditions, the black residents of Richmond fought vehemently to prove the unconstitutionality of the Vonderlehr ordinance. As early as May 1912, almost a year after the passage of the statute, black Richmonders began their legal protests. One of the first cases was brought by the African American attorney William L. Royall on behalf of five blacks convicted under the statute. Royall argued that the segregation ordinance violated Section 1 of the Fourteenth Amendment to the U.S. Constitution. Despite the reassurances of white Assistant City Attorney Anderson that the "ordinance tended to the promotion of peace and happiness of both races," the court did not dismiss the charges out of hand.[113] Instead, this case marked the beginning of a long legal fight before a variety of courts.[114] More than two years later, in September 1914, opponents of the ordinance received a major setback when the ordinance was held valid by the Hustings Court of Richmond.[115] Judge Wells argued that residential segregation was "a legitimate police power for the general good of the community" and declared that he regarded "the law as thoroughly impartial and nondiscriminatory."[116] He based this decision primarily on the fact that the ordinance was worded to apply to both races, but as the *Richmond Planet* noted: "It does not matter if a white man is denied his privileges and immunities and a colored man is treated in the same manner. The law says that neither shall be denied these privileges and immunities, and because both are equally robbed of their rights, the mandate of the law is no less violated."[117]

Firmly believing the ordinance was unconstitutional, a group of African American lawyers carried the case to the Virginia Supreme Court of Appeals.[118] Upon losing, the NAACP along with local black attorneys chose the white attorney Alfred E. Cohen to lead their suit. Cohen joined forces with contingents from other states fighting similar segregation ordinances and filed an amicus curiae brief in a case against Louisville, Kentucky's ordinance (modeled upon Richmond's example) to be heard before the United States Supreme Court.[119] The Supreme Court heard this case, *Buchanan v. Warley*, in March 1917, almost six years after the passage of the Vonderlehr ordinance.[120] Black Richmonders joined together in the segregation fight and formed the locally organized Community Improvement League to fund Cohen's role in the case almost entirely through individual donations.[121] The white *Richmond Times-Dispatch* criticized the case, arguing that "our colored friends are making a serious mistake in continuing their fight against Richmond's segregation ordinances."[122] Not intimidated, the *Richmond Planet* only responded calmly that all "we ask is the right to live in peace and harmony with our white neighbors."[123] Turning the tables on whites' paternalistic references to the historical loyalty bonding the two races, the African American newspaper explained: "We may be making a mistake in contending for our constitutional rights, but those of us who were born upon the plantations of the old aristocrats and who played and romped with their children and studied our 'three R's' with the best type of humanity that GOD has ever created, will not falter in our onward march now for those rights and privilege to which we are justly entitled. . . . Mr. Editor, that segregation is unconstitutional, from any angle from which it is viewed."[124] African Americans hoped their references to the paternalistic relationship between the two races would remind whites of their promises of black autonomy and help them to recognize the extent to which residential segregation obliterated the pretense of that ideal.

In November 1917, the Supreme Court handed down its decision on the Louisville ordinance. Although the Court refused to overturn the 1896 *Plessy v. Ferguson* decision and declare segregation unconstitutional, the justices did agree that residential segregation ordinances infringed too closely on a citizen's personal property rights. Justice Day explained "that there exists a serious and difficult problem arising from a feeling of race hostility which the law is powerless to control and to which it must give a measure of consideration may be freely admitted. But its solution cannot be promoted by depriving citizens of their constitutional rights and privileges."[125] Black Virginians were ecstatic. Although the Louisville ordinance had been the lead test case, the decision would also apply to Richmond's Vonderlehr ordinance. The city's African American residents hoped that they could now expand into the racial border areas where many houses stood vacant because of legal restrictions. Hoping to quell white fears about black intrusion, the *Richmond Planet* urged its readers to "be conservative and not attempt to take undue advantage of this degree" and prove that "colored people in the South land have never intruded upon their white neighbors, but have suffered themselves to drift along and occupy houses that had been vouchsafed to them by white owners, who had chosen other parts of a city for their residences."[126]

Despite the momentous ruling, most black and white Richmonders did not believe it would substantially change the racial status quo in the city. Black activists hoped that many white people, especially those with whom they frequently worked on benevolent interracial causes, would see the justice of the Supreme Court's action and trust the intentions of their black neighbors. But realistically, they expected little to change. While whites were far from happy about the setback to their newest segregation policy, they believed that the current racial order would prevail. The *Richmond News Leader* reflected, "Richmond had little race trouble before it adopted the segregation ordinance and it will know how to protect itself."[127] Although whites feared that "the radical element of our Negro population" may misinterpret the Court's decision, they had faith that the city's "sensible Negro leaders" would understand that only the ordinance, not custom, had been upended.[128] The editor of the *Richmond News Leader* declared: "Race segregation is a fixed principle in the South. It rests not upon prejudice but upon a correct understanding of our peculiar problems."[129] Able to see the situation more clearly without the blinders of racial prejudice, Mitchell criticized his white colleagues for their faulty logic: "Because race segregation is a fixed principle does not imply that it is a fixed right principle. We are so mixed up now that we cannot tell 'which from [the] tother [*sic*].'. . . . *The segregation plan is a joke.*[130] While whites, convinced of their superiority, believed Jim Crow to be the "natural" and logical social order, African Americans understood the arbitrary separation of the races to be a cultural, political, and economical perversion of common sense.

The 1917 Supreme Court ruling changed little in the state of Virginia. Whites simply worked to stay ahead of the courts, amending and rewriting residential segregation ordinances frequently to meet the letter if not the spirit of the law. For example, in 1928 Richmond passed another Jim Crow ordinance that prohibited individuals from living next to each other who were not allowed to marry under the Racial Integrity Act of 1924. The law did not mention race, but its intent was clear. African Americans again waged a legal battle and won for a second time in 1930, when the United States Supreme Court ruled, in the *City of Richmond et al. v. Deans,* that "the right of the Negro race to purchase and live in homes of his choice in any part of American cities just like any other United States citizen" could not be infringed upon.[131] Although this decision clearly pronounced this practice to be unconstitutional, de facto Jim Crow and discriminatory real estate policies kept Richmond neighborhoods largely segregated throughout much of the twentieth century.

Councilman A. L. Vonderlehr was defeated when seeking reelection in 1914, but the legacy of his segregation ordinance not only marked boundaries of black and white neighborhoods in Richmond for most of the twentieth century but also stunted the city's economy and rate of urban growth.[132] By physically limiting the expansion of African American neighborhoods, the legislation stymied African American residential areas in the city. City managers compounded the problem by not providing adequate sewage, water, and street maintenance or cleaning services to these areas, preferring to spend public funds on white neighborhoods. In addition, these same whites maneuvered for the placement of most city dumps and crematories in black residential sections. Not surprisingly, health and sanitation concerns remained paramount. These conditions led elite African American leaders to reevaluate their emphasis on class over racial alliances. Despite white paternalists' willingness to cooperate with "better class" blacks, whites made no class exceptions when enforcing Jim Crow. Unlike earlier public transportation segregation laws, elite blacks could not simply distance themselves from discrimination. Instead, residential segregation diffused (though did not eradicate) class divisions among African Americans by forcing the wealthy and poor alike to live under shared inequities.

Against these odds and despite the broken promises, white and African American activists still sought to promote cooperation efforts between the races. They persisted as they had in the past because such initiatives remained the most promising means to improve inequitable conditions. Although African American leaders were wary of white promises, they continued to seek the goodwill of liberal-minded whites. Some believed that, over time, whites could be convinced that their black neighbors deserved better treatment because of their respectable behavior. Others simply hoped to make the best they could of a bad situation, believing that even unreliable white friends were of more use than race-baiting white haters of the African American race. Thus, some black leaders, like Giles Jackson, devoted enormous energy to cultivating white approval.

Jackson, born during the days of slavery, had long been a prominent public figure and lawyer in Richmond. He understood the advantages of playing into whites' stereotypes of a loyal but dim-witted "Sambo."[133] This policy brought Jackson power, because Virginia whites frequently turned to him first as the appointed (by whites and Jackson himself) leader of his race. Many African Americans resented Jackson's Uncle Tomism, but, regardless, his tireless activism for racial uplift could not be ignored. He subscribed to Booker T. Washington's example and believed that in order to fight discrimination, blacks must first prove their worthiness as individuals and as a race. Accordingly, in 1915, Jackson planned an extravagant show of African American progress since Emancipation in a national Negro Exposition to be held in Richmond. This event showcased the ongoing efforts of white and black leaders alike to stress interracial goodwill in an era of increasing racial strife.

Although the Negro Exposition of 1915 was an interracial endeavor from its inception, the project, unlike many others of its kind, was ultimately directed by African Americans. Beginning in 1914, Giles Jackson appealed to Congress for financial support for a national fair celebrating the progress of the black race in its first fifty years of freedom. Various legislators were skeptical that enough examples of success could be found to justify a large exposition, but Congress commended Jackson's proposal and appropriated fifty-five thousand dollars to offset some of the expenses. Black Virginians appreciated the weight of the task before them. "The colored people of Virginia as well as the whole colored race are now on trial,"

Giles Jackson. (Courtesy of the Virginia Historical Society)

the *Richmond Planet* pronounced; "If the celebration fails, the light of dishonor will fall not on one colored man, or set of colored men, but on all."[134] In the face of this enormous pressure, Jackson went about his plans. He procured promises to send exhibits from African American schools, businesses, and individuals across the nation and declared that the exposition would be held in Richmond in July 1915.[135]

This action by Jackson and the appropriation of funds were not without opposition among the African American community and white leaders. In particular, the Negro Civic Improvement League of Virginia came out against the plan, arguing not that the exposition was not a worthy endeavor but that it was a frivolous action when more immediate needs were going unfunded. In support of this viewpoint, a self-titled "White Taxpayer" wrote the *Richmond Times-Dispatch* in February 1914:

> The Civil League wisely points out to the General Assembly needs of the negro paramount to the holding of any expositions. Here are a few: Increased appropriation for Central State Hospital . . . the erection of building on the farm in Hanover . . . more money for the negro reformatory for boys . . . dormitories at the Virginia Normal and Industrial Institute . . . increased appropriation for the colored deaf, dumb, and blind school, increased appropriations for the negro elementary schools of the state, and the establishing of rural high schools for negroes, there being only one in the state; last, but not least an appropriation for the establishing of a tuberculosis sanatorium to save the negro from the ravages of the great white plague, which not only threatens his extinction, but which will eventually produce as great a death rather among our people as the negroes, as they are our cooks, house maids, nurses, butlers, coachmen, chauffeurs, office boys, waiters, and employes [*sic*] in hundreds of different ways.[136]

Yet the concerns of this anonymous letter writer and the Negro Civic Improvement League of Richmond were ultimately dismissed, and the plan for funding went forward.

Jackson, always a brilliant strategist in navigating racial interaction, understood that the fair's success depended in large part on whites' perceptions and involvement. First, he determined that Governor Stuart needed to make an executive proclamation "exhorting the general public to give moral and financial support to the enterprise launched in the interest of the negro race in America."[137] He prepared a statement in favor of the exposition and hand-delivered it to the governor. Jackson commented in a self-deprecating manner that he knew Governor Stuart would understand: "Yes, sir, your excellency, we would mightily like for you to proclaim this proclamation. I composed and wrote it myself, and I haven't left anything out that ought to be in."[138] His tactics worked, and the governor accordingly issued an executive proclamation in June 1915.

Although it is unclear whether Stuart used the exact copy written for him by Jackson, he was effusive in his support, declaring that "the [white] people of Virginia and of the nation desire to encourage the negro in his efforts to solve his industrial problem, and . . . to this end the white people of this State have given their cordial support and encouragement to the enterprise." He praised the "friendly relations" between whites and African Americans in Virginia as "a source of gratification to both races" and traced this goodwill and "enduring bonds of friendship" to the "fidelity displayed by slaves during four years of [Civil] War."[139] The white editor of the *Richmond Times-Dispatch* also encouraged his readers to support the exposition, arguing that its setting in Richmond would illustrate that "nowhere in this country is the negro as a race better housed, better employed or more generally prosperous and contented than he is here in the old capital of the Confederacy."[140] Turning a blind eye toward the skyrocketing African American death rate and crippling residential segregation ordinances that were earning the city national criticism, the white editor believed the fair would instead demonstrate to northerners how wrong they were in their assumptions about how the city treated its black residents. Although this support was patronizing, it was also the advertising and goodwill that Jackson needed.

Giles Jackson also went straight to the leading white American at the time, President Woodrow Wilson, to ask for his commendation of the Negro Exposition. In this endeavor, leading white Virginians felt it was their responsibility to take a larger role in "helping Jackson." Although Wilson had already promised through correspondence to attend the July fair, a delegation of Virginians traveled to Washington, D.C., in early June 1915 to invite the president in person.[141] The group of prominent whites including Mayor George Ainslie, William M. Habilston, John Stewart Bryan, Harry M. Smith Jr., L. H. Kemp, and Henry Fairfax, along with Jackson, were met in the capital by Senator Thomas S. Martin and John Skelton Williams, comptroller of the currency, and escorted to the White House to meet with President Wilson.[142] After the invitation was extended, Giles Jackson, the only African American present, spoke as president of the Negro Exposition and delivered a small address, in response to which Wilson "expressed his thanks for the invitation to visit the capital of Virginia, and said it would afford him pleasure to address the negroes of the State."[143] Jackson was granted the privilege of accompanying the delegation and speaking to the president in recognition of his long history of accommodation to whites. Playing up as he always did his performance of black subservience, Jackson convinced whites to support him in his efforts to take his appeal to the most powerful man in America. Several weeks later, in early July, Wilson, according to the *Richmond Planet*'s coverage, issued a proclamation to encourage "the active interest of the nation in the exposition and trust that every facility will be extended to the leaders whose earnest work has made the undertaking possible."[144] Despite this favorable response, Wilson found various excuses throughout July and never attended the exposition.[145] However, the constant promise of his presence, as Jackson had counted, fueled white interest in the Negro Exposition throughout its duration.

Jackson personified the progress that he hoped to display in the exposition. Born into slavery in Goochland County on September 1853, Jackson was still a boy when he had to follow his master, Charles F. Dickerson, a Confederate cavalry colonel, into the Civil War as a body servant. Then, starting from nothing after the war, he worked to gain an education; first just to read and write and then eventually studying law under a Richmond attorney, William H. Beveridge. In November 1887, Jackson became the first black Virginian to be certified by the Virginia Supreme Court of Appeals. Not surprisingly given his path and age, Jackson became a great follower and supporter of Booker T. Washington. He stressed the importance of self-uplift—a goal he had worked so hard to achieve.[146]

Jackson was known as an accommodationist, and thus he rather easily succeeded in enlisting white support, in part because of his willingness to work behind the scenes and downplay the extent of his efforts. Although an educated man with years of experience as a lawyer and social leader, he chose to play the role dictated to him by racial mores and address whites with a deference that deftly hid his remarkable intelligence and unparalleled political skills. Asked by a reporter for the *Richmond Times-Dispatch* to describe the upcoming exposition, Jackson sighed dramatically and began his performance:

> Can I tell you anything about the big negro fair? Well, I reckon I can. I don't know anything about anything else right now. It is the subject of my thoughts by day and of my dreams by night. I tell you, boss, I wouldn't undertake such a proposition again for all the money on Main Street, as much as there is down there, and as well as a nigger loves money. *It's a big strain on a plain colored lawyer to have so much responsibility,* to keep so many odds and ends together, and to have to interview so many big white folks all over the country to make 'em think just like he does on the proposition that the niggers ought to have a big fair to show the folks what they have been doing since the s'render. *Take it from me, boss, to talk like you white folks, it's some job.*[147]

Although the reporter noted that Jackson did not appear as weary as he claimed and that "his robust physique showed no sign of weakening and his mental acumen seemed as acute as ever," he never questioned Jackson's deprecating manner.[148] The white reporter found Jackson charming and believable, unaware that

Jackson's exaggerated minstrel-like performance was designed as a larger joke on the white man's limited understanding.

Some African Americans believed Giles Jackson went too far in his "Uncle Tom" act before whites, but his manner was effective. By heartily playing into whites' own claims of racial harmony, Jackson put on the fair he wanted, designed to advertise African American advancements not only in industry (as whites encouraged) but also in arts, literature, and other areas of higher learning. He achieved this goal during a time when black Virginians daily faced new discriminations and did so with the support and financial backing of whites. Jackson hoped to exhibit the tremendous progress African Americans, including himself, had made in the years since Emancipation and provide evidence on a grand scale that his race had proven their worthiness as American citizens. The fair did fulfill Jackson's vision of a grandiose demonstration of African American uplift, but it only fueled whites' paternalistic sentimentality rather than encouraged them to reconsider their commitment to white supremacy.

The Negro Exposition proceeded according to Jackson's plans and was declared by white and black papers alike to be a success by all measures except for having a lower visitor turnout than expected. The large fair building held exhibits from across the country, demonstrating African American advances in every conceivable field of learning and industry.[149] The two-week extravaganza included several large parades, and the fairgrounds hosted a midway with the usual popular fair oddities and attractions. One evening even showcased a large pantomime featuring three hundred local schoolchildren in "The Answer to the Birth of a Nation," a visual demonstration of the progress of African Americans from their arrival as slaves in Jamestown to the new opportunities of the twentieth century. Keeping to Jackson's policy of white appeasement and respect for the Lost Cause, the pantomime depicted one idealized scene of happy slaves working the fields of a plantation but focused primarily on post-Emancipation advancements, particularly the opportunities of higher education and the refinements of black middle-class life.[150] These later scenes of modernity focused on the dynamics of African American homes and communities, offering a visual argument for the benefits of black autonomy.

Despite a spattering of grumbling by a few white Richmonders about the lack of financial success, whites were generally enthusiastically supportive of the fair.[151] Mayor Ainslie addressed the audience during the opening exercises, and whites visited frequently, not only on the specially designated "White Folks Day" but throughout the exposition's duration.[152] Whites wrote numerous letters of support to the daily newspapers and even encouraged white women to arrange for their black housekeepers to attend.[153] One white woman, Avis Barney Stewart, wife of the Presbyterian minister J. Calvin Stewart, declared that all Richmonders should "again urge all who are conscientiously laboring for the uplift of their race to show their interest by their attendance."[154]

Although Jackson intended the Negro Exposition of 1915 as a demonstration of African American uplift, self-help, and capability of autonomy, whites used the event as an opportunity to claim that any African American progress was the product of whites' paternalistic supervision. Regardless of the theory of segregation, many white Virginians had little use for black autonomy. They believed monitoring the lives of black Virginians to be necessary to the protection of both the black race and the white racial order. "The well-being of the colored population of this city is a matter of deep and intimate concern to the white race," explained the editor of the *Richmond Times-Dispatch:* "The Southern white man is the friend of the negro, both from sentimental considerations, bred of long association, and because of his perception of the fact that negro prosperity, negro health and negro happiness are related inevitably and inextricably to his own."[155] White paternalists supported African American uplift and enthusiastically joined interracial reform efforts but were extremely leery of black culture becoming too independent. They applauded the progress exhibited by the exposition but viewed the success to be, in large part, the result of white influence. The fair represented to whites more a testimony to their own moral guidance than a demonstration of the fruits of black autonomy. They encouraged the growth of a separate black space, but only if whites retained the ultimate authority.

Despite of false claims of racial harmony, black and white Virginians realized that the lives of the two races within the state, even under numerous segregation statutes, were intricately intertwined. African American leaders as well as many whites believed that cooperative interracial relations were essential to maintaining social order. Whites, with an eye toward the building and protection of segregation, believed their interest in black Virginians was the most efficient method to extend (in what they saw to be an inoffensive benevolent manner) white control over the supposedly insular black world. African American leaders sought to hold on to their diminishing rights by any means possible, hoping that friendly relations with whites would offer them some citizenship advantages or at least material gains for blacks. "The liberal minded white men of the Southland," John Mitchell Jr. explained, "must be encouraged in their efforts to aid us in our march forward. . . . God is on our side, but these kind of white folks can do much to better our condition before He gets to work punishing these agents of the Devil who are so active in this world of sin and sorrow."[156] Practicality necessitated alliances across the color line. Interracial cooperation attempted to camouflage a central contradiction of segregation; the system of white control allowed, at least in theory, a degree of black autonomy.

3

Public Welfare and the Segregated State

Richmond negroes are among the best and most law-abiding in the world. They suffer from the misconduct of the disreputable element, but in the main, they are prosperous, self-respecting and thrifty. Moreover, they are being decimated by disease and are suffering from the lack of medical attention. . . . Heart disease, bronchial complaints, and other ailments without number afflict them. From a purely selfish viewpoint, we must protect ourselves by caring for our Negroes; from a broad standpoint of humanity, we must give them better sanitation and abundant hospital facilities.

— Editorial, *Richmond News Leader,* 1913

RIDING THE Progressive wave, Virginia in the early twentieth century, like many other states, began to adopt new public welfare functions of the government. These initiatives encompassed issues such as child welfare and public health that had been primarily handled, if at all, by private charities. Virginians viewed these issues in racial terms that needed to be resolved in accordance with the politics of segregation. But these problems never adhered neatly to racial lines and clearly illustrated the extensive interconnection between black and white communities. Poor health and inadequate sanitation, although mostly prevalent in overcrowded African American neighborhoods, could not be neatly segregated. Many whites brought black domestic workers into their homes on a daily basis and had a personal stake in improving the living conditions of black Virginians. Apart from any assumed responsibility of noblesse oblige, whites desired to protect themselves from communicable diseases. Health and sanitation were frequent topics of discussion among Virginian activists along with other pressing concerns such as penal reforms and care of delinquent children — issues that became more urgent as Richmond, Norfolk, and other Virginia cities grew.[1] These problems did not hold to a color line, and, thus, interracial communication became essential in seeking answers and crafting effective state policy. Life-threatening issues forced white activists to move past nonbinding effusions of racial harmony and work together with black leaders for tangible solutions. With the shared goal of a healthier Virginia, black and white reformers worked together to build a segregated public welfare state.

One of the major figures in the public welfare initiatives in the state was Thomas Calhoun Walker. An African American born in 1862 and coming of age in the post–Civil War South, an era fraught with both dangers and opportunities, Walker had years of experience in effectively managing his interactions with "well-meaning" whites. Writing his memoirs in the mid-twentieth century, Walker shaped a past for himself similar to the one Booker T. Washington related in his *Up from Slavery*. For example, Walker stressed that from a young age, he placed enormous importance on education to ensure not only personal success but the advancement of the race as a whole. He told a dramatic story of how he ran away from home against the wishes of his father to attend Hampton Institute. Once there, he struggled for several years to both earn the money for tuition and also fulfill the educational prerequisites. Finally, he attended the school and was heavily influenced by his opportunity to study under Washington. Walker graduated in 1883 changed by his experience.[2] After becoming interested in racial uplift campaigns during his hard-won education at Hampton, Walker decided he could best help his race by obtaining a law degree and fighting for the rights of African Americans throughout the state. Without any accessible, nearby law school open to him, however, he decided to look instead for unconventional opportunities closer to home.

Determined to further his education, Walker appealed to Maj. Benjamin Bland, an elderly white lawyer and former Confederate soldier who lived near Walker. Aware that Bland would be hesitant to tutor an African American student, Walker began a roundabout campaign to secure his assistance. One afternoon, Walker walked by Bland's house and recognized his opening when he saw Bland, in lieu of his ill servant boy, out trying to cut wood. "Of course," Walker later recounted, "I stopped and offered to do this chore for him but he refused, saying he did not want any college man waiting on him."[3] Walker waited patiently, and, when Bland was too tired to finish, he took the axe from the white man and chopped a large box full of wood. He refused pay but instead spent the evening sitting in Bland's office discussing "race problems."[4] The following morning, Walker fed Bland's horse and then returned "without permission" in the afternoon to do more chores. Again, he refused pay but stayed for a long discussion with Bland. This continued for a week when, finally, in the midst of a comfortable chat, Walker "felt the time had come to say to him" that he wanted to study law.[5] Bland, grateful for Walker's humble help, gave him his extra law books and, likewise, refused payment. Walker then appealed to the elderly white man, saying "Major Bland,

Thomas C. Walker and his second wife, Ellen Young Walker, at
their home in Gloucester, Virginia. This photograph was taken
by Jackson Davis. (Jackson Davis Papers, Albert and Shirley
Small Special Collections Library, University of Virginia)

now that you have got the books for me, I don't know how to study them. Will you
give me a start?"[6] Bland happily agreed.

Walker convinced Major Bland to provide him with law books and tutor him
despite Bland's dislike of educated blacks. He achieved this by enacting a traditional role of African American subservience expected by whites and appealing to
the Confederate veteran's sense of paternalism. Knowing from the start what he

wanted to gain from the relationship, Walker first gained Bland's favor and then presented his ambition as an afterthought that he could only achieve with white aid and guidance. In this manner, Walker found the tutor he needed. Moreover, he received both the books and education for free because accepting payment would have offended Bland's sense of noblesse oblige and racial order. Walker knew perfectly the rules of racial decorum and manipulated them brilliantly. He studied with Bland for three years until the old major became too feeble to continue. Walker then successfully appealed to Gen. William B. Taliaferro, another white Confederate veteran, to continue his education.[7]

After years of study, Walker passed the bar examination in May 1887 and was certified to practice law in Virginia.[8] As a black man virtually alone in a white man's profession, Walker did not ignore his racial heritage but instead dedicated his life to African American uplift by becoming a leading reformer within the state. Throughout his long career, he preached the gospel of African American progress. He also stressed the utility of cooperating with whites. Although Walker was frustrated by constantly having to prove himself worthy as lawyer and capable of appearing before white courts, he valued the whites who had helped him. He worked frequently with white lawyers, particularly Taliaferro, and had white as well as African American clients.[9] By working within the framework of expected racial decorum, he built a remarkable career and refused to accept notions of African American inferiority. Walker encouraged other African Americans to not discount the opportunities that might be found in working with whites. In 1887, the evening after having won his first case, Walker went to visit Major Bland to discuss his experience. "He was so proud," Walker recalled, "that he actually put his arms around me and hugged me — he a southern major in the Confederate army and I born in slavery."[10] Although Walker romanticized his experience for his memoirs written late in life, his interactions with whites had undoubtedly proved fruitful. His accommodationist stance never curtailed his reformist fervor.

Walker, among other interracial activists, became integral in encouraging the white public and white officials to recognize the value of including African Americans in the state's Progressive public welfare initiatives. In terms of improving health and sanitation, the convincing was fairly easy, because liberal-minded white reformers could appeal rationally to whites' sense of self-preservation. Yet, these activists also argued that the state should assist not only white Virginians who were handicapped, mentally ill, destitute, elderly, or juvenile delinquents but African Americans as well. In the early twentieth century, when the role of state and national government was being redefined to encompass Progressive reforms, Virginian leaders, white and black, engaged in a debate about how to incorporate Jim

Crow ideals into the new order.[11] The Virginia Conference of Social Work was one the first forums for negotiating these concerns.

Around 1905, a number of white reformers, headed by Dr. Roy K. Flannagan, organized the Virginia Conference of Social Work to discuss and promote reform initiatives, especially those regarding the improvement of health conditions.[12] Thomas Walker saw the event as advantageous to black Virginians: "Walls of prejudice shut off all efforts to reach the causes of trouble. But now it seemed that there was at least recognition that something must be done lest worse befall us."[13] Although the Virginia Conference of Social Work was formed as an all-white organization, Flannagan, later the health officer for Richmond, encouraged the group to widen its scope to include African American concerns. He believed, in the words of Walker, that as long as black Virginians were "cut off from opportunities to learn about how to deal with health and other problems, just that long would we [black Virginians] be an increasing menace to the health of all."[14]

Two other influential whites, Joseph T. Mastin (Methodist minister and later secretary of the Board of Charities and Corrections) and Douglas S. Freeman (later editor of the *Richmond News Leader* and member of the Board of Charities and Corrections) supported Flannagan in his agenda. These three men tried to convince the white organization of the necessity of providing black Virginians with better information about disease prevention. In his memoirs, Walker recounted that Freeman insisted "the Negroes would be a great help if they were included in the conference and educated to co-operate intelligently in movements already being inaugurated by white people."[15] Many of the other white leaders, however, dismissed the idea that blacks would be "interested." Despite this initial reluctance, the Virginia Conference of Social Work began to hold informational meetings about problems of health and disease in various black churches to test African Americans' response. They were overwhelmed by the result. The meetings were packed, and numerous individuals had to be turned away. Blacks not only came to listen but surprised the white speakers with questions and requests for further information.

Although the Virginia Conference of Social Work officially only had white members, Flannagan dismissed the racially exclusive rules as a "benevolent mistake."[16] By 1911, he had successfully incorporated six black leaders into the organization. Two years later, Thomas Walker and Janie Porter Barrett served on the executive committee. Walker, Barrett, and others were active members of the organization, even though their participation was prohibited by the by-laws. This clause was not officially changed until sixteen years later. Walker, grateful for his opportunity to contribute, viewed the situation in a positive light, concluding that the slow inclusion gave him, Barrett, and others the opportunity to demonstrate their "interest and capacity." He defended Flannagan as a protective benefactor who believed "white people needed education as to the competency of their colored fellow citizens to help solve social menaces."[17] Despite the urgency of deteriorating health conditions, some white reformers viewed interracial cooperation as a gradual process that required time for African Americans to prove themselves capable and for whites to recognize the intellectual capacity of blacks to converse about complex issues. A number of these white Progressives were white supremacists as well as liberals who had to reconcile their racial preconceptions of African American inferiority with the practicality of joining forces with like-minded reformers across the color line. The scope of these cross-racial efforts was limited at times by whites' willingness to work with black leaders and their continued incomprehension of African Americans' aptitude and interest. African Americans like Walker and Barrett were forced to be patient and accommodating to white prejudices in order to be in positions to bring about change. Their patience, however, did not mean they were immune to the racial abuse.

Walker picked his battles carefully and sometimes stood up to whites. At an informational meeting of the Virginia Conference of Social Work held in an African American church in Richmond, Douglas Freeman (executive secretary of the Anti-Tuberculosis Association and director of publicity for the new State Board of Health) decided to lecture the primarily African American audience on their reluctance to pick up the "excellent leaflets and pamphlets on health subjects [that] had been published for free distribution."[18] Freeman chided the group for not caring more that statistics proved tuberculosis, typhoid fever, and other communicable diseases to be highest among the African American population. Irritated by these remarks and undaunted by the "many prominent white conference people" present, Thomas Walker stood up and challenged Freeman. He recounted his experience several days previous of going to the Board of Health's office to pick up some informational materials for distribution: "As I came up the steps someone in the office yelled out: 'Hello, Tom! What you doin' hyeh?' as if there were something funny about a Negro's wanting to learn about health. I said my people did not like to be treated that way in public or in private either and self-respecting Negroes just stayed away from the offices. It didn't do any good, I said, to publish things for Negroes if they were going to be insulted when they showed an interest in reading them."[19] Clearly, concisely, and ridiculing the office worker's poor grammar in contrast to his own impeccable diction, Walker claimed the right of African Americans not simply to be included in reforms but to be treated with respect. Furthermore, he explained that blacks' limited access to proper health care was, in part, a result of their reluctance to be placed in situations where they would be humiliated and treated as inferior. "I finished by saying," he concluded, "that when Negro mortality went down it would be because the manners of white health workers has gone up."[20]

Walker claimed that his remarks "of course . . . were all said in the friendliest way," but his act of defiance challenged the rules of proper racial decorum by openly questioning the assumed authority of white Virginian elites, who believed they had a nuanced understanding of African Americans. Freeman, speaking in a venue where he was a minority, was placed in the unusual position of having to defend himself to blacks. He had little choice but to claim regret for past lapses and promise to try his best to ensure that African Americans would receive better treatment in the future. Despite his willingness to accommodate to Jim Crow when necessary and acceptance of his status as an unofficial member of the Virginia Conference of Social Work, Walker forced the issue and demanded that African Americans be treated as courteously as whites. In these forums, whites like Freeman listened civilly to the concerns of black leaders, even if the incidents did little to change the white Virginians' overall treatment of African Americans.[21]

This unique inclusion of blacks in social welfare initiatives gained widespread attention. Activists from other states traveled to Virginia to witness firsthand the interracial cooperative work. The work was a learning process, and yet, Walker later remembered, it "began to expand and to become better organized as we went along feeling our way."[22] The members of the Virginia Conference of Social Work, however, were always handicapped by never having enough money to address all their concerns. Not surprisingly, African American projects were often the first to have their funding cut. Black activists in Virginia made considerable strides in including their agendas in state reform efforts but could not, despite their advances, ever make separate equal.

Activists, across the color line, believed that improved health conditions required cooperation toward new standards of cleanliness and health care. Accordingly, these men and women organized assorted "clean-up" initiatives. In 1914, for example, the Negro Organization Society (NOS) called for a General Clean-Up week from April 27 to May 2. John M. Gandy, the African American principal of the Petersburg Colored Normal School and executive secretary of the NOS, encouraged black preachers to spread the word across the state through special "health sermons" and to observe the cleaning period "agreed upon by the white people."[23] The following year in Richmond, the second week in May was designated by the mayor for citywide clean-up. In support, the *Richmond Times-Dispatch* noted that "the co-operation that these movements have received from citizens in all parts of the city attests public approval of them."[24] Although designed to encourage improvements on both sides of the color line, whites focused on these cleaning initiatives as opportunities to encourage better hygiene and housekeeping within black neighborhoods.[25] Failing to see segregation's role in creating poor health conditions, many white Virginians simply assumed African Americans' life-styles and innate natures were the cause. Rather than blaming city administrators for refusing to provide black neighborhoods with adequate municipal services such as sanitation and street cleaning, whites reasoned that African Americans, without the aid of whites, simply did not practice sanitation and were content living in overcrowded, disease-infested areas.

Fear of tuberculosis pervaded both black and white communities. Prevention and help for sufferers of the disease were frequent topics of discussion. Care un-der quarantine was the common treatment for tuberculosis, but few sanatoriums existed for African American patients. Accordingly, white and black activists alike argued that adequate facilities for black Virginians were needed. White reformers believed such places were necessary to fulfill the rather empty promise of separate but equal. African Americans, on the other hand, accepted the proposal of segre-gated sanatoriums in the hope of securing whites' financial and political influence in fighting the deadly disease. In 1914, the *Richmond Times-Dispatch* printed an ar-ticle entitled "Richmond's Duty to the Negro and Herself," lamenting that while nearby Pine Camp had been converted into a "haven of refuge" for working-class white sufferers of tuberculosis, the "city makes practically no provision" for indi-gent blacks. "There is gross inhumanity," the article argued, "in permitting the ravages of tuberculosis among this dependent race, without every effort being made to check its spread, but there is something more. For the white people of Richmond to neglect this constant menace, always at their doors, involves many of the elements of self-destruction."[26]

Apart from a plethora of humanitarian appeals, whites had a selfish interest in these reforms because they knew that the disease did not respect the color line and feared that the black contagion would be brought into white homes. Undeniably, African Americans suffered from tuberculosis at a far greater rate than whites. In 1914, statistics released by the State Board of Health revealed that 270.5 of every 100,000 blacks in Virginia died of consumption, as opposed to 119.5 whites. In the state's ten largest cities, the death rate was slightly lower for whites, 102.2, while considerably higher for blacks, 316.5.[27] Deeming African Americans an inferior race, many whites blamed the increased numbers among blacks on their supposed substandard sanitary and moral habits. Regardless, white reformers agreed with black leaders that an African American sanatorium was needed to stem the tide of contagion.

The African American–run Negro Organization Society and the primarily white Virginia Anti-Tuberculosis Association cooperated to establish the needed institution. For years, the Negro Organization Society had worked to improve the housing and health conditions of blacks through lectures, health bulletins, and other programs, such as supporting the Clean-Up movement.[28] In 1914, however, they focused attention on the tuberculosis epidemic after Miss Agnes D. Randolph, a white reformer and executive secretary of the Virginia Anti-Tuberculosis Association, addressed a meeting of the NOS and described how her organization had spearheaded an effort to establish a sanatorium for black patients.[29] Together the two organizations began a fund-raising campaign that included selling Red Cross Christmas Seals. White women from prominent Virginian families headed the effort for the Virginia Anti-Tuberculosis Association. In 1915, these women, including Janet Randolph (wife of Norman V. Randolph), the author Kate Langley Bosher, Avis Barney Stewart, and Francis Scott, among others in addition to Agnes Randolph, headed a statewide letter-writing initiative to elicit contributions.[30]

News of these efforts was advertised in both white and African American newspapers. As a measure of support for the proposed facility, the Board of Charities and Corrections resolved that "this work promises alleviation from suffering and the prevention of death . . . [and] the spread of this disease in a way that deserves the hearty co-operation of the citizens of the State."[31] In 1917, to encourage greater awareness of the disease, the Richmond Anti-Tuberculosis Association declared a "Tuberculosis Day" on the fourth Sunday in April and organized myriad lectures throughout the city. The group worked with a committee of African American leaders, including Ora. B. Stokes and Miss Adela F. Ruffin, to arrange events within black neighborhoods.[32] Finally, on April 22, 1918, in Burkeville, Virginia, the Piedmont Sanatorium opened its doors for black tuberculosis patients. The second state-sponsored sanatorium in Virginia, the institution catered only to African American sufferers of the disease. The white director, H. G. Carter, reflected, "It is up to the white man who controls his destiny to see that he [the Negro] gets the proper treatment when sick; for the sake of humanity first, from an economic point of view second and for his own sake and that of his family if he sees no other reason."[33]

All these numerous efforts played a role, yet the Board of Charities and Corrections, more than any other organization in Virginia, determined how Jim Crow would be implemented in the new public welfare state. It transformed private acts of interracial cooperation into governmental policy. In March 1908, the General Assembly created the board (forerunner to the Virginia Department of Public Welfare) to help restore Virginia's image as an innovative leader rather than a reactionary follower.[34] In the words of the historian of the board, Arthur James, white Progressives hoped the new venture would address concerns about Virginia's "unprivileged classes — those who for one reason or another were not able to provide for themselves, and those who needed the protection of the state."[35] Board members understood that many difficulties would hamper their efforts, foremost being the widespread poverty, destitution, and poor health conditions plaguing the state, particularly in African American communities. In the words of one member, their work "seemed all but helpless," with "one-third of the population consisting of Negroes" whose poverty illustrated the need for "fundamental changes in the economy and government of the State."[36]

The board, an outgrowth of the state's involvement in the National Conference of Charities and Corrections, sought to update, regulate, and reform the state's health care and correctional facilities, as well as charitable organizations such as orphanages and maternity homes. The historian and board member Arthur James recalled that the organizers, reminiscent of an era when Virginia had been "one of the leaders in social thought at the time of the formation and development of the Union," had argued that new approaches were needed within the state to solve the modern problems of the twentieth century.[37] Charged by the General Assembly with "the general supervision of charitable and correctional activities, state and local," as well as with developing an investigative study and educational campaign of statewide physical and mental health concerns, the board defined and molded one of the state's first sustained ventures into public welfare and broke ground by opening meetings to all races.[38]

The Board of Charities and Corrections had an open-door policy in terms of sex as well as race. Women often participated in meetings, and though no African American woman ever became an official board member, several white women held that distinction.[39] Although this interracial cooperation work occurred in the public and male sphere, nearly half of the individuals involved were women. This liberal inclusion of females stemmed from the desire among white reformers to segregate by sex as well as race in the belief that rehabilitation could only be achieved through categorization and separation. The white board members believed that individuals could not be reformed until separated into proper categories — the deaf and blind from the insane, the insane from the criminal, blacks from whites, men from women. Accordingly, women tended to manage charities that catered either exclusively to women, such as maternity houses and female reformatories, or that could be classified under maternal responsibilities, primarily orphanages and other child-centered initiatives. A number of white and black women founded and managed institutions of these types. In the 1910s, the board began to appoint female parole officers, white and African American, assigned exclusively to work with female parolees of their own race.[40] Segregationists' professions of "separate but equal" necessitated Virginia women's inclusion in cross-racial reform efforts.

While they never debated the eradication of segregation as one of those needed changes, the white board members fervently believed it was their Christian obligation to bring about modern Progressive reforms and include African Americans in new state-supported services. Some of the more liberal white board members, such as the secretary Joseph T. Mastin, argued that although black Virginians were second-class citizens, they were still citizens who paid taxes and had a right to receive a fair share (as determined by whites like himself) of governmental aid. The politics of expanding public welfare programs were intricately connected in Virginia and throughout the South with the simultaneous process of creating segregation. While African Americans in some southern states were, for the most part, simply left out of these developments, Virginian leaders across the color line openly discussed who would benefit from public welfare initiatives. The Board of Charities and Corrections, drawing on established interracial practices, became a forum where black and white reformers came together to negotiate these issues. This organization was not merely a token committee to discuss vague reform ideals. Responsible for overseeing numerous private charities as well as public reformatories and corrections facilities, the Board of Charities and Corrections had real power to bring about change. In 1908, the year of the board's founding, the cost of government in Virginia was about $6 million, and a little over $1 million, or one-sixth of these expenditures, was appropriated to the public welfare institutions under the board's supervision.[41] In a very public and visible manner, the Board of Charities and Corrections molded the course of segregation and Progressivism in Virginia.[42]

The board, as well, illustrated an important change that was occurring in terms of charity and social welfare. In the late nineteenth century, the majority of welfare-aimed organizations in Virginia (and most of the United States) were private charity-minded clubs, church groups, fraternal organizations, or other like groups. In the commonwealth, several major charity efforts were Lost Cause–motivated mothers', soldiers', and widows' programs of the United Daughters of the Confederacy. This type of aid focused much more on relief than on seeking solutions for the causes of poverty, and the organizations delivering the aid often blamed the poor for their circumstances.[43] Around the turn of the twentieth century, this approach began to change and slowly be replaced by charity organization societies that focused more on planned and larger-scale efforts than on a haphazard giving of alms. As with most change in Virginia, this transition was balked at by some who viewed these new groups as impersonal and less in touch. As the Progressive movement reached Virginia, these reformers brought yet another stage in social welfare. As the historian Elna Green noted, "Virginia's twentieth-century political leadership has been famously—even infamously—conservative, and historians have frequently stressed how essentially conservative its progressives were as well."[44] Change was not swift in Progressive Era Virginia, but gradual.

The new charity organization societies format began to prevail in the early decades of the twentieth century, yet the leaders of these organizations were relatively wary of social welfare progressivism because they distrusted governmental involvement — a concern particularly strong in the Lost Cause–dominated South. Regardless, the Virginia state government (like state governments across the country) became increasingly involved in social welfare programs. The Board of Charities and Corrections was a product of this transition — reflecting the interests and influence of private charity organization societies to make recommendations to the General Assembly on these myriad groups and adequate appropriations. The board grew in power as the state increasingly took over the work once fully in the realm of private charities. Perhaps more than anyone else, Dr. Joseph T. Mastin helped oversee this transition.[45]

As secretary of the organization for more than a decade, Mastin, a white Methodist minister, organized the board with evangelical fever into an effective vehicle of reform that shaped, for better and worse, Virginia's public health and correctional policies until its absorption into the Department of Public Welfare in 1922.[46] The General Assembly authorized the board to supervise state and local charitable and correctional facilities and initiatives. In this capacity, the group studied numerous public welfare concerns including mental health care, tuberculosis treatment, maternity care, juvenile reformation, and placement of abandoned or neglected children.[47] The board visited facilities across the state, checked for signs of misconduct, and then served as an advocate to the General Assembly for increased funding to organizations deemed worthy. These responsibilities led the board to contemplate the implications of enacting public welfare reform in a Jim Crow society.

The early work of the board was closely controlled by Mastin, who was a dynamic figure in early public social welfare in Virginia. Born in May 1855, Mastin did not have a charmed childhood. His father died when he was only four, and his mother subsequently lost most of the small estate in a family conflict over the inheritance. She later scraped together the money to send her son to Randolph Macon College, yet money lost in a bank failure prevented his graduation. Instead, he worked as a traveling Methodist minister, becoming increasingly concerned about social problems facing the state.[48] Described by the historian Samuel C. Shepherd as lean and tall with a "thick brown mustache and a serious countenance," Mastin believed his social work to be part of his mission as a Christian and fervently felt that the Gospel of Luke as "the best thing . . . [written] about the story of social work."[49]

Joseph Mastin. (From Lafferty, *Sketches and Portraits of the Virginia Conference*)

The board developed simultaneously with the culture of segregation in Virginia. As reformers, Mastin and others believed, perhaps naively, that separate could be equal and hoped to use their positions of power to mold Jim Crow into their idealistic vision. They defended their decision to cooperate with African American leaders not as an attempt to undermine the region's new racial structure but as necessary in making segregation work. They believed their welfare work was essential to ensuring a racially harmonious future, in which all Virginians could lead more productive and well-informed lives within their appointed social realms. The white board members foresaw their own limitations reaching into African American communities and developed a dialogue with black leaders in order to diagnose social problems and then offer their own (white) expertise in ameliorating these concerns. In turn, African Americans helped to determine their race's participation in and access to reforms by actively working with whites rather than solely having whites advocate on their behalf. The board provided a forum not only for discussion but also for oversight to ensure that African American and white charitable institutions and associations were fulfilling their stated purpose. In this manner, Mastin and other white board members hoped to use their power to strengthen Jim Crow.

These individuals, members of some of Virginia's most prominent white families and descendants of slaveholders, saw their work to be a natural extension of the "ethos of paternalism" instilled in them as children and reinforced by Lost Cause remembrance.[50] Their positions with the Board of Charities and Corrections gave them the opportunity to reconcile their "Old South" ideals with their "New South" goals. They believed fervently in the sentiment expressed by Henry Grady, the quintessential "New South" promoter from Georgia, when he proclaimed in regard to the descendants of his family's enslaved men and women, "May God forget my people if ever my people forget them!"[51] Paternalism held on in Virginia long after it had dwindled in other southern states. In a state where vigilante or mob violence (outside of the bounds of the legal system) was relatively uncommon, white Virginians stressed the importance of paternalism in solving the "race problem" rather than overt violence. They chose this more peaceful method of managing white supremacy, not because they were less racist but because they found it more effective and more in line with their Christian beliefs. Mastin and his fellow board members hoped to implement these paternalistic ideals into state policy, believing this to be the most efficient method to not only conduct personal relations but also structure governmental administration. By extending key public welfare reforms to black Virginians, these white reformers sought to ensure the longevity of the white-directed social order.

The Board of Charities and Corrections became a unique venue to frankly discuss the problems and needs of all Virginians across the color line. It became one of the only public organizations of its type to encourage such open dialogue between the races. Although the members of the board were always white (both male and female), associates and occasional employees were frequently African American. These included longtime committee member Thomas C. Walker and also Emma Bailey, a social worker employed to assist with the overwhelming child welfare caseload. Never state-appointed board members, Walker and Bailey, along with a number of others, were accredited agents of the board who fulfilled similar duties to Mastin and his colleagues. Although without the prestige and political clout of the official white board members, Walker and Bailey were often more directly involved with the organization's daily operations. Although some individuals, such as Secretary Mastin, did work on board business on nearly a full-time basis, others were essentially figureheads of prominent Virginian families who appeared when required to fulfill their civic duty. Racial diversity was common at these gatherings as various groups appealed to the board for assistance, financial or otherwise, for numerous welfare causes throughout the state.

Mastin and the white board members generally accepted the principles of segregation to be central to their building of a modern Progressive public welfare state. They engaged African Americans like Walker and Bailey to help oversee black institutions and charities. In 1918, when the General Assembly, upon the recommendation of the Board of Charities and Corrections, provided in Chapter 349 for the expansion of parole services throughout the state, the board jumped at the opportunity to appoint a number of African American probation officers to handle black parolees. These individuals included Ora Brown Stokes and W. H. Sharps in Richmond, W. B. Jennings in Portsmouth, Mrs. I. N. Paey and Estelle Tate in Norfolk, Rev. L. L. Downing and Lawrence Franklin in Roanoke, and Rev. J. T. Jordan in Suffolk.[52] Mastin's insistence on adhering to Jim Crow ideals ironically aided a handful of black Virginians by creating new governmental positions in fields previously closed to their race.

The Board of Charities and Corrections stressed the need to extend racial segregation at any cost. In 1908, Jim Crow statutes across Virginia applied primarily to public transportation. White reformers, however, believed that health, correctional, and reformatory facilities would be more efficient and successful if segregation were implemented. After one unsatisfactory inspection of the Prince Edward County jail and almshouse in January 1910, Mastin chided the clerk, Horace Adams, on the conditions. Upon inspection of the building designated as a pauper house, Mastin found that not only were the rooms dirty, but "the colored and white, male and female, were gathered in the same rooms." As a result of this disregard for the ideals of segregation, Mastin reported the institution to be in poor condition.[53] Nine years later, Mastin was still frustrated by the lack of segregation in some of the state's convict camps. He complained: "Public sentiment, especially in the South, is very pronounced as to the separation of the races. Yet we force white men who have been convicted of slight offenses, some of who are held for nonpayment of fines, to associate in intimate terms with the colored criminal, to work in the same group, to eat and sleep in the same tents with practically no separation. . . . We recommend the adoption throughout the prison system of a classification of prisoners with reference not only to race but to physical, mental, and moral conditions."[54] Casting a harsh light on his declared racial goodwill, Mastin believed that even white criminals deserved the "dignity" of segregation.

Despite white Virginians' professed dedication to segregation, Mastin had to prod the state relentlessly to extend Jim Crow into mental hospitals, jails, and reformatories. The battles had less to do with the principles than cost. Legislators were concerned about the increased expenses and were not very sympathetic about the conditions facing African American criminals, juvenile delinquents, and mental patients. The General Assembly was forced to listen to Mastin, however, because they worried that any lapses in racial decorum, even behind prison walls, could create bad publicity and make public officials, like themselves, vulnerable to defeat. By encouraging the legislature to consider the rights of white criminals and mental patients, Mastin also quietly secured provisions for the better care of African American criminals and mental patients. Problematically, these divisions entailed increased costs for separate facilities. Additional funding for the four state mental hospitals (three white and one black) became necessary as Mastin oversaw the transfer of numbers of mentally ill prisoners in jails to health care facilities. The board members believed that proper segregation according to racial, gender, physical, and mental characteristics was well worth the added expense. Separation, they argued, brought peace and order to their envisioned modern and Progressive Virginia.

Segregation ultimately resulted in inferior conditions for African Americans, but the Board of Charities and Corrections along with individual activists, like Thomas Walker, attempted to alleviate some of the inequity by extending state services to black Virginians. For example, Central State Hospital had the reputation of being one of the most efficiently run in Virginia. Founded during Reconstruction in Richmond in 1868 as Central Lunatic Asylum, the facility was the first mental hospital for African Americans not only in the state but in the country. It relocated to Petersburg in 1885, where it was renamed Central State Hospital. Dr. William Drewry, a nationally renowned white doctor and alienist, ran the hospital as superintendent from 1896 to 1924. In 1910, Drewry was elected president of the

American Psychiatric Association.[55] Despite offers to move to one of the state's three white facilities, along with a higher salary, Drewry chose to dedicate his career to improving Central State. Under his guidance, the facility became one of the first in the country to modernize its care of the mentally ill by discarding all physical restraints (irons, cages, straitjackets, etc.).[56] The white mental hospitals gradually adopted the innovations first implemented at Central State Hospital.

The success of Central State illustrated the efforts of the Board of Charities and Corrections to enact its vision of segregation as the key to improving the welfare of all citizens — black or white, rich or destitute, sane or mentally ill. Yet, despite these efforts, the pursuit of parallel equality was futile. When choices had to be made, services for whites were always the priority. While Progressive reformers congratulated themselves on the success of some black institutions, they faced criticism when the white public learned of the comparative circumstances. For example, when various tales of medical mix-ups, mismanagement, and fund misappropriations at the white Eastern Hospital in Williamsburg erupted into a scandal in 1906, the relative conditions of Central State were brought into the investigation. "When the testimony was at its height," the *Richmond Planet* lamented, "the poor Negro had to be dragged into it, if only by comparison and the result of this was to show that the inmates of the colored hospital at Petersburg are better treated than those of the white institution at Williamsburg."[57] Activists, black and white, had to deal not only with the question of whether or how separate could be made equitable but also public white backlash if African American initiatives were too outwardly successful. Although most white Virginians approved of the goals of interracial cooperation and the ideal of noblesse oblige, they were quick to resent any suggestion of reforms benefiting blacks over whites. Regardless of some white board members' personal desires to make separate equal, they were agents of the state and had to answer not only to public sentiment but to the governor and General Assembly as well.

Race became a central consideration of the members of the Board of Charities and Corrections in carrying out their work. In a climate of racial suspicion and growing segregation, board members had to evaluate the racial implications of every charity and institution they oversaw. They delegated and discussed segregation on a daily basis, recommending racial policies in the state's penitentiaries, reformatories, orphanages, and numerous other facilities. While the General Assembly and local governments passed Jim Crow laws, the Board of Charities and Corrections worked perhaps more than any other state organization to apply segregation to the rudimentary facets of a modern society. Every action taken by the board was studied through a racial lens to determine not only its feasibility and application but also the white public's reaction. But the white board members found that compliance to white Virginia's standards of racial propriety was not always congruent with effective management policies.

In 1913, race became the central contention in a controversy at the Virginia Home and Industrial School for Girls, the white girls' reformatory in Bon Air, Virginia. The school had a long history of bad relations with its neighbors. Incidences of escaped girls, riots, rock throwing, and other vandalism contributed to the facility's reputation as a poorly managed den of immorality. By 1913, however, the situation had improved with the employment of an African American laborer, Beverly Banks, who supervised the girls during their fieldwork. He developed a good rapport with the inmates and served as a stabilizing force and "a great protection to the Home" as his presence kept male "visitors" at a distance from the farm.[58] Yet, the trouble began when a girl with a long history of disruptive behavior escaped the facility. She was quickly found and detained by state authorities, but her actions had long-lasting consequences. When attempting to ease her punishment, the girl complained of the injustice and impropriety of having a black overseer. Word of her accusations soon reached Governor William Hodges Mann. In response, Mann ordered the Board of Charities and Corrections to account for the situation.[59]

Mastin headed an investigation into the incident. Speaking for the board, he stated, "We are of the opinion that the feeling which called for complaints to your Excellency had its origin in the employment on the farm in the capacity of general assistant of a negro named Beverly Banks."[60] Mastin and others interviewed numerous witnesses including some young female inmates as well as the matron, Mrs. M. M. Light. He found that "the officers of the home, the matron and the inmates expressed the utmost confidence in the integrity of this negro" and that no evidence could be found that he had "violated the trust imposed in him or had taken the slightest advantage of the girls under his charge."[61] Regardless, the board determined that Banks's position of "virtual control of these unfortunate girls" during their hours spent in field labor was unacceptable and against the standards of proper racial decorum.[62] They had no problem with Banks working closely with the white matron, Light, but feared that his unsupervised interaction with young white girls of questionable morality might result in improper sexual liaisons. The fact that Banks was well liked and credited with a sterling reputation was immaterial. The color of his skin disqualified him for the position. Censuring the actions of the white officers of the home, Mastin concluded, "We feel that proper race sentiment would have forbidden the employment of a negro in such a capacity and we are convinced that in so doing the Board made a mistake."[63]

The Board of Charities and Corrections caved in to the white newspapers' and politicians' denunciations of Banks, without consideration of how his removal would affect the long-term stability of the institution. Thus, the board promptly ordered the reformatory's administration to fire Banks despite the lack of any evidence of wrongdoing and set a new policy against employing any African American men in the future. In his place, they hired a white man, W. H. Turpin. African Americans were outraged. John Mitchell, editor of the *Richmond Planet*, exclaimed, "We cannot understand how Virginians of this type and calibre [*sic*] can bow to the prejudices of the age . . . and discharge not only a colored man who has stood the test and whose record is as white and as pure as the Winter's snow, but also all other colored people."[64] Contrary to the rules of racial propriety, the majority of the white reformatory girls protested the loss of Banks, insisting that he had never done anything to offend and had provided a needed sense of security to the facility. They remained loyal to Banks and, outraged at his dismissal, soon drove Turpin away. Turpin reluctantly came back only to be beaten by the inmates (the "helpless" girls whom the white leaders were trying to protect), forced into a wagon, and left soaking in pouring rain miles away from the institution. He refused to return a second time. The aggression of the girls proved that white women were not all the delicate and sheltered individuals stereotyped by white southerners and also contradicted the belief that white girls should "naturally" feel more protected by a white man than by a black one.[65]

Although the board had decreed that no more African Americans would be hired by the Bon Air reformatory, they were forced to recant because of pressure from the school leaders and allow the administrators to rehire Banks, among others, though only in the extremely limited positions of day laborer with little contact (and none unsupervised) with the inmates. But the behavioral problems of the institution again degenerated. Unable to restore order, the trustees of the Home and Industrial School for Girls (many of whom were also involved with the Board of Charities and Corrections) faced legal charges brought against them by the residents of Bon Air for "maintaining a common nuisance."[66] Although Mastin and other white board members worked diligently to extend segregation in public health and reformatory institutions across Virginia, they occasionally found, as in the white girls' reformatory, that racial decorum and effective management did not always coincide. Throughout the board's existence, white members worked to negotiate on a case-by-case basis how to successfully shape segregation in a manner fair to both races as well as financially and administratively beneficial. Moreover, they had to justify these policies to a reactionary white public.

The Board of Charities and Corrections frequently felt the pressure of public criticism over the money and attention they directed toward African American concerns, most particularly the care of delinquent or orphaned black children.

Throughout the 1910s and 1920s, the biggest and most time-consuming challenge the board faced was their care of orphans and other juvenile dependents of the state.[67] The work was wrought with racial implications. While the Children's Home Society of Virginia, a privately funded organization, helped to place many white children, black children were often left in inadequate state facilities, usually local prisons. In 1910, whites operated twenty-five orphanages throughout Virginia catering to about 1,800 white children, but African Americans had only four small homes caring for around seventy children. To compound the problem, African American juvenile dependents of the state always outnumbered whites. The escalating poverty among black Virginians along with the racist tendency of white policemen to single out African American children and take them into custody for minor offenses, among other factors such as the greater number of private white charitable orphanages, led to a consistently higher number of black than white children being committed to the board's custody each year. Mastin believed that "much of the help [for black dependents] must come from the state" and spent enormous time and resources in caring for these children.[68]

The placement of African American children became a major responsibility for the board. In 1916, 756 of the 929 juveniles committed to the board's care were black.[69] Despite the fact that African Americans were statistically a minority in Virginia, throughout the 1910s, courts and judges consistently placed more black than white juvenile dependents in the care of the Board of Charities and Corrections. In response, the white newspapers and politicians spoke out against the board's seeming preference for black children, envisioning white children left starving in cold, dark alleys because of the board's favoritism for black children. Over the years, the board continually faced this criticism and struggled with their inability to adequately justify this practice to white Virginians. Some years, judges deliberately committed only black children to the care of the board because white children could be helped elsewhere and the board's resources were already overtaxed.[70] "This is a dangerous policy and we believe deserves much consideration," Miss Gay Shepperson of the Children's Bureau (an outgrowth of the Board of Charities and Corrections) warned in 1926; already they had faced the "criticism of the Board [for] caring for colored dependents in preference to white."[71] Nevertheless, Mastin and his board continued their struggle to aid and find homes for the state's orphans and declared delinquents, regardless of their skin color.

Although they defended the necessity of caring for all of Virginia's juvenile dependents, board members had different racial standards as to what constituted acceptable care. Mastin believed that the best solution for dependent children was to place them in "proper" private homes rather than public institutions.[72] Although the board did not record details about these children, many of these individuals were probably not actual orphans with no living parents. Instead, Virginia courts followed the prevailing practice of the time for declaring troubled youth as dependents of the state, blaming delinquency on the economic and racial family background or being raised by a single mother.[73] Many truly orphaned African Americans, in fact, were never committed to state care and instead were informally taken in and raised by neighbors and extended family.[74] Although many of the African American youth who found themselves in the custody of the board were guilty of only minor infractions that would have been ignored if they were white, Mastin and his counterparts argued that it was their moral duty to "save" these individuals and, thus, determined to put them into board-approved foster homes that would teach not only morality and hard work but also racial etiquette. This decision stemmed in part from the belief that private families provided a more Christian upbringing than did institutions but also from the lower cost to the board of placing a child placed in a foster home.

In the early years of the board, home placement was conducted in a random, haphazard manner. Although white children were always put in white homes, the board experimented with placing black children in white homes, hoping to solve not only the concern of juvenile dependents but also the ever-present "servant problem." Minutes from a July 1911 meeting proclaimed that "the experiments have, so far, proven remarkably successful and every indication goes to show that we will be able to supply Virginia families, who may need servants, by placing our own delinquent children with them."[75] This policy was plagued with difficulties. Interestingly, the board cited one of their success stories as Carrie Cook, an African American youth who was placed with the white family of Robert E. Payne of Remington, Virginia. Cook "was mad at something one day and the barn was found afire. Again something crossed her and one of the family members happened to go upstairs and found that the mattress on one of the beds [was] afire." Despite these obvious conflicts, the family kept Carrie because Mrs. Payne needed "help."[76] Whites cared about securing inexpensive black domestic help in addition to nurturing troubled youth. African American children, unlike their white counterparts, were more often seen as economic commodities to be trained for a life of service rather than as neglected children in need of emotional support. In response, the black reformer Thomas C. Walker worked to change the white board's practice of placing black children with white families as servants.

Surviving historical accounts tell dramatically different versions of Walker's decision to join forces with the Board of Charities and Corrections and, in particular, Dr. Joseph Mastin. According to the official white historian (and member) of the board, Arthur James, Mastin believed that black children should only be placed in African American homes. James claimed that Mastin always disliked the practice of putting black juveniles into white homes for both reasons of racial propriety and for fear that white families would misuse the children. James recounted that Mastin, concerned about the welfare of these children, convinced Walker to work with him.[77] Walker's autobiography, on the other hand, offers a different perspective. In his memoirs, Walker delineated carefully the gradual process through which he became a leading advocate in the state for juveniles' rights. Walker's story is one of African American agency in the midst of one the most staunchly white supremacist arenas of Jim Crow Virginia — state bureaucracy.

Although involved in numerous black uplift causes, Thomas Walker dedicated much of his time to Virginia's troubled African American youth. In a distinctly paternalist manner, Walker believed these black children, judged delinquent by the courts, must be saved from the blight of their background. Around 1910, Walker first became involved with juvenile reforms. His work began in earnest with a tour of a Richmond jail to witness the situation firsthand. In that facility, he found thirteen young African American boys living under unsanitary conditions and in the same area as older, hardened criminals. Outraged, he appealed to a number of his white colleagues including the attorney Henry Pollard, Judge Crutchfield, and Judge Richardson, demanding that the thirteen boys be released into his custody. When told that no precedent of such an action existed, Walker countered, "You know that when you white folks haven't got a law you need, you just make one."[78] He soon left Richmond with the thirteen boys. Within a few days, he used his networks within Gloucester County's black communities to place all the children in private homes.[79] These thirteen were only the first of hundreds of children he eventually aided.

These events convinced Walker of the need to streamline the legal process in order to reach a greater number of children. Thus, he sought out Dr. Joseph T. Mastin, an old acquaintance (through Walker's legal career and work in temperance campaigns) and newly appointed leader of the Board of Charities and Corrections. Walker praised Mastin as "one of the best friends our race ever had" as well as "my good friend and co-worker."[80] The two allies, drawing particularly on Walker's legal training, worked together to draft a child welfare law.[81] With the help of other white advocates recruited by Mastin, the law passed the General Assembly in 1912, stipulating that "any child adjudged dependent or delinquent by a court might be committed to the Board and the Board might place the child in either an institution or private home."[82] In the first year, Walker and Mastin worked together to place 142 black children in private African American homes.

Grateful for his assistance, Mastin appointed Walker as an official, accredited agent of the board. The secretary, however, assumed Walker did not need any compensation apart from the black man's assumed appreciation at being included.

Supporting himself through his law career, Walker worked diligently, without receiving any pay apart from partial reimbursement of his travel expenses.[83] Despite
his dedication to the work, Walker could not do the work alone. Thus, with Mastin's help, the board appealed to the General Assembly and secured additional
funding in 1918—a four-thousand-dollar annual appropriation—to aid in the children's work. Recognizing that a salaried employee was needed, Mastin used some
of the money to hire the social worker Emma Bailey to help Walker by performing
the day-to-day casework of supervising, visiting, and, when necessary, investigating the care of black children in foster homes.[84] As a black woman, Bailey was paid
a pittance despite her dedication and heavy workload, a salary that barely covered
her living expenses. As a longtime agent of the Board of Charities and Corrections
and later the Children's Bureau, Emma Bailey, by 1926, earned only nine hundred
dollars a year for her work investigating cases and visiting homes. She was paid
significantly less than her white counterparts. In 1926, Miss Gay Shepperson, director of the Children's Bureau, requested a raise of sixty dollars a year for Bailey.
"She has been with the Board many years," Shepperson pleaded; "I know that she
can hardly meet her expenses in her home and this small amount of money is not
sufficient to affect our budget one way or another."[85] No evidence suggests that
Bailey ever received this raise. Mastin believed it was important to include African
Americans in new state public welfare services, but, like most white Virginians, he
did not challenge the practice of paying African Americans less than whites.

Although the hiring of Bailey and the increased appropriation helped, the growing number of African American state dependents convinced Thomas Walker that
more aid was necessary. Realizing he would receive only limited help from the
white legislature and even his supporter Mastin, Walker turned to a traditional
center of black communities—local African American schools. Drawing on this
resource, Walker organized through his associations with the Hampton Institute
and the Negro Organization Society a network of African American supervisors of
rural schools across the state. These eighteen officials became integral in assisting
Walker in identifying Virginia's black children in need and placing them in approved homes (financially stable, Christian, two-parent families).[86] The board paid
the Negro Organization Society fifty-five dollars a month to help screen and in-
spect potential foster homes as well as provide quarterly reports to the board.[87] As
an agent of the Board of Charities and Corrections, Walker developed this efficient
procedure to reach as many African American children as possible throughout the
state. In a paternalistic attitude similar to that of Mastin, Walker believed that this
process not only saved many children from the vices of their own poverty-stricken
(and single-mother) backgrounds but also encouraged racial pride and confidence
in foster families.[88]

Thomas Walker and three of the hundreds of children he helped
through the State Board of Charities and Corrections. An unidentified
county jail is seen in the background. (Jackson Davis Papers, Albert and
Shirley Small Special Collections Library, University of Virginia)

Arthur James later described Walker as an "able lieutenant for the difficult
task of extending public welfare services to the Negro in [an] effective, intelligent,
and harmonious manner," yet Walker's memoir shows that he was more of an
innovative leader than an "able lieutenant."[89] Throughout the 1910s and into the
1920s, Mastin and Walker worked together successfully to place hundreds of children, white and black, with families across Virginia. James recalled with pride one
case where Walker and Mastin rescued a three-year-old African American girl
who had been born in the State Penitentiary and then forgotten by the system.
James reminisced that after being retrieved by the two men, "she was adopted by
a family in Gloucester City, grew up, married a respectable Negro, and became

the mother of a better class Negro family."[90] As elitists, Mastin and Walker alike assumed the girl would live a better, more moral life as a member of the respectable middle class, often stressing that environment was the key to curbing poverty and crime. Despite the quiet assumptions of white supremacy of Mastin and other white board members, the board's work with dependent black children illustrated their belief, in defiance of contemporary assertions, that African Americans were not innately inferior but capable of progress. They believed that nurture, with their "enlightened" help, would triumph over nature.[91] With Walker's influence, African American children were placed in African American homes where they at least had the opportunity to grow up within a family environment rather than be sentenced to a life of early servitude. "It is our policy," the board reported in 1925, "to place colored children in colored homes."[92] Walker had brought about this turnabout in policy.

Even with an efficient system of placement, Walker, Bailey, Mastin, and others struggled to find enough households deemed socially proper for placing the ever-growing number of children declared delinquent. "Many investigations prove to us that a large number of children are being taught at home or not at all and that they are being neglected in other respects," the organization reported in 1925; "Effort is made to find kindly families who will work sympathetically and intelligently with us. The number of these families is small. We need money to board children in order to find a higher type of family to suit the needs of children with special problems."[93] Bailey, in particular, spent countless hours investigating foster families and working to ensure that no black juvenile dependent would be neglected or exposed to "inappropriate" influences. But there were never enough acceptable and willing foster families (often defined in class terms). Influenced by the concern and dedication of the African Americans with whom they worked, the white board cared about the well-being and opportunities of these juvenile dependents rather than simply ridding themselves of unwanted charges. Mastin and Walker were committed to putting as many children as possible in private homes and only placed their charges in public detention homes when no other options were available.[94] Although the board members faced complaints about the preponderance of black juvenile dependents helped by the state in comparison to white dependents, they remained dedicated to helping Virginia's dependent children, across the color line, throughout its existence.

Escalating economic and social inequality necessitated greater cooperation between the white board and black leaders in Virginia. The board members, despite their self-assumed expertise, had a limited understanding of the state's black citizens and the problems they faced. They often declared their "approval of any effort that may be made for the uplift of the colored race" yet had little practical understanding of the means to work toward that goal.[95] Thus, the white reformers, by necessity, turned to established African American associations and leaders. They listened to proposals sent to them by black citizens, such as a plan from Rev. R. L. Peters to found an orphanage for black children in Stuart, Virginia. The board declared it was anxious to "assist in the effort to establish such an institution for colored children" yet ultimately denied certification to Reverend Peters following the investigation and advice of Walker.[96] While the board's interracial conferences usually resulted in the approval of black institutions, resolutions such as that with Reverend Peters were not uncommon. For example, in November 1915, the board denied approval to African American minister S. P. W. Drew's plan to establish an "old folks' home and orphanage" on a farm outside Richmond. The decision was only made "after conference with the leaders of the colored race in Virginia, the State Board of Charities and Corrections . . . [deemed] it unwise to lend its influence to the proposed scheme."[97] Although anxious to create and support as many reform agencies as possible in order to spread relief services throughout the state, black and white reformers held these welfare institutions to a high degree of scrutiny.

State regulation of Virginia's numerous private charitable institutions required frequent visitations by agents of the Board of Charities and Corrections (an almost impossible task with its few employees) as well as an open line of interracial communication. For example, when the board found irregularities in African American Rebecca Violet (Crawford) Phipps's management of the Christ Mission Workers' Working Woman's Industrial Home and Nursery, they turned to black community leaders for help in the inquiry.[98] In November 1918, Mastin, Peter Winston, and H. D. Coghill, all white agents of the board, began their investigation of the Richmond establishment, primarily a home for neglected black children, following an unsatisfactory visit in October by Coghill. Coghill had found the place unkempt and unsanitary, noting that the "bedrooms had not been swept or otherwise put in order for the day, and the odor was very bad in some of the rooms — the ones not ventilated by missing panes of glass."[99] Moreover, Mrs. Phipps did not appear to have kept any records books. Phipps stated that she had no time to keep accounts but instead merely took her tambourine downtown and begged for money when it was needed. Coghill found Phipps's behavior very unprofessional and potentially a dangerous influence for the children in her care.

For answers, the Board of Charities and Corrections turned to Ora B. Stokes, wife of the prominent black minister William Stokes (who led dissent in the public park controversy) and an activist in her own right. Phipps had told Winston that Stokes was the vice president of the Board of Christ Mission Workers, but Stokes denied this claim when questioned. She explained that she and several of the other black board members had left the Christ Mission Workers several years prior. At the time, Phipps had explained to Stokes that her services were no longer needed, because Avis Barney Stewart, a white minister's wife involved in interracial reform and Lost Cause efforts, became president of the charity.[100] Stokes stated that while she had "always been of the opinion that it was doing effective work," she had not "visited the institution for several years."[101] Stokes gave her testimony not only in the form of a letter but also in various interviews with Mastin, Coghill, and Emma D. Kessnich, a white agent for the board.

After many delays, Phipps finally appeared in person at a Board of Charities and Corrections meeting but failed to produce any further paperwork. Her cause was further hurt by Mastin and Janet Randolph, a white Richmonder, both testifying to seeing one of Phipps's charges, a young crippled boy, sitting in the street holding out his hat to beg for pennies. Upon testimony from both black and white reformers, the board decided that Phipps was "not a suitable person to have the custody of destitute children" because of her lack of housekeeping, her encouragement of the children to beg for money, and numerous financial irregularities including the potential embezzlement of collected funds. To deal with the situation, the board drew on the authority given it by the General Assembly and recommended to the Richmond Board of Health that Mrs. Phipps lose her license. The Board of Health responded by closing the institution.

Although the Phipps case was not particularly unusual in its particularities, the amount of time and effort the Board of Charities and Corrections put into its investigation of a small African American children's home illustrates the white board's commitment to maintaining high standards for black as well as white institutions. Mastin and the other white board members did not view their responsibility to help neglected or delinquent African American children as an afterthought or secondary concern. They conducted numerous investigations of white charities that were also well documented, but, perhaps surprisingly given Virginia's climate of suppression and white supremacy, Mrs. Phipps was treated fairly in a similar manner to her white counterparts. She was given ample opportunity to speak for herself, appeal her case before the board, and take steps to correct the situation. Moreover, she was referred to politely with the title "Mrs." or by her full name, in the same manner as the board would have used for a white woman. The Phipps investigation was not a case of black versus white. Rather, Mastin, Coghill, and other whites sought the testimony of black leaders like Ora Stokes, whose many years in social work and status in the community made her a respected and unimpeachable witness. Although African American children's homes and other institutions were often handicapped by the lack of funds and resources as a result of the inequity of segregation, the Board of Charities and Corrections made a sincere attempt to include African Americans in the new public welfare state. This work never came close to eradicating racial inequity but did include blacks in Virginia in the discussion of Progressive reforms and the governmentalization of public welfare.

Through interracial cooperation, new public welfare reforms encouraged by Progressive leaders were extended into African American communities across Virginia. Black activists like Thomas Walker, Emma Bailey, and numerous others worked with white reformers to ensure that African Americans received some portion of the services offered by the ever-expanding state government. Although these black leaders protested the discriminatory nature of segregation, they, by necessity, knew that their best opportunity for achieving material gains was to work within the Jim Crow system and remind civic-minded whites of the promise of separate but equal. In this manner, they were able to free delinquent children wasting away in prisons and place them in more enlightened juvenile reformatories, find homes for troubled or orphaned children, provide proper sanatorium care for tuberculosis patients, establish a school for the state's deaf and blind children, and initiate numerous other initiatives to improve the lives of African Americans across the state.

Disregarding occasional criticism from white Virginians and politicians, board members and employees of its offshoot, the Children's Bureau, took pride in their achievements and sought aid to extend their work. The commissioner reported in 1925 that "the Board of Public Welfare in Virginia [the former Board of Charities and Corrections] . . . [was] the only public institution in the South that undertakes to handle extensively dependent, neglected and delinquent colored children."[102] As a result, the Child Welfare League of America, a national organization, worked to secure the board additional funding through philanthropic groups such as the Commonwealth Fund of New York. Dr. James Gregg of Hampton Institute and Thomas Walker as agent of the board lobbied for these grants to further their capabilities to place and supervise black children in foster homes as well as develop more extension services specifically targeting African American children. "All of us believe," the board reported, "that a plan of this sort thoroughly worked out can be used as a demonstration not only for the State of Virginia but for the whole South. The persons in the North interested whom we have been able to reach are enthusiastically in favor."[103] Interracial cooperation networks made public reforms in Virginia possible that were often neglected in other southern states. Through the Board of Charities and Corrections, black and white reformers across the state ensured that African Americans would at least be included in the new expanded public welfare state.

Despite these efforts, separate became increasingly unequal. Interracial cooperation could better the situation, but never in this pre–civil rights movement era address the crippling effects of segregation. Even the eternal optimist Thomas Walker, trained directly under Booker T. Washington during his days at Hampton, lamented that "our Jim Crow cars would have disappeared years ago if . . . [our] white friends had made such unobtrusive but persistent protest by riding them."[104] Walker and his colleagues realized that although their forays into interracial cooperation had substantially bettered certain public welfare conditions across the state, segregation had only strengthened as a result. Most of their white associates, despite their professions of friendship, showed little interest in attacking the root of many of these social problems—segregation. In fact, some of their declared friends, like Joseph Mastin, ultimately used cross-racial cooperative efforts to legitimate the existing racial hierarchy. Interracial public welfare initiatives offered opportunities and achieved some needed reforms in Virginia, but the work ultimately extended segregation into a new realm—state bureaucracy.

4

Women and Cooperation

The white women don't work for us, — they work with us.
— Maggie Lena Walker

IN THE FIRST three decades of twentieth-century Virginia, white and African American women frequently joined forces to confront social welfare concerns. The story of their efforts offers unique insight into the intricacies of the culture of segregation where white and black spaces were rarely clearly divided. The most common interaction across the color line occurred daily within the confines of white homes.[1] But the experiences of those women, black and white, who met in the public realm tell a different story. These individuals came together not in the traditional roles of mistress and maid but to address concrete problems of health, housing, and citizen welfare that became increasingly acute as the new century brought further urbanization and industrialization to the region. Interracial cooperation was motivated by separate agendas. White women desired to mold and strengthen the developing system of segregation in what they considered was a socially responsible manner.[2] African American women fought to retain what rights they could and claim a share of the state's limited public resources. Despite seemingly irreconcilable goals, white and black activists found it beneficial to cooperate on shared projects.

The career of Ora B. Stokes, wife of the Richmond minister William Stokes, offers one poignant example of how African American women in Virginia took advantage of the activism opportunities ironically created by segregation in order to combat increasing racial discrimination. Ora was born in 1882 in Chester, Virginia, but raised in Old Town Fredericksburg. Her father, Rev. James E. Brown, had been Booker T. Washington's first Sunday school teacher and highly valued education — a mind-set he instilled in his children. Ora proved to be a remarkable student and was at the top of her class at all the institutions she attended. Graduating from high school at the young age of thirteen as a medalist for highest grades every year, Ora went to the Virginia Normal Collegiate Institute in Petersburg. After graduating from that institution at the age of sixteen as a high performer and with a prize in oratory, she taught for two years at a school in Milford. On September 2, 1902, Ora married William Stokes, the prominent pastor of Ebenezer Baptist Church in Richmond. Although she became very involved in all aspects of his church, she also attended Hartshorn College (now part of Virginia Union University) and later took classes in sociology and anthropology at Chicago University. Stokes was a brilliant women who ironically had access to the extensive education that was denied to her wealthy white colleague Mary Munford.[3]

Stokes became involved in social causes at a young age, long before she met her reform-minded husband. At the young age of twelve, she organized her first temperance society. Throughout her life, she took on many different roles and projects. She worked twenty years as a probation officer with the Richmond juvenile court. She organized the National Protective League for Negro Girls and a local chapter of the Council of Colored Women, served as president of both the Southeastern Section of the National Association of Colored Women's Clubs and the Virginia Negro League of Women Voters. During World War I, she acted in a number of new roles as chairman of the Colored Woman's Section of the Council of Defense of Virginia, secretary of the Fifth Liberty Loan, and secretary of the Food Conservation, as well as field agent for the Virginia War History Commission, Negro Collaborators. In addition, she served as a regimental mother for Camp Lee and organized the Camp Fire Girls, known as the Regimental Sisters, at Camp Lee. These were just a few of her accomplishments and activities. Ora Stokes was a busy woman with a passion for service.[4]

Around 1911, Stokes, along with several other African American community activists, founded the Richmond Neighborhood Association to address the problems of poor African American girls. The organization created a sewing department to train young women in domestic employment skills and also opened a nursery for working mothers. Its motto, "Not Alms, but a Friend," encouraged destitute women to help themselves in order to build not only financial security but also self-esteem. Wanting to expand training opportunities for black women, Stokes turned to a white acquaintance, Orie Latham Hatcher, then head of the Virginia Bureau of Vocations for Women. Stokes convinced Hatcher to redirect that organization's focus to include the needs of blacks as well as whites. The result of this cooperative endeavor was the Home for Working Girls, a segregated organization for black girls. Stokes served as president. By 1921, the Richmond Neighborhood Association had more than 1,400 members and an excess of ten thousand dollars in property.

Stokes became well known throughout the state for her ability to communicate

Ora Brown Stokes. (From Caldwell, *History of the American Negro and His Institutions*)

with and for the underprivileged and often neglected members of society, as well as for her rapport with white activists. In 1917, Governor H. C. Stuart chose Stokes to represent Virginia at the National Conference of Charities and Corrections meeting in Indianapolis.[5] When the state Board of Charities and Corrections, in line with its segregationist views, convinced the General Assembly to hire black probation officers (both male and female), the board recommended Stokes in acknowledgment of her years of service. In 1918, she became one of Richmond's first African American probation officers, along with W. H. Tharpe.[6] The parolees under her guidance were all black females. By choosing to work with white segregationists for the expressed purpose of helping black women, Stokes found new opportunities and venues to carry out her own social career. These contacts offered her official sanction as well as occasional funding, which she utilized to carry out her own uplift programs within the African American community.

Stokes was not alone. Both men and women, white and African American, participated in this cross-racial activism, yet the fact that women composed approximately half of this group in the era before woman suffrage is remarkable. Men typically held the top positions in organizations connected directly or indirectly with cooperation work, such as the Virginia Board of Charities and Corrections or the Negro Organization Society, and ran the major state newspapers, such as the white *Richmond Times-Dispatch* or the African American *Richmond Planet*, that helped to shape the discussion of how race would structure southern society. Women, however, became equally involved, working across the color line to found charities, raise money, and lobby state institutions when necessary.[7] Although they typically followed societal rules of "proper" racial behavior, white and black women found it easier to work together because white society saw their interaction as a natural replication of the mistress/maid relationship with none of the sexual undertones that would have been present with black women working with white men, or far worse, black men working with white women. Elsa Barkley Brown's research on southern African American women and Virginian Maggie Lena Walker, in particular, outlines these women's strategies for reform, concluding that they acted out of race-specific "womanist" motivations.[8] A study of the cross-racial activism of black and white women, however, suggests that while African American women did act out of differing racial motivations than white women, their strategies and interests in terms of project goals contained more parallels than differences. Social reform work such as improved health care, sanitation, and child welfare fit within African American women's concern with racial uplift as well as white women's stated beliefs in noblesse oblige and maternalism.

The building of a Jim Crow culture stymied Virginia's social and economic development in countless ways, but, ironically, segregation created a public space where both white and African American female activists could gain influence and respectability. White progressives believed segregation and scientific classification of all citizens to be the most efficient methods of addressing social problems. They desired to broaden the definition of segregation, which they considered to be an effective modern reform, in order to organize all individuals into neatly controlled societal categories. In terms of social welfare initiatives, this meant dividing Virginians into four subsets: white men, white women, black men, and black women. Whenever possible, separate state institutions, particularly reformatories, were established for each group. Even in institutions that combined men and women (divided by race), the two sexes were separated and were administered under differing guidelines. In a state concerned with budget shortfalls, these divisions increased costs. Separating women from men, however, created opportunities for women interested in public welfare work. The segregation of races necessitated interracial communication to make the system function. Taking on seemingly nontraditional roles for women in a male-dominated realm, female reformers of both races claimed for themselves a unique feminine space for public work and interracial dialogue by supporting and promoting facilities and charities that served women.[9]

Women, white and African American, played central roles in the segregation of Virginia. The few but influential white women who became interested in addressing the problems of the African American communities typically did not desire to overthrow the social order or challenge white supremacy. Rather than seeking a dramatic overthrow of the social system, white activists wanted to maintain a dialogue between the races in order to recapture what they "remembered" as a history of peaceful racial harmony in Virginia. White women such as Mary Munford and Elizabeth Cocke, full of paternalistic fervor, went into African American communities looking for reforms needing their support. African American women pushed as well, identifying their own concerns before turning to Munford and her allies for financial and political assistance.[10] The negotiations between these white and African American women in debates over access to state resources also provided opportunities to discuss the daily realities of racial separation and helped shape the culture of segregation. The clearinghouse for much of this work in Virginia, as discussed in chapter 3, was the state Board of Charities and Corrections.

In addition to Stokes, Mary Munford and Janie Porter Barrett established themselves as two of the most prominent female reformers in Jim Crow Virginia. During the first half of the twentieth century, the two women, both separately and together, participated in countless social welfare initiatives. Munford and Barrett were well known by Virginians across the state, male and female, white and African American. Both women were considered members of the "better class" of their race. Mary Cooke Branch Munford, white, boasted a lineage connected with the most aristocratic of Virginia's old families. Janie Porter Barrett, African American, also grew up in a wealthy white home (in Georgia) but as the daughter of the family's housekeeper. Munford was a devotee of the Lost Cause and a fervent believer in the superior gentility of the Old Dominion. She carefully modeled herself on her father's image as a benevolent paternalist. Barrett also valued herself among the state's elites, relishing the fact that she used fine silver rather than tin forks like most of her neighbors. Yet unlike Munford, Barrett lived under the veil of discrimination and an increasingly restrictive culture of segregation. Although neither was representative of the average Virginian woman, each was a representative of her race and class. Black women elected Barrett the first president of the Virginia State Federation of Colored Women's Clubs.[11] Munford held offices in numerous organizations, including the Richmond Education Association, National Consumer League, and later the League of Women Voters. Both women brought credibility to any project they took up. Interracial efforts, particularly the founding of the Virginia Industrial School for Colored Girls, brought the two women together on a frequent basis.[12] They entered the work out of vastly different motivations: one inspired by the spirit of white paternalism and Progressivism, and the other by a desire to uplift her race. Yet both believed interracial cooperation was the best way to achieve their goals.

White and black women often held vastly different opinions on racial discrimination and the justice of segregation, but they found themselves with similar agendas when facing such concrete concerns as improving hospitals and promoting a cleaner city to cut the skyrocketing death rate among African Americans. In particular, they collaborated on issues concerning children and child care reforms. These white women did not routinely enter black neighborhoods and attempt to dictate "white" standards, unaware of what black women realistically needed to improve the health of their children. While this practice did occur in Virginia, cross-racial activism more often led to demonstrations of African American agency, not only within the black sphere but on the front line of racial interaction. Historians including Tera Hunter and Glenda Gilmore not only have documented the experiences and achievements of African American women but have also highlighted the "agency" or control they exerted over their own lives even under the oppressive restrictions of segregation.[13] This work has focused primarily on actions within black communities. A reconsideration of interracial cooperation, however, reveals evidence of African Americans' agency outside of the more comfortable enclave of black neighborhoods. Often black women spearheaded reforms based on their own assessments of needs and then sought the help of whites to fulfill their plans. For their part, white women joined such causes as long as they fit within their own understanding of a properly ordered society. In practical terms, the groups' contrasting motivations were of little relevance if the projects' goals fit their shared reformist vision.

The most prominent and successful interracial effort of Virginia women in the early twentieth century was the Virginia Industrial School for Colored Girls. Although Janie Porter Barrett initiated the fund-raising campaign and eventually became superintendent of the institution, the project would not have succeeded without interracial cooperation. Barrett sought to save young African American girls from a life of crime and poverty. And whites supported the venture not only to support the Progressive order of getting delinquent black girls off the streets or out of overcrowded jails but also because the institution proposed to train its inmates for domestic service, thus, in the eyes of whites, turning a social blight into a solution to the ever-present servant problem. Janie Barrett successfully opened and ran the school to the satisfaction of white and black activists by skillfully lobbying for white support while assuring black Virginians that the project would live up to their own uplift goals.[14]

Barrett was known throughout the state as a prominent African American reformer and club leader long before she conceived the idea of the Virginia Industrial

Janie Porter Barrett with her husband, Harris Barrett, and their children at home in Hampton, Virginia, in 1903. The photograph was taken at the time she ran her Locust Street Settlement. (Courtesy of Harvard Art Museums/Fogg Museum, Transfer from the Carpenter Center for the Visual Arts, Social Museum Collection, 3.2002.231.2)

Children playing in a sandbox at Janie Barrett's Locust Street
Settlement in Hampton, Virginia, in 1903. (Courtesy of Harvard
Art Museums/Fogg Museum, Transfer from the Carpenter Center
for the Visual Arts, Social Museum Collection, 3.2002.232.3)

School for Colored Girls. Although she first developed an interest in the work as
a student at Hampton Institute, she did not become actively involved in reform
efforts until after her marriage to Harris Barrett, a bookkeeper for Hampton, in
1889. The Barretts were not wealthy, but they were financially comfortable and
prominent members of the African American community in Hampton. Unlike
many married African American women, Janie Barrett did not need to work outside the home. Instead, she dedicated her life to social welfare reforms. Around
1890, Barrett founded a settlement house at her home in Hampton, Virginia,
which was the first of its kind in the state. She built the Locust Street Settlement
House in her own front yard as a center of community uplift. With the aid of
volunteers, Barrett provided child care for working families, taught the virtues
of domesticity and sanitation standards, and also held cultural and artistic programs. In addition to this pet project, she, in the words of the white reformer
Lily Hammond, "built a bridge between the races" by making friends with white
women living in Hampton and starting an interracial "Clean-Up" campaign.[15]

She participated in a variety of women's clubs, most prominently the Virginia State Federation of Colored Women's Clubs, which she helped to found and then served as president.[16] Her work with this latter organization took her across the state and allowed her to establish contacts with numerous white and black activists.

Barrett became deeply interested in the plight of abandoned or neglected children and determined that the state needed a reformatory school for delinquent black girls. Similar institutions already existed for white and black boys as well as white girls, yet state officials had little initiative or financial appropriations to begin a similar project for black girls. Such facilities were popular nationwide among Progressive reformers, who sought to remove troubled children from jails and offer them the opportunity for education and rehabilitation. In 1912, Barrett presented her idea at the biennial meeting of the National Association of Colored Women held that year in Hampton. At her request, committees and clubs across Virginia began to raise money for the project. Knowing the importance of influential supporters, Barrett enlisted the fund-raising skills of Maggie Lena Walker, the prominent African American banker and club leader in Richmond. In addition, she appealed for advice and funds from the white philanthropic Russell Sage Fund in New York.[17] Only months after her proposal, Barrett received promising support from both African American groups across the state and her northern white contacts.

Barrett realized, however, that white Virginians' approval of her reformatory was critical to its success; thus, in November 1912, in the midst of her fund-raising frenzy, she presented her plan to the Board of Charities and Corrections. Drawing upon Barrett's reputation as a dedicated social worker within the black community, particularly her work in Hampton, the board passed a resolution of support, pronouncing: "This Board wishes very heartily to commend the movement to establish a reform industrial school for colored girls. The present situation is one discreditable to the Commonwealth and unjust to our colored population, in that for want of an institution for the care of the delinquent colored girls, the Commonwealth is forced to commit these girls to jail, where they are subject to immoral influences and cannot hope for reform. We trust heartily that this condition will be changed and that an institution will be opened where these girls can be given a fair opportunity to reform and to lay the foundations for future usefulness."[18] The white board members recognized the advantages of assisting Barrett and the Virginia State Federation of Colored Women's Clubs of Virginia. Simply, their goals meshed. The proposed Virginia Industrial School for Colored Girls supported segregationist policies. Furthermore, the removal of these young women from jails would considerably reduce the board's caseload. The Board of Charities

Playground at the Virginia Industrial School, illustrating how overcrowded
the school became in the 1920s. (From Virginia Industrial School
for Colored Girls, *Pictorial Record of the Virginia Industrial School*)

and Corrections' commendation of Barrett's plan validated the project in the eyes
of many white activists.

Interracial cooperation became the key to the school's success. By 1913, Barrett's cause had widespread support from white and black individuals and associations across the state. She raised $5,300 and soon bought a 140-acre farm in
Peake's Turnout, Virginia, about eighteen miles outside of Richmond. To bring
the project to fruition, she assembled a board of trustees comprised of two leading
white clubwomen in Richmond (one of whom was Mary Munford), a well-known
white minister, a white businessman, and several African American community
leaders, including Maggie Walker. With the support of this prominent board of
trustees, the endorsement of the Board of Charities and Corrections, and, perhaps
most important, the legislative lobbying by the two well-connected white women,
the 1914 General Assembly granted an annual appropriation to the school of three
thousand dollars. Munford and the other white woman promised two thousand
dollars more annually.[19] Historical record has lost the name of this second white
woman, but from the description of a well-to-do white clubwoman from Richmond who was part of this interracial reform generation, it was most likely either
Martha McNeill or Elizabeth Cocke. McNeill is the more probable choice, considering that she worked with the school for years. Regardless of this unnamed

woman's identity, this widespread support from activists on both sides of the color line, the Virginia Industrial School for Colored Girls opened in January 1915, leading Barrett to declare that "we cannot do the best social welfare work unless, as in this school, the two races undertake it together."[20]

Although whites played a major role in ensuring the opening and later longevity of the institution, Barrett remained firmly in control. She became superintendent of the school in 1916 to stem protests from neighboring whites who declared that they would accept the institution only if it were under her "respectable" guidance. Initially, Barrett had made a point of resisting the position publicly, stressing the great sacrifice involved. She recalled that when one of her white female associates first proposed the idea, she exclaimed, "I, go to Peake! I, give up my pretty home to live in a dormitory and eat from thick plates with a tin fork?"[21] In fact, the 1915 death of her husband was probably the central factor in her decision to accept the position, for financial as well as altruistic reasons. Barrett, however, always insisted that her employment was solely an act of moral duty. She often reminded her white patrons of her sacrifice and worked to cultivate the image of herself as a "lady," a privilege typically reserved for white women. She demanded respect because of her decision to take on the responsibilities of the daily running of the school and stressed that it was a decision made out of civic duty, not necessity. Many whites recognized her dedication and piety and trusted her ability to shape the school into a beneficial institution. Barrett relied on this influence to retain the support of white patrons and develop friendly relations with the school's neighbors. Unlike the white girls' reformatory at Bon Air that frequently found itself engaged in lawsuits with surrounding residents, the Virginia Industrial School for Colored Girls was well liked by the black and white citizens of Peake's Turnout. When the state took over the organization a few years after its founding, no one questioned Barrett's management skills. She remained in charge of the daily running of the school and worked with, rather than for, the interracial board of trustees.[22] By behaving impeccably within and beyond the roles defined for black women by white society, Barrett cultivated the support from influential whites to run her institution under her own terms.

Barrett declared herself a "lady" to demonstrate her respectability while quietly defying white assertions of superiority. But this designation was also a product of class identification, identifying herself as a leader and an elite of her race. Very light-skinned, Barrett grew up in a wealthy white home in Georgia, treated not as the housekeeper's daughter (which she was) but as a pampered child among the family's white offspring. As Barrett grew older, her mother and the white mistress of the household fought over her future. Barrett, in fact, remained with the white family after her mother remarried. The white woman wanted her then former housekeeper to give up all rights and custody of her daughter, in order for Barrett to be sent north to school, where she could pass as white. Barrett's mother refused, sending her to Hampton Institute. Barrett frequently retold this tale of her childhood to cultivate and perpetuate her image of refinement and sacrifice as well as to illustrate her appreciation of white paternalism. As an adult, she placed enormous value on material luxuries, particularly china, silver, and fine linens, which she regarded as emblems of her privileged status. Although concerned about the needs of her community, Barrett never let her neighbors forget her good fortune. When living in Hampton, she sent meals to different poor families every Sunday on her finest china, expecting the dishes and accompanying silver utensils to be returned promptly and in good order.[23]

Barrett's race enabled her to identify with the underprivileged African American masses far better than her white counterparts. But like those white reformers, her activism stemmed in part from paternalistic benevolence, reinforcing a sense of social superiority. In quiet defiance of whites' core racial beliefs, Barrett felt she had more in common with the white women on her board of trustees than with the troubled young women sent to her school. She believed her status morally obligated her to cooperate with members of that "better class" of whites in order to help less fortunate members of her race. Thus, she concluded that the most important lessons her charges needed to learn were those that would teach them how to behave as proper "ladies," according to the standards of white society. By using a detailed honor system that offered a graduated system of rewards and privileges for good behavior, Barrett taught her charges, some of whom had committed egregious crimes, the values of virtuous womanhood that she upheld in her own life.[24] Barrett dedicated herself to helping these troubled young African American women out of a sense of class obligation and desire for control apart from her concern with racial solidarity.[25]

Barrett, along with the interracial board of trustees, wanted to prepare the students of the reformatory to assume a respectable "place" in segregated society upon their release. Thus, apart from providing a general education of reading, writing, and arithmetic, the institution focused on teaching the girls proper homemaking skills. For Munford and her white colleagues, this curriculum illustrated perfectly how their benevolent support of African American concerns bolstered their own ideals of a racially ordered society. They were not only saving neglected black girls but also training servants for white homes. Barrett cooperated and, in fact, encouraged this agenda because she believed it to be the most practical course of action to teach her charges to cope with the difficulties of living in a Jim Crow society that offered African American women few employment options apart from domestic service. Barrett foresaw some students using their training to one day manage, like she had, their own "proper" homes, but she acknowledged that most of them would be servants in white households. Although she was the daughter of a woman who spent her life keeping house for a white family, Barrett believed she had risen above that existence through money, marriage, and community service to establish herself as one of the "better class" and never entertained the idea of herself or her daughters working as domestic servants. However, she argued for the need for dignity and proper training for those less fortunate than herself. In alignment with Booker T. Washington's philosophy, she stressed the importance of hard work, polite behavior, and racial pride.[26] Barrett never approved of the limitations of Jim Crow, but she believed practicality demanded that individuals, at least outwardly, accept their place in society (in terms of both class and race) and find realistic means of survival. As such, she defined her place as an influential elite with the power and benevolence to assist in the uplift of the less fortunate black masses.

Given her upbringing, Barrett was not blind to the frequent incidences of poor treatment of domestic servants. Thus, she attempted to educate white women on employers' responsibilities to their employees. She stood up for the rights of her students despite the potential for white reprisal. "Such a terrible creature as I am thought to be," she once exclaimed, "You see, I must know where my children are going [once paroled], since until they are twenty-one they are under my care."[27] She demanded references from white employers as well as assurances that each of her girls would be provided a private bedroom inside the protection of the home with a bed properly equipped with linens and bedding, facilities for bathing, fixed hours, and the opportunity and encouragement to attend church. Moreover, Barrett explained: "I insist also that she have a wage. My girls are not to be paid in board and old clothes only."[28] She wanted them to have the opportunity to save their earnings and build better lives for themselves. "At first the women were angry at this," Barrett reflected; "they couldn't understand the demands I made upon them."[29] She successfully convinced these white women of the efficacy of her guidelines because these requirements fit nicely with whites' elitist concern with overseeing through proximity and influence the morality of social inferiors, and also, quite simply, because good maids were hard to find.

Barrett believed that the key to surviving segregation regardless of one's occupation or wealth was the ability to understand and work with whites. Although courageous in making demands, she always remained concerned with white public perceptions and proffered at least lip service to the subscribed racialized and gendered role assigned to her by societal conventions. Despite Barrett's tenacity and Maggie Lena Walker's outstanding fund-raising skills, the Virginia Industrial School for Colored Girls would never have achieved the success it did without the political and social connections of Mary Munford and the other whites on the board of trustees. They helped Barrett access a world of power denied to her by segregation, and she gave them credit for her success: "I could never have succeeded as I have in my demands, except that my Board has stood loyally back of me. Such wonderful white women!"[30] Such behavior enabled Barrett to pursue successfully her own agenda—a lesson she hoped to teach to her students. She attributed many of her charges' problems to their families' failure to teach them how to interact properly with whites. For example, Barrett blamed the infamous Virginia Christian case, in which a young black girl was executed for killing a white woman, on the girl's mother, who had instilled in her daughter the maxim, "Don't ever let a white woman touch you!"[31] Barrett argued that black women undoubtedly had the right to protect and defend themselves but sought to show her charges that racial cooperation was the safest path to follow in an increasingly inequitable and often violent world. She reminded the students of the debt they owed the patrons of the institution. One member of Barrett's staff later reflected, "We constantly told them of the good women (Negro and White) who were laboring for them and striving to have them help make the world better by having lived in it."[32] Barrett taught them the advantages of viewing white women as potential allies rather than certain adversaries.

The complex relationships between these white and African American women were marked by both mutual manipulation and respect. Although race remained a dividing factor, Barrett appreciated and valued Mary Munford, who remained on the school's board of trustees for many years. When Munford left the board in the mid-1920s for health reasons, Barrett confided: "I am heartbroken. I just cannot get over it, not having you on our Board, you who have meant so much to us through the years. . . . It is a real comfort to know that you will keep up your interest in our cause. Mrs. Munford, you have been a wonderful help to us through the years, for which I am very, very grateful."[33] Mary Ovington, a northern white woman prominent in the NAACP, stressed the importance of this interracial dynamic when reporting on the success of Barrett's reformatory. Ovington emphasized that although black women outnumbered white women on the institution's board of directors, the white women were "not figureheads but hard, devoted workers."[34] Although she privately disapproved of segregation and southern white women's expressions of white supremacy, Ovington praised their work, arguing that "too much credit cannot be given to the white women who first entered upon the work at the plea of the colored women, and who now hold their positions as appointees of the governor."[35] Munford gave not only her prominent name to Barrett's project, but her time and energy as well. Apart from the Virginia Industrial School for Colored Girls, Munford and Barrett served in numerous organizations together in the 1920s, including the Richmond Community House for Colored People, the Richmond Urban League, and the Commission on Interracial Cooperation. In spite of their social differences, the two worked closely together for over a decade. In fighting for similar social reforms, they developed a mutual appreciation.

Accustomed to a rather privileged life, Barrett never accepted white claims of African American inferiority. She understood and experienced the inequities of racial discrimination, but Barrett had full confidence in her own social prominence and accomplishments. She and her friend Maggie Lena Walker (also a trustee of the school who worked with Munford) believed their positions within the "better class" of African Americans led to shared interests with "better class" white women, even with Mary Cooke Branch Munford whose very name bespoke Virginia's white aristocracy. Barrett and Walker considered Munford their partner, not their benefactor. As Maggie Walker observed, "The white women don't work for us, — they work with us."[36] Barrett and her counterparts had an unshakable sense of their own respectability as southern women that defied white society's attempts to exclude them from the role of "ladies."

White women continued to take an active role in the school throughout its first decades of service. Another leading figure who worked closely with Barrett in the running of the school during its first years was Annie Moomaw Schmelz of Hampton, who served as chairman of the board of trustees and, later, board of managers for a number of years. Schmelz spent much of her life involved in interracial and educational reforms both in Virginia and in New York, where she moved in her later years. Born near Roanoke in September 1886 to family of considerable financial means, Schmelz learned from a young age to place a great value on education. She graduated from Hollins College and remained very active in the school's alumni group throughout her life. In 1904, Annie married Henry L. Schmelz, a widower, who was one of the most well-known and successful financiers in the state, serving as president of the Bank of Hampton and also president of the Virginia Bankers' Association. Although Henry had children from his first marriage, he and Annie never had any of their own. Instead, Annie devoted her life and employed much of her substantial means to social and political causes.[37] In addition to Annie, Henry L. Schmelz's business partner, Frank W. Darling, and his wife, Mollie, worked closely with Barrett, both serving in various positions on the board of managers. Frank acted for a number of years as treasurer. Darling was one of the richest men in all of Virginia in the early twentieth century, with his wealth deriving from both his career as a financier and his work as head of his family's business, J. S. Darling and Son, the third-largest oyster packer in the United States. Mollie, like Annie, devoted her life to social causes. Later, her granddaughter Ann Tormey, who grew up in their home, recalled fondly that many found Mollie to be "quite aggressive" because of her exuberance and crusade to share her family's wealth. Tormey remembered her grandmother welcoming anyone in to sit down and join them at dinner regardless of race.[38] Yet another member of this group who served on the board was Martha Chamberlayne Valentine Mc-Neill (sister-in-law of the leading suffragist Lila Valentine and also the probable unnamed fund-raising advocate mentioned earlier), who devoted much of her life as well to interracial causes, particularly through the YWCA.[39]

Munford, McNeill, the Darlings, and Schmelz all remained very active in the Virginia Industrial School for Colored Girls for years, working closely with Barrett to ensure the school's success. The institution became a source of enormous pride for both races as an example of what interracial work could accomplish. In her 1921 annual report to the governor as chairman of the board of managers, Schmelz boasted of her opportunity to share "the shining light" of the school at the interracial conference of southern women held that year in Memphis, reporting that "this institution was brought to the attention of women in every Southern state and brought always as the work of the colored women of Virginia, who we, the white members of the Board, are helping."[40] She made sure to praise the agency of black women, namely Barrett, in leading the project. Barrett expressed her appreciation of help she received as well, acknowledging her "sincere thanks to the Board of Managers for the large-hearted way they have helped me. . . . It would have been impossible to do what has been done had they not stood so completely behind me."[41]

This help of the white members of the board was not just ceremonial or in name only. These white men and especially white women put considerable time and effort into their responsibilities. Although Barrett was in charge of the daily administration of the school, these whites worked largely on securing the appropriations necessary for the school's success. Mary Munford, Annie Schmelz, and Martha McNeill, in particular, frequently petitioned the governor and members of the legislature for funds, believing, like many Progressives, that success lay in great governmental support of the school.[42] In 1919, these individuals influenced the Virginia General Assembly to delay its adjournment in order to have time to pass additional appropriation of twenty thousand dollars to help with construction of two needed new buildings. One white supporter was Harry C. Beattie of Richmond, who himself was a member of the House of Delegates.[43] These whites were not alone but were aided by fellow African American board members, including Maggie Lena Walker, T. C. Walker, Rev. William Stokes, and, later, Virginia Randolph. In the annual reports of the school, the lists of the board of managers always applied the honorifics Mr., Mrs., Dr., or Rev. to all names with no separation in terms of race. This use of courtesy titles regardless of race was atypical of Virginia in this era. Yet, leaders across racial lines saw the Virginia Industrial School for Colored Girls to be one of the greatest successes on interracialism and a point of pride for Virginia. Speaking in 1923, Schmelz declared that "in the great problem of the adjustment of race relations . . . this school has offered a worthy contribution in practically demonstrating what can be accomplished by conference and co-operation between the white and colored races, and it has helped in both North and South to place Virginia in the forefront as a State leading in fine race relationship."[44]

This school was not only a point of pride for black and white leaders in Virginia, but the project gained attention across the nation. African American Charles E. Stump reported about the school to the Chicago paper the *Broad Ax* in early summer 1920. After visiting Lynchburg and Richmond, Stump traveled to Peake's Turnout to visit the Virginia Industrial School for Colored Girls. He argued that, "while the white men in politics in Virginia are fighting to make the republican party a party for white men, the women are joining hands with our women trying to help save our girls." His experience convinced him that women were able to work together across the color line in a way that men would or could not do. Speaking to his Chicago readers, Stump proclaimed, "There is no question about it in my mind now, the white woman has a soul, a heart, and her sympathy goes out for her sister in black." He concluded that these white women had realized that they "can come among us without our black rubbing off."[45] Stump praised both the black and white women for committing to action and not just discussion.

Barrett's reformatory illustrates how segregation unexpectedly expanded opportunities for female activism within the supposedly "males-only" public domain. Across the nation in the early twentieth century, "New Women" pushed the boundaries of gender roles to articulate social welfare concerns.[46] Since reforms were usually divided by sex as well as race, female activists claimed the right and the responsibility to advocate for causes such as maternity homes, female reformatories, and women probation officers. Virginia women across racial lines often found that the best way to address these concerns was through interracial cooperation efforts. White and black women had the freedom to work together without any of the scandalous sexual undertones that similar encounters with black men would have evoked. Their interactions were easily accepted and encouraged by the white populace as replicating, at least publicly, the benevolent mistress/grateful servant paradigm praised by devotees of the Lost Cause. Women were not the only leaders of interracial cooperation efforts, and the work never became a strictly feminine endeavor, but these female activists made history by claiming their space as equal participants within reformist circles despite living in one of the most restrictive and discriminating societies in twentieth-century America. These reformers used the limited space created by segregation to publicize the need for cooperation across gender as well as racial lines. Female activists, black and white from across the state, understood the importance of this work and thus became unlikely allies in efforts to reform and modernize Jim Crow Virginia.

5

Race and War

We have proven our fidelity to the government, [but] what will the government and its officials prove to us? We do not like to put this subject in this way, but what else are we to do? We get talk and promises from white citizens, *who have not the power to do else than give us talk and promises.*
— *Richmond Planet*, 1917

JOHN MITCHELL JR. was not the only influential African American editor in early twentieth-century Virginia. While Mitchell was one of the leading black voices out of Richmond, Plummer Bernard Young became a similar voice out of Norfolk. Young, born on July 27, 1884, in Littleton, North Carolina, began working in publishing at the early age of fifteen. After his marriage in 1906 and the birth of a son the following year, he decided to move his young family to Norfolk for a new job as plant foreman at the *Lodge Journal and Guide*, the newspaper of the fraternal organization the Supreme Lodge Knights of Gideon At this job, he gained some experience in writing and decided to buy the paper after the Lodge folded in 1910. He renamed his new newspaper the *Norfolk Journal and Guide*, which became one of the largest African American weekly newspapers in the country.[1] In such close proximity to Richmond, it was perhaps inevitable that he would have a somewhat contentious relationship with Mitchell, the editor of the *Richmond Planet*.

Mitchell and Young had very different ideas about how to handle encroaching segregation in the late 1910s. Deteriorating conditions played directly into a statewide debate about the Great Migration. Many black Virginians grew tired of working and living within a discriminatory system that they had little power to change and chose instead to leave. This emigration movement had a profound impact on Virginia, not only in terms of numbers leaving but on the debate and rhetoric concerning race. White and black Virginians alike had strong opinions about the advantages and disadvantages of leaving. The trend alarmed whites, who worried that their societal structure and the ample labor force that they had worked so hard to cultivate were in trouble. Migration was a form of protest that whites had little means to combat. African Americans fed up with the ever-tightening strictures of segregation and lack of political rights could simply leave Virginia in the hope of securing a better life farther north.

Whites were generally unified in their fear of black migration. Although Virginia was deeply segregated, most of its white residents never desired an all-white state. Instead, their culture was based on their ability to exert control over blacks. This power was central to securing a cheap and readily available labor source to fulfill the domestic and manual labor jobs that many whites considered inappropriate for their superior race. This racial order also validated whites' paternalistic mind-sets and imagined past where contented slaves lived under the benevolent and uplifting care of their white masters. Migration was a very public and extremely embarrassing rejection by African Americans of whites' claims of Virginia as a haven of idyllic racial harmony. White newspapers across the state desired to halt the outflow of the state's labor force but disagreed on the methods acceptable. Some editors called for the arrest of blacks attempting to leave as well as the northern labor recruiters who sought to entice them. Most publications, however, approved of licensing fees for recruiting agents but decried any efforts to arrest migrating blacks. "Such a policy," explained the *Richmond Times-Dispatch*, "founded in mingled folly and injustice, and in open violation of law, is certain to do more harm than good."[2] White Virginians needed black labor and were willing to make some concessions to discourage the northern exodus. Rather than expanding the political rights of blacks, whites hoped interracial cooperation with "better class" blacks would stem the outflow, making promises of reforms and reassuring blacks of white elites' credentials to advocate African Americans' concerns.

Not surprisingly, black leaders throughout the state were deeply divided on the emigration issue. P. B. Young was steadfastly against blacks chasing dreams of a more prosperous life up North. Although Mitchell certainly supported and promoted interracial work and fostering goodwill with whites, his stance on race relations was generally more militant than that of P. B. Young. This difference, in large part, was a result of the Norfolk editor's close alliance with Booker T. Washington, a man he considered not only his idol but his friend. Washington and Young first met in August 1907 and grew to know each other well over the years.[3] Young often traveled the state with Washington during Washington's frequent trips to Virginia. Young, like Washington, placed enormous emphasis on the need for the rise of a black entrepreneurial class, even taking Washington's philosophy of "Build up, don't tear down" as the *Norfolk Journal and Guide*'s motto.[4] In other words, he believed that black Virginians should accommodate segregation for the time being and use the separation as an opportunity to build businesses in black communities. This perspective aligned quite well to goals of white paternalists

P. B. Young, circa 1943. (Courtesy of Library of
Congress, Prints & Photographs Division)

engaged in interracial activism. This emphasis on economic progress of African Americans within the South convinced Young, like Washington, that northern migration was a mistake and a false hope. Both believed the best future for African Americans was their economic advancement within the segregated South.[5]

Thus, P. B. Young argued that promises of a better life outside of Virginia were false. Instead, he worked with whites to encourage blacks to stay. Young believed that black Virginians would meet similar discriminations wherever they went and, thus, would prosper more in an area where they understood the situation and knew the social rules expected of them. Within a Jim Crow culture, blacks could find a comfortable niche where work was readily available and competition from foreign immigrants was negligible.[6] John Mitchell Jr., editor of the *Richmond Planet*, held a more nuanced view, believing the decision to be an acutely personal choice. He argued that the experiences up North could not be nearly as bad as southern whites claimed or the migrants would write their families encouraging them to stay at home rather than join them.[7] Although Mitchell, as a prosperous banker and editor, never considered leaving Virginia, he wished his black neighbors well who hoped they could find greater economic, social, and political opportunities elsewhere.

By mid-1917, however, Mitchell began to advocate the advantages of remaining in Virginia and using whites' fear of migration to negotiate for better conditions. This was their home, he argued, and black Virginians should manipulate the concerns of whites to address the inequities of Jim Crow. "Segregation," he lamented, "which has floated like a dark pall over the southland, is one of the leading causes advanced for the disposition of the colored people to seek other climes." Informal segregation, he explained, "has always been in operation throughout the Southland, but it was not legal, forcible segregation."[8] Mitchell contested correctly that residential segregation laws, then in effect throughout much of Virginia, were the primary cause for poor housing throughout the South. In Richmond in 1917, houses stood empty, with whites prevented from selling and blacks prevented from buying because of disputes over whether particular city blocks were designated white or black. Although Mitchell did not think that segregation would be eradicated from Virginian society, he believed some whites, like the paternalists with whom he worked, might support a return to de facto segregation and encourage the Richmond City Council to remove its tedious restrictions in order to improve living conditions and encourage blacks to stay.[9] Mitchell hoped black Virginians could use whites' concerns about losing their labor force to bring about some real political change. And although whites' fear of black migration never actually lessened racial discrimination, many African Americans responded to the appeals of black leaders like Young and later Mitchell by choosing to remain in Virginia. Thousands of blacks left the state in search of greater opportunities but many more stayed, believing that Virginia was just as much their home as the whites who dictated state policies.

African Americans outside of the South had difficulty understanding why any blacks would want to stay and live in a segregated society and, at times, criticized southern black leaders for failing to encourage greater migration. From New York City in January 1917, African American Henry P. Lipscomb wrote a letter to the *Richmond Planet* openly admonishing black leaders in Virginia for working with whites to stem "the Negro exodus from the Southland to the North."[10] Lipscomb believed that the cooperation practiced by individuals like P. B. Young was only a tacit acceptance of inferior treatment. He despised the policy of accommodation perfected by Booker T. Washington, who, though deceased for two years, still influenced "race relations" throughout the nation, to the resentment of some and the admiration of others. He concluded that African Americans in Virginia were naïve to think that they could fight discrimination without any direct political power. And he was angered by the indifference of supposedly "friendly" whites to the real reasons for the black migration. "It seems to me," Lipscomb argued, "the white people are appealing to the wrong source. They should appeal to those who have created and are creating such an intolerable condition that makes it impossible for the Negro to live in peace among them."[11] Thus, he encouraged black Virginians to take the one real positive action open to them to fight segregation, and leave. Lipscomb spoke with many blacks recently arrived from the South and determined that all agreed on the cause, "viz: that they are lynched, Jim-Crowed, disfranchised and segregated, given bad police protection and rough justice."[12]

From an outside perspective, Lipscomb found it easy to condemn the seeming "Uncle Tom" actions of Virginia's African American leaders. These individuals, particularly P. B. Young of Norfolk, Giles Jackson of Richmond, and Thomas Walker of Gloucester, swallowed their pride and played the stereotypical "loyal darkey" role when it suited their purposes. At least outwardly, they at times accepted segregation and even found some advantages such as building up African American businesses and leadership within black communities. They believed it was impossible to stop segregation and, instead, decided to work to better conditions within its confines. Undeniably, these men, especially Jackson, were at times accommodationists. Yet, accommodation did not mean simply surrendering in the face of every demand of white men. Instead, this role gave these leaders a voice among white policy makers and activists. Although it never resulted in equality, accommodation, on one level, meant negotiation on both sides of the color line. Through interracial cooperation, African American leaders in Virginia accepted many segregationist policies, while white paternalists, in exchange, listened to their concerns and assessments of needed reforms. This work kept the lines of negotiation and discussion open. Walker, Mitchell, Young, and others cared less about being labeled "Uncle Toms" than improving conditions for African Americans within Virginia and preserving their own class authority as black elites.

Black Virginians hoped that the interracial goodwill fostered by whites' attempts to stem emigration and the state's participation in World War I would lead to an extension of their civil rights. Community leaders saw the war as a golden opportunity to prove their patriotism and convince whites of the injustice of the current system. Understanding the Lost Cause culture and white paternalists' idealization of the "remembered" fidelity of slaves to their ancestors during the Civil War, blacks speculated that the new war could enable their race to demonstrate their worthiness as loyal American and Virginian citizens. They hoped that whites would appreciate their willingness to set aside their anger at discrimination and wholeheartedly join the war effort. "White folks have no need to inquire about the patriotism of the colored folks," John Mitchell Jr. declared sardonically; "According to their past treatment, they should all be traitors, but as a matter of fact, there has never been any mass of humanity more loyal. Their motto to the white man has always been, 'though he slay me, yet will I trust him.'"[13] Mitchell believed that African Americans' loyal participation alongside southern whites in the world war would encourage a rethinking of the current system of discrimination. Although calling boldly for equal rights and color-blind justice, Mitchell concluded in accordance with the traditions of interracial cooperation in Virginia that progress could only be made with the help of "better class" whites.

While some white Virginians did debate whether blacks would remain loyal and feared their defection to the German cause, most whites, particularly the upper class, who controlled the newspapers throughout the state, expressed their confidence in black Virginians' patriotism. The support of these elite whites was not surprising. Any suggestions otherwise would have shattered the justifications for genteel paternalism on which they based their worldview. If "their" blacks were not faithful or willing to step in and help white folks, then white paternalists' facade of idyllic racial harmony in Virginia, that they had worked so hard to cultivate, would be questioned. Accordingly, the *Richmond Times-Dispatch* declared its faith in "where the Negro of the South stands, and will stand, in this war, despite all the efforts of propagandists and trouble-makers to lure him from his allegiance."[14] That position, they argued, would be one of loyalty, fighting beside the southern white men. "Other nations," the paper declared, "have extended greater recognition to the Negro as an individual, but the race has never prospered and advanced as it has in America. The Negro will stand firm because he is neither an ingrate nor a fool."[15] The *Richmond Evening Journal* echoed this sentiment, even promising the possibility of future extended rights if African Americans stopped worrying about obtaining access to the vote. "Let him be patient," the journal counseled, "even as the brave women are patient, and time will cure the legal defect at which he now rebels."[16] In response, the African American *Richmond Planet* ignored the white newspapers' admonitions about acceptance of current inequality. Instead, the paper pondered the war's potential for improving the lot of blacks throughout the state. The *Planet* sought to reassure its readers: "We do not like our treatment, and some of us feel some resentment, but we do not carry it to the point of being guilty of treasonable conduct. What we want is fair treatment and a chance to show just what we can do, and we shall demonstrate that we can forgive an injury when our country is involved just as quickly as we can resent a wrong."[17]

When the United States entered the world war, black Virginians rushed to prove their patriotism — conducting Liberty Bond drives, joining the Red Cross, and turning out in droves, in some areas outnumbering white men, when service registration began on June 5, 1917.[18] They made their activism a very public matter. John Mitchell Jr. wrote Governor Stuart offering his services to the state in any manner needed. Mitchell, by 1917, was long past fighting age, but he wanted to demonstrate the support of African Americans, particularly the black elite, in organizing war efforts. He printed both his and Stuart's correspondence in his newspaper. Stuart suggested that "it occurs to me that in your position a vigorous campaign among the people of your race to buy Liberty Loan bonds would be of great value."[19] In response, Mitchell appointed himself one of the leaders in Richmond of bond campaigns. The Liberty Loan movement received support in African American communities throughout the state. In Richmond, several mass meetings were held where a number of whites, including Hon. Oliver J. Sands and Col. William T. Dabney, spoke to black audiences praising their patriotism and also encouraging the buying of bonds.[20] Although interracial cooperation had for years played a prominent role within the state, the work reached a new high point during World War I as cross-racial efforts such as the Liberty Bond meetings became increasingly frequent.[21]

In Richmond on June 17, 1917, a massive Red Cross parade brought whites and blacks together on the streets of the city in a communal declaration of patriotism. The coming together of the two races in a public forum in mutual support for a shared cause led African Americans to hope that whites might also recognize the injustice of segregation. "For the first time in half a century," the *Richmond Planet* praised, "colored people were accorded a place in line with the white people."[22] Afterward, many residents gathered in the city auditorium to hear an inspirational speech delivered by Congressman Carter Glass. He made a particular point of praising the African American residents, many of whom listened to the speech from segregated seating. The parade was a success except for a minor incident involving Maggie Lena Walker, who led the Red Cross organization in the state among black Virginians. Police prevented Walker from riding in the parade, for dubious reasons, by forcing Walker's chauffeur to exit the parade line in the midst of the procession. White authorities encouraged African Americans' public support of the war effort but kept a careful eye on the color line. They were happy to have African Americans to demonstrate their support but were uncomfortable about Walker's exhibition of her automobile, which they perceived as too ostentatiously expensive for any African American to own, much less a black woman. Whites, despite the atmosphere of goodwill, were vigilant against any displays of African American equality, or, in this case, superiority.

Whites attempted to use these interracial demonstrations to their advantage by trying to "instruct" blacks on issues like migration. In August, Hon. William T. Dabney, white, of the Richmond Chamber of Commerce spoke at a meeting of the Independent Order of St. Luke — a national mutual benefit society headed by Maggie Lena Walker — praising the group for their efforts in supporting the war.[23] Dabney unexpectedly took the opportunity to lecture the audience on the "dangers" of migration and how much better life was in Virginia than in the North. He professed that the "relationship between the white and the colored people here was most friendly" and that "there were less handicaps to colored people in this community than anywhere else."[24] Either unaware of or indifferent to how quickly he dismissed all the legitimate concerns of black Richmonders, Dabney singled out several black leaders to praise for their cooperative work with whites. The audience applauded John Mitchell Jr. and Maggie Lena Walker, but when Dabney named Giles Jackson, loud hissing broke out in the auditorium. While Mitchell and Walker frequently worked with whites in an accommodationist manner when necessary, they were also known for their avid support of black rights and pride. Jackson, however, had the reputation of being too old-fashioned (though he was about the same age as Mitchell and Walker) and an "Uncle Tom." The African American crowd expressed vocally their frustration that years of work from men like Jackson had only resulted in increasingly limited political and civil rights. The situation reached a critical point when Dabney defied the jeering and intensified his praise of Jackson, who was present and, in fact, had introduced him. A reporter present recounted that Dabney "stuck to his guns" and "asserted that no colored man in the United States could so readily secure the ear of President Wilson, members of Congress and high public officials at Washington as could Giles Jackson." In response, many members of the audience walked out. Maggie Walker salvaged the evening by rising and tactfully changing the subject. Yet, the incident demonstrated that blacks remained angry at the inequities of discrimination despite this era of public demonstrations of interracial goodwill.[25]

Although disruptive incidents were unusual at these events, they reflected a growing unrest with the status quo among African Americans. For years, white interracial activists had promised better conditions if blacks only trusted whites' guidance and expertise in advocating African American concerns to state and local governments. When the war began, blacks hoped their displays of patriotism would convince their white "friends" of their ability to speak for themselves. Yet, only a few months into America's war effort, black Virginians were beginning to wonder whether all their efforts were for naught. "We have proven our fidelity to the government," the *Richmond Planet* reflected, but "what will the government and its officials prove to us? We do not like to put this subject in this way, but what else are we to do? We get talk and promises from white citizens, *who have not the power to do else than give us talk and promises.*"[26] Blacks were tired of assurances by white activists like Mary Munford and Elizabeth Cocke who spoke endlessly of reform but who themselves could not vote and had only indirect access to the power structure. Even those like Joseph Mastin and William Dabney who held prominent positions within the state could accomplish little in the large scheme of what needed to be done. Mastin and Dabney, as well as Munford and Cocke, had some power but not enough support among the white public and governmental officials.

Despite this fear that the situation would never improve, African Americans continued to support the war efforts. On October 26, 1917, black Virginians held a large parade and mass meeting in Richmond to bid farewell to all the black soldiers mustered into service from that region. In addition to the soldiers, local African American and white bands joined the procession. The event became a fantastic display of goodwill. The *Richmond Planet* reported: "White people were as enthusiastic in cheering the marching throngs as were colored. . . . Race lines disappeared for the time being and all symptoms of race prejudice were lost in the era of general good feeling that prevailed in this city. White citizens marched side by side with colored ones, fraternizing together in this time of the nation's peril."[27] The reporter clearly saw the situation through rose-tinted glasses, perhaps hoping this event would mark the beginning of a new era. While his view may have been overly optimistic, no violence of any sort occurred, not with the fifty thousand black and white residents who lined the streets for the parade or afterward, when the city auditorium was packed beyond capacity with people eager to hear reassurances that America, and Virginians in particular, would emerge victorious from the world war. The meeting featured a speech by Mayor Ainslie of Richmond. His address was followed by speeches from numerous black and white leaders seated together in front on an elevated rostrum. These speakers included Maggie Walker, John Mitchell Jr., John Stewart Bryan (white owner of the *Richmond News Leader*), Judge J. C. Pritchard (U.S. Circuit Court), and Judge

George L. Christian, among others. According to the newspaper, Mary Munford, from the audience, added her praise of the African American soldiers and "for a few minutes stirred the audience with her fervid utterances."[28]

African Americans hoped the event with its ostentatious exclamations of racial goodwill marked a real change in their relative position within the state. Afterward, the *Richmond Planet* reflected: "Some people seem never to tire in saying that the Southern white people are the best friends of the colored people. This war against the Teutonic allies has brought to these same people the full realization of the fact that the colored people are the best friends of the Southern white people."[29] Mitchell felt exhilarated by the event, appreciating that African Americans were receiving the public respect of their white neighbors. "We have been deeply touched by the evidences of general esteem and solicitation on the part of the best white people in Virginia," he declared; "We shall never forget it. . . . We feel like calling to our people, who have gone North to seek better wages and more congenial surroundings, 'Come back home. Conditions have changed.'"[30] Mitchell understood that the racial advancements resulted from a perhaps temporary wartime fervor, yet he believed African Americans had a real chance to "receive the encomiums of the nation and be welcomed to receive all of the rights and privileges of any other citizens" if they continued to exhibit their patriotism and if the war lasted long enough. Only slightly satirically, he declared, "From a short, quick war, Good Lord, deliver us!"[31]

White newspapers also provided extensive coverage of the parade and mass meeting celebrating the African American soldiers' departure for Camp Lee. The *Richmond News Leader*, whose owner, John Stewart Bryan, spoke at the rally, offered its readers both pictures and articles concerning the local display of patriotism. In addition to complimenting the enlisted men and the Red Cross workers who staged the events, the *News Leader* praised the actions of the white public in supporting the African American war effort. Not only was Richmond the only city in the country with an African American chapter of the Red Cross, "the News Leader feels that no city in America has given a more earnest God-speed to its troops than was given the colored selects last night and this morning."[32] Like Mitchell, the reporter considered the implications of these developments on the future rights of African Americans: "It is a very solemn responsibility that a Southern state assumes in sending to fight the nation's battle men whom *grim necessity has forced it deny the franchise*. The law of noblesse oblige applies . . . and it is for us who give the sanction of our ballot and our influence to the system of universal service to see to it that patriotism is rewarded with justice—no matter by whom that patriotism is displayed. Even the most ignorant boy of the Selects must be made to see that he has a stake in a country worth fighting for!"[33] Although the editorial comments were patronizing and based on the assumption that whites had the responsibility of determining what was best for black Virginians, the white reporter did offer vague promises of future rights in exchange for current loyalties. Reattainment of the right to vote was held tantalizingly before the young soldiers. "There is nothing that a colored man likes so well," Mitchell advised his readers, "as to see white folks in trouble and to be able to help them out of that trouble."[34]

This hope faded as the war ended. Promises of racial concessions were quickly forgotten as the emergency ended. Yet, interracial efforts still continued. Not surprisingly in a state so obsessed with its own history, one of the first postwar attempts at interracial cooperation was through the Virginia War History Commission.[35] This committee created by the state legislature sought to record all the accomplishments of Virginian soldiers on the battlefields of Europe as well as the work of loyal citizens on the home front. Both male and female members were appointed to the commission, but white women became some of the primary motivators behind the movement. Arthur Kyle Davis, president of Southern Female College in Petersburg, headed the commission, but white women filled many of the important posts. Experience with the United Daughters of Confederacy and the Daughters of the American Revolution prepared these women for the work, particularly since the nature of the project was to praise the heroes of the conflict rather than to critically analyze the legitimacy of the war itself.[36] Two of the leading white women involved were Mary Munford and Mary Stanard. In the vein of the interracial understanding Munford had advocated for years, they worked to include African Americans in the study.

But the question of how to include blacks quickly became an issue of concern. On February 24, 1919, Mary Munford organized a meeting to "further the plan of collecting data showing the part played by the colored people of Virginia to win the war."[37] Like the majority of biracial conferences, it was held in an African American venue, the Community House for Negro People, a service organization founded through interracial cooperation. Munford hoped the meeting would settle several organizational concerns including whether African American experiences should be recounted separately or not from whites and also the establishment of a committee system for gathering data. Opinions varied. Rev. A. A. Graham, an African American minister from Phoebus, Virginia, wanted a black man to be given a position on the commission with official status. T. B. Williams, an African American professor at Hampton, suggested that blacks form a separate organization. The African American lawyer J. Thomas Hewin agreed with Williams that a separate organization was needed that would cooperate with the Virginia War History Commission. The group voted on and accepted this last proposal, appointing Professor Williams as chairman and Mary C. Carter, from Richmond, as secretary.

Once this decision was reached, Munford yielded the floor to Williams. Speaking for the African Americans present, Maggie Walker and a Dr. Morris of Norfolk thanked the whites for attending—Munford as well as Col. Charles R. Keiley of the Virginia Council of Defense and Mary Newton Stanard. Since their portion of the business was completed, "the white friends withdrew" in accordance with racial decorum and left the remaining committee to decide their next course of action.[38]

This initial gathering only began the discussion. The white members of the Virginia War History Commission were happy for blacks to form a separate organization, an action that aligned with their segregationist beliefs. However, they assumed that the black committee would remain under white control. Following an additional meeting a few days later, the black committee sent a proposal for action in the form of a letter to Mary Munford. They declared their "sincere gratitude and pleasure that the Virginia War History Commission . . . [were] planning to include in their record the part the colored people of the state have played" and pledged "our hearty support."[39] After this socially proper profession of gratitude, the black delegation detailed what they believed to be acceptable terms of cooperation. They desired to have a central committee appointed with "official designation" to oversee and organize the collection of data throughout the state.[40] They requested the authority to set up local county or city agencies to work under the direction of the central committee and also using the resources of the Negro Organization Society when appropriate.[41] Fearing that material gathered from industrial plants where both whites and blacks worked would not fairly represent both sides of the color line, the delegation insisted particularly that "care be taken to separate contributions of colored people from those of white people in order that the contribution of the colored people may be known and credit given therefor [sic]."[42] Maggie Walker, T. C. Erwin, T. B. Williams, A. A. Graham, and the other committee members encouraged a complete separation of the African American history from the white whenever possible. They believed that only through this division could black Virginians fairly represent their contributions in helping to win the world war. The group proposed to gather the materials, write the African American history themselves, and then submit the completed product to the Virginia War History Commission.[43]

The white members of the state commission feared the consequences of this proposal even though it aligned with the supposed tenets of segregation. The system the African American representatives presented to Munford called for a division of the project in a separate but equal manner, where blacks operated under the same authority as whites with full editorial control of their work. Yet, despite theoretical professions otherwise, whites never intended Jim Crow to create a separate and independent black world. Instead, segregation meant partitioning African

Americans into defined "black spaces" that operated under white supervision. Although supportive and encouraging of including African American experiences in their study, Munford, Stanard, and the other whites involved were concerned with the request to leave African American affairs solely to African American leaders. Thus, it was not surprising that the white activists found portions of the blacks' proposal to be unacceptable and potentially dangerous.

Arthur Kyle Davis, chairman of the Virginia War History Commission, informally assigned Mary Munford and Mary Stanard to oversee the organization of the African Americans' involvement. While Mary Munford had much experience in interracial work, Mary Stanard, the wife of William G. Stanard, secretary of the Virginia Historical Society and editor of the *Virginia Magazine of History and Biography,* had published considerably on Virginia history both alone and with her husband.[44] Preparing to put the project in motion, the two white women discussed the blacks' proposal extensively, hoping to work out most of the disagreements through personal negotiation before presenting the concerns to Davis. Finding their phone conversations inadequate to discuss the matter in any depth, Munford invited Stanard to dinner. In preparation, Stanard decided to air her thoughts in a letter to Munford, so they could reflect on various concerns before their meeting. "As I told you," Stanard confided, "I think the statement describing the informal conference was objectionable, and am sure it would produce a bad effect if it were necessary to present it to the Commission."[45] She had several major concerns about the African Americans' response. First, Stanard was offended by the lack of racial protocol exhibited. Four white members of the commission attended the meeting, but no special acknowledgment was made of that fact. Stanard argued that those individuals should have been thanked and singled out rather than "jumbling the names of these visitors with their own without discrimination."[46] While many interracial meetings of this sort listed the names of those in attendance separately by race, the report sent to Munford and Stanard offered no such distinction. "As the meeting was to further *their* interests," Stanard continued, "that much respect should have been paid especially in a case like that of Bishop Denny, who was there to help them at considerable sacrifice of his own convenience."[47]

Although she claimed to find the plan in general "entirely unobjectionable," Stanard had several specific qualms about the details. The idea of giving official commissions to African Americans troubled her. "In the shrewdly worded clause," she explained to Munford, "asking that their committee be so 'designated' as to give them authority there is suggested a plea for commissions for negroes." The African American delegation made no actual demands for commissions, but Stanard read between the lines of racial decorum and realized that much of the interracial communication remained unstated. Stanard claimed not to object, but Davis had instructed her "not to hold out any idea of commissions." Instead, Davis preferred an informal system where "one or more their committee [would be] invited to our meetings at proper times to report progress of their work." Stanard respected Davis's position and felt it was her and Munford's duty to represent the wishes of the chairman, who "at great sacrifice is giving a vast amount of his time" to the project and who "will be held responsible for its gigantic work."[48] The issue of commissions involved more than simply a title. The African American committee sought official recognition of their work and responsibilities. Understanding their involvement to be equally as important, they desired to be accorded the same rights and sanction as the white members of the Virginia War History Commission.

But the final organizational decisions were not agreed upon until later that spring. Following the recommendations of Munford, Stanard, and other whites, a separate agency was created to study African American war efforts. Yet, rather than giving the black leaders the autonomy they desired, the Virginia War History Commission appointed Father Charles Hannigan, a white priest active for years in interracial work in Richmond, as director of the new agency. Hannigan worked throughout his career in spreading Catholicism among African Americans in Virginia and was involved in numerous interracial endeavors like Barrett's Virginia Industrial School for Colored Girls. In a dedication of a building on that campus in May 1916, Hannigan declared: "At no time has there been a more sympathetic coming together of the races than there is now. We are about to demonstrate in Virginia that we can make good, that we can draw out of the colored people the qualities we believe are in them—honesty, fidelity, and an undying affection for their friends."[49] Hannigan's words underlined his belief that it was the Christian duty of whites to aid African American uplift. In concession to blacks' requests, Hannigan had the authority to offer commissions to "as many negro collaborators as the director thinks it wise to appoint."[50]

Father Hannigan, through his personal contacts, recruited a number of additional black leaders throughout the state to work on the project, including Rev. L. L. Downing of Roanoke, Mrs. Janie Porter Barrett (then president of the Virginia State Federation of Colored Women's Clubs), Rev. W. T. Johnson (Red Cross), Rev. J. E. Jones (Virginia Union University), and J. H. McCrew (YMCA), among others. Under Hannigan's authority, the committee of African American collaborators appointed several black leaders to represent their interests to the director. They chose John Mitchell Jr. as chairman, T. C. Erwin as secretary, and Ora B. Stokes as assistant secretary.[51] This solution gave the blacks involved the official commissions they wanted but not the control. The plan called for them to gather the data and write their history, but they never had full editorial discretion. Guidelines stipulated that the final product of the African Americans' work would be revised "if necessary," first by Hannigan and then by Mary Stanard as chair-woman of the Committee on War Work Activities.[52] Despite these restrictions, the black collaborators dedicated themselves to the work. Black newspapers across the state ran frequent ads calling for information.[53] John Mitchell Jr. used the pages of the *Richmond Planet* to promote the project and its importance. Calling for the support of black Virginians in gathering data, he declared, "It is important in the interest of the race and as irrefutable evidence of the high quality of our rapidly developing civilization that the history of the deeds, both military and civil of the Negroes of the state should be as full and as accurate as it can possibly be made."[54]

Like most interracial work, the Virginia War History Commission was an imperfect enterprise structured upon inequality, but this fact did not rob the venture of its utility. Although forced to work under white control and on white terms, the African American committee members gained official sanction and support to preserve their history not simply as African Americans but as Virginians in a time of crisis. This contribution was important, especially in the post–world war era, when racial tensions within the state reached a new straining point. The tedious issues of negotiation and committee control that the Virginia War History Commission faced were the heart of interracial cooperation initiatives.

Power struggles shaped not only the results of the work but the manner in which it was conducted. Stanard and Munford tried to iron out these delicate concerns before presenting any plan of action to the executive committee. These two white women took on the sometimes uncomfortable position of middlemen between the concerns of black and white Virginians. Their interests were defined by a white perspective, yet Stanard and Munford also had strong motivations for offering concessions to make the relationship with African Americans work. Apart from an embedded understanding of benevolence, their sense of honor and pride compelled them to find a solution. Moreover, they enjoyed the power they derived from acting as liaisons and spokeswomen on behalf of black Virginians. They did not want Davis or others to doubt their ability to act as contacts with the black citizenry. Their key to success was negotiation. African Americans activists also recognized the need for compromise. They attempted to push the terms of cooperation and challenge discriminatory practice, as they did with the Virginia War History Commission, but realized their inclusion was due only to the goodwill of selected paternalistic whites. Activists across the color line engaged in a strategic give-and-take interplay, ironing out not only the issues of particular interracial ventures but the larger dynamics of race in a segregated society.

The paramount success of interracial cooperation in this era, however, was the ability of white and African American activists to work together to minimize racial violence and deal with individual incidents in a practical manner that discouraged mob action. During these post–World War I years, Virginia, like the rest of the nation, was wrought with signs of racial tension. The outbreak of war in Europe in 1914 virtually halted immigration and left a number of jobs unfilled, especially in the Northeast and Midwest.[55] In response to this development and the discrimination and humiliations forced on them by white segregationists, nearly a half million African Americans fled the South from 1914 to 1917. The heightened presence of blacks in northern cities sparked both economic and racial fears among whites. Although ignored and glossed over during the national emergency of war, racial strife intensified across the nation after the war. The arrival of peace brought an increase in lynchings and race riots. Returning African American soldiers who had fought for democracy abroad were met with ignorance and prejudice. Rather than accepting the situation, they were outraged and refused to be demeaned from proud veteran in immaculate uniform to a white man's "boy." In response to these assertions of black equality and manhood, whites worried about the sanctity of white supremacy. The experiences and horrors of the first modern world war convinced many white Americans that they needed to return to isolationism and be more vigilant against foreigners, especially those attempting to "invade" the United States through immigration. Thus, whites in the North and South united under the banner of 100 percent Americanism, proclaiming that "American" meant only Anglo-Saxon and Protestant.[56] Writing in the late 1920s, William Faulkner captured this fear through his character Miss Jenny, a white Mississippian upset at the "uppity" ways of black veterans: "Who was the fool anyway, who thought of putting niggers into the same uniform with white men? Mr. Vardaman knew better; he told those fools at Washington at the time it wouldn't do."[57]

After armistice, the summer of 1919 became known as the Red Summer as dozens of race riots broke out nationwide.[58] Virginians, across the color line, were shocked by news of the bloody race riot in Tulsa, Oklahoma, the discovery of the mass murder of African American workers on a peonage farm in Jasper County, Georgia, as well as daily accounts of grotesque lynchings across the South. Virginians, black and white, kept a careful eye on these national stories of racial violence. The Richmond NAACP, for example, issued frequent pronouncements condemning the outrages.[59] Several of the largest race riots were outside the South. In early July 1917, a riot erupted in East Saint Louis in which a mob of whites burned alive, shot, and assaulted estimated hundreds of blacks.[60] Another riot occurred the same year in Houston. Two years later, in 1919, a total of twenty-five race riots flared across the nation within six months that killed at least two hundred people, the majority of them African Americans.

While interracial cooperation did much to stem racial violence in the state,

Virginia was not entirely immune from the nationwide wave of violence. In keeping with the continuing interracial efforts, the Norfolk City Council organized a
week-long celebration and with a concluding ceremony to recognize its returning
black soldiers. Violence erupted, however, after the arrest of one black soldier,
Alexander Moore. The resulting clash left five blacks and two white policeman
wounded, mostly from gunfire. Despite this, the ceremony was still held. White
and black leaders attempted to downplay the incident, but the violence indicated a
trend where the grandiose promises of goodwill and potential extended rights that
had been spoken in the excitement of national emergency slowly ebbed away.[61]
Yet, this was not isolated. After a 1917 hanging ended an eighteen-year period
without lynching in the state, white mobs hanged one black man in 1920 and
another in August 1921.[62]

   In each incident, whites throughout the state were quick to denounce the vigilante acts.[63] Although staunch supporters of white supremacy and segregation, the
majority of white Virginians found lynching to be unacceptable. In *Lynching in the
New South*, the historian W. Fitzhugh Brundage offers a comparative study of the
history of lynching in two southern states, Virginia and Georgia. He found that
there were significantly fewer lynchings in Virginia largely because of both the
different economies in the two states as well as white opposition to vigilantism in
the Old Dominion. In addition to the economic factors, he argued that white Virginians, particularly state officials, emphasized the importance of working within
the legal justice system, believing the racial order could be implemented through
other means besides violence. Paternalism in Virginia, as well, helped to cultivate
this emphasis on "polite racism" rather than violence as a means of social control.
The state indeed had the lowest number of killings among the twelve states where
lynching occurred. According to a 2015 comprehensive study of the Equal Justice
Institute, 3,959 lynchings have been documented as occurring between 1877 and
1950.[64] Of these, Virginia witnessed 76 people lynched. The state with the next
closest was North Carolina with 102 victims. In contrast, the highest were Mississippi at 576 and Georgia at 586 during the same time period.[65] Although Virginia
certainly had a lower rate of vigilante violence, it did not mean that lynching was
unknown in the state.[66]

   Throughout the early twentieth century, Virginia governors typically took
public stands against vigilantism and threatened the use of military force to ensure order. In December 1920, for example, Governor Westmoreland Davis sent
troops to Wise County to protect an African American man accused of attacking
an elderly white man. "Virginia has no place for mob vengeance," Davis proclaimed; "It will not brook, however provocative the cause."[67] This commitment
to order, however, did not mean that African Americans, particularly males, were

in less danger of unjustified accusations of violence, including stories of rapes of white women. Instead, Virginians prided themselves on their swift justice system. Vigilantism had less appeal when the same ends could be achieved both quickly and legally. Thus, white Virginians boasted about their civilized and "humane" handling of alleged African American criminals.[68]

A number of white paternalists in the state were outspoken opponents of lynching. In 1923, the best-selling novelist and social activist Mary Johnston reached a national audience with the publication of "Nemesis," a gripping short story about the lynching of an African American man in a small southern town. "Nemesis" grabbed the attention of the NAACP. Guilt or innocence, she argued, meant little to the white mob — only the color of the accused man's skin. She not only wrote about the injustice of the act for the victim but depicted the entire white mob as victims as well for succumbing to such barbaric behavior. The tale, which appeared nearly seven years before Jessie Daniel Ames founded the Association of Southern Women for the Prevention of Lynching, offered a unique perspective, focusing on the events that followed the lynching and on its psychological impact.[69] Arthur Spingarn, vice president of the NAACP, wrote to thank Johnston for her "brave and beautiful" story and informed her of a NAACP press release to all African American newspapers in the United States announcing publication of the story. "It will mean much to them to know that there are white women like Mary Johnston in Virginia."[70] His colleague, Walter White, agreed: "[I have never] read any story on this national disgrace of ours which moved me as yours did."[71] Johnston was only one of several white paternalists in Virginia to speak out against lynching, stressing the importance of whites' benevolence and civility.

These publicized condemnations of lynching were not empty threats to appease national public opinion. Governors and other public officials encouraged local police to take stands against any potential white mobs. In Houston, Virginia, in April 1921, John H. Draper, white, was fined five hundred dollars and sentenced to twelve months in jail for attempting, in the midst of a white mob, to break into a jail and lynch an African American prisoner named Coleman, accused of murdering a white man.[72] John Mitchell Jr. saw enormous hope in the conviction. He reflected: "Southern white people are now viewing conditions from twentieth century angles and with them rest the prospects and hopes of the colored people. . . . The time will come when both black and white, rich and poor in our beloved section will stand together and the lawless elements of both races will come to understand that the day of unrest and misunderstanding between the races has gone never to return."[73] Within the tragedy of the lynchings, African Americans found hope in white officials' public support of the black victims and not the lawless white mobs.[74]

Mitchell was not the only newspaper editor to take such a forcible stand on lynching, yet he was the most active in doing so in the early 1920s. The white editor Louis Isaac Jaffe would also use the *Norfolk Virginian-Pilot* to publicize and discourage the violence. Jaffe, in fact, later became one of the leading critics in the South of the KKK and vigilante violence. Unlike many others in this study, Jaffe was not one of the elite white class in Virginia and possessed no useful First Family of Virginia connections. However, as editor of one of Virginia's largest newspapers, he grew to be one of the most influential men in the state. Yet, in 1920, Jaffe still had a relatively low profile, having only moved to Norfolk to accept the editor position at the *Norfolk Virginian-Pilot* the previous year.

Louis Jaffe was born in 1888 in Detroit, Michigan, to orthodox Jewish Lithuanian immigrants but moved to Durham, North Carolina, when he was only seven.[75] So, although Louis was new to Virginia in 1919, he was not new to the expectations of segregation and the complex southern social structure. As Jaffe's biographer Alexander S. Leidholdt noted, "Interestingly, given the intensity of his editorial assault on the practice as the decade wore on, he did not respond directly to specific lynchings that occurred in Virginia early in his tenure as editor."[76] Eventually, Jaffe would become an instrumental figure in the successful campaign for the Virginia General Assembly to adopt an antilynching law in 1928. This work helped lead him to win the Pulitzer Prize on May 12, 1929.[77] Yet, although he spoke against lynching and in 1921 characterized the vigilante violence as an "abomination that cannot be too severely dealt with," his more direct and vociferous attacks would come later.

These efforts to maintain at least a facade of racial goodwill during the rocky post–World War I period paid dividends in stymieing vigilante violence during crises when racial tensions were heightened. For example, in March 1921, white and black leaders worked together to prevent a well-publicized rape of a white woman in Richmond from leading to a race riot. Early one morning in Fulton, a section of Richmond, two men, reportedly black, entered the home of John E. Heisler, a respected working-class white. After robbing Heisler and his wife, the men threatened Mr. Heisler with a gun, forced him to face the wall, and then took turns raping his wife. The savagery of the crime stunned the community, particularly that the horror had occurred in such a crowded area where cries for help, if heard, should have brought numerous citizens to the couple's aid. Yet, the threat of the gun and the efficient manner in which the intruders invaded the home and overtook the occupants gave neither Mr. Heisler nor Mrs. Heisler the opportunity to cry out. Instead, the crime occurred in brutal silence with other Richmonders only steps away, unaware of their turmoil. Whites were terrified, and throughout the following week filled the offices of city hall requesting gun permits. Although themselves afraid of the possible backlash, black residents stayed away from city

Louis I. Jaffe. (Papers of Louis I. Jaffé, Albert and Shirley Small
Special Collections Library, University of Virginia)

hall, realizing any attempts on their part to gather weapons could provoke mass rioting.[78] And race riots were a common concern in 1921, sparked across the country by much more minor instances than a brutal crime.

The African American newspapers expressed as much shock as the white dailies. The *Richmond Planet* questioned how such a tragedy could occur and declared that it "did not believe that there were in this city two colored men who would have permitted a woman to be so assaulted without having made some outcry or without having offered his life to prevent such a fiendish crime in his presence."[79] Editor Mitchell, a confirmed bachelor who never entirely trusted the sensibilities of women, found it difficult to believe that any white woman in Richmond "with her innate horror of the male members of the darker race, who would even under threat of death submit to such an indignity when there were within calling distance hundreds of white and colored men, who would have risked their lives to save her from such a disgrace."[80] He agreed that a crime had occurred but did not entirely believe the Heislers' version of the story or that black men could have been the culprits. Black elites feared that the incident challenged their constant assurances about the irreproachable morality of the black masses. They understood that the crime could end white support of African American uplift reforms and threaten the relative peace in which the two races lived in Virginia.

After the initial frenzy, white Virginians tried to dismiss the possibility that the rapists were African American. Mrs. Heisler's family physician, Dr. B. L. Beams, white, came forward with his story to the press. The white *Richmond News Leader* reported that Beams had been called the morning of the attack to treat Mrs. Heisler and, at that time, also took her statement. He confirmed that she had indeed been violated and also assured the public that it was through no fault of her own. Mrs. Heisler, Beams explained, was "a moral, honest woman though in very, humble circumstances."[81] Beams, however, offered his opinion that the house was too dark for either of the Heislers to see whether or not the attackers were actually black. Although Beams's statement was less than concrete evidence, the white newspapers accepted his interpretation, and fervor over the crime subsided. In the following weeks, the police continued to search for culprits with no success. With their minds eased that no crazed African American criminals were on the loose (only white ones), the white public, at least according to the newspapers, forgot about the incident.

Apart from Beams's statement, racial tension was diffused by white paternalists working with African American leaders, drawing upon the ties of years of interracial cooperation. Whites asked African American leaders to release statements denouncing the violence, reassuring frightened whites, and expressing their desire for racial peace. According to the *Richmond Planet*, "this request was complied with although the colored people resented an imputation that any colored resident of this city would be guilty of such a crime." The paper predicted that once "the facts were investigated under the impartial and unprejudiced searchlight of public opinion," those conciliatory statements issued by black leaders would be proven unnecessary and seem "ridiculous."[82] Although African Americans resented the necessity to issue assurances of their "peaceable nature," the actions of the black and white leaders successfully prevented any vigilante action. "Conditions have improved," the *Richmond Planet* reported, "and the bond of friendship and esteem is now stronger between the two races than it was before."[83] In a time of escalated racial tensions nationally, interracial dialogue in Virginia worked to the benefit of both races and stopped large-scale outbreaks of racial violence. The delicate balance of racial understanding in the state held. Discrimination continued, but whenever possible it was mitigated by a lingering code of civility.

This reaction was not an indication that there was less racial prejudice in the state than in the Lower South or, in fact, the nation as a whole. Many white Virginians were as ardent white supremacists as ever lived. Yet, they believed thoroughly in a code of organized racial order based on "civility." Paternalist whites saw themselves as the benevolent guardians of the black population of the state and approved of interracial efforts that sought to improve racial understanding. In turn, they concluded that black Virginians were superior to African Americans throughout the rest of the nation. Whites clung to Lost Cause myths of loyal slaves saving their white mistresses and the family plantations with its buried silver while the white men of the manor were off in glorious battle. Accordingly, they convinced themselves that "their" blacks loved and respected them. They preferred to believe that the rapists were white rather than have their illusions of racial harmony shattered. African Americans leaders, particularly the prominent spokesmen editors P. B. Young of Norfolk and John Mitchell Jr. of Richmond, fed into this image by repeatedly declaring their devotion to the "better classes" of whites. Despite the obvious hypocrisy of both sides, the complicated system of negotiation and flattery worked. In some other states, the Heisler incident would have sparked mass mayhem, but in Virginia public interest in the rape dwindled after the white press decided that the attackers were probably not black. African American leaders, however, remained indignant and hurt that their race had ever been suspected.

This mind-set successfully undermined the second Ku Klux Klan's recruitment efforts in Virginia. Nationally, the post–World War I climate of racial tension proved fertile ground for a resurgence of the Ku Klux Klan.[84] Inspired by D. W. Griffith's heroic portrayal of the first Klan in the movie *Birth of a Nation* (1915), the second Ku Klux Klan formed in 1915 on top of Stone Mountain, outside Atlanta,

Georgia. Despite the film's enormous popularity, membership remained low until post–World War I racial tensions encouraged a national recommitment to white supremacy. Tapping into this unrest, the Ku Klux Klan expanded to approximately 5 million members nationwide in the early 1920s.[85] Middle-class whites across America united in their fear and prejudice of "others," whether blacks, immigrants, Catholics, Jews, communists, or socialists. The KKK updated Populists' concerns in terms of 1920s rhetoric tapping into whites' fears about the power of big business and their marginalization via consumerism that, they believed, perverted the nation's moral compass and ignored the centrality of Protestant values. The group opposed evolving gender roles, particularly those that offered women new sexual, social, economic, and political freedoms. Disgust with irresponsible displays of sexuality extended to men as well, leading the group to employ vigilante tactics to stop domestic violence and stem adultery. Klan ideology transformed Populist concerns along racial lines, insisting that the "international Jew" controlled big business and blaming Catholics and African Americans for becoming dependent upon an evil industrial system. Attacks on American (Protestant) values, the Klan argued, came from both the upper and lower segments of society, and middle-class white America must stand up and fight for their privileges of whiteness, with violence if necessary.

In Virginia, as in the rest of the South, the Klan campaigned primarily on the protection of white supremacy. The dangers of miscegenation with blacks and the blurring of racial identities were considered far greater threats than any posed by immigrants or non-Protestant religious sects. On those grounds, the KKK worked to expand its membership base within the state. They began their first major recruitment effort by appealing to whites' fears that Virginia might soon succumb to African American control.[86] Unfortunately for Klan organizers, while this rhetoric did resonate with a number of the more radical racists within the state, this outlook ran directly counter to the vision of racial harmony that many white Virginians believed still prevailed. Convinced of their aristocratic pedigree and the superiority of their state, these whites argued that their relationship with the Commonwealth's exceptional breed of "Negroes" was an idyllic model of racial order to be envied by the rest of the nation.[87] While white Virginians most assuredly believed a "race problem" existed, paternalists, in particular, agreed it was best handled through vigilant segregation where whites could keep a benevolent eye on their darker-skinned neighbors who they felt needed their guidance. Although Virginia was as racist as states farther South, Virginians cultivated their own unique brand of "polite racism." While whites worried about maintaining a careful control over blacks, most white paternalists still believed in the early 1920s that they were successfully handling their "Negro Problem." They saw no need to turn to the newly reorganized Ku Klux Klan, which many whites viewed as a crass organization unworthy of Virginians.

In this atmosphere of opposition, the Ku Klux Klan, in 1920, intensified its efforts to recruit members throughout Virginia. It was most successful in attracting members in growing cities like Norfolk, Newport News, Portsmouth, Lynchburg, Danville, Hopewell, and Roanoke where new industrial jobs led whites to fear potential economic competition from blacks. Yet, the group also made some headway in more rural towns in the Shenandoah Valley, like Staunton and Winchester, where African Americans comprised a much smaller percentage of the population than in the Tidewater area.[88] When possible, the Klan held public demonstrations of their strength. In early December 1920, Klan leaders led a large procession through the streets of Richmond, proclaiming their organization to be a righteous, vigilante force sanctioned by God. The event ended with a mass meeting at the city auditorium where emotional appeals were made for white Virginians to join the "cause" and protect white supremacy.[89] The following September, the KKK held another march in the state's capital. This parade drew a crowd of eight thousand to ten thousand spectators to watch the masked participants.[90]

Due to the secret nature of the organization, exact membership numbers or socioeconomic data on those who joined is unknown. Some white Virginians, particularly those from the working and middle classes, eagerly embraced the KKK, but membership was not as widespread as elsewhere in the nation. From the beginning, the Klan met opposition in the state. As early as the fall of 1920, Richmond's two major white daily newspapers spoke out against the KKK. The *Richmond Times-Dispatch* criticized the new Klan for its anti-American (in the editor's opinion) support of lynch law, promotion of "racial rancor and hatreds," and efforts to arouse "religious passions . . . [in order] to set creed against creed." The organization, the editor argued could not "measure up . . . to the 100 per cent American gauge."[91] He concluded that these irresponsible tactics proved that "there is neither room or need for this Klan in America."[92]

Although the *Richmond News Leader* initially printed a recruitment ad for the KKK on Saturday, November 20, the newspaper issued an apology the following Tuesday stating that no further advertisements for the group would be printed in their paper.[93] The editor Douglas Freeman (himself active in paternalistic interracial reforms) conceded that he agreed with the goals of white supremacy promoted by the Klan but not with their methods, which could potentially endanger class order among whites. Support of violent mob rule contradicted white Virginians' aristocratic and benevolent self-image. Freeman feared that the Klan's appeals might strike some resonance among Virginia's working-class whites who were concerned about economic competition and were beginning to lose faith that elite white paternalists were really effective in supporting working-class whites' interests. Freeman worried that these disaffected whites would ruin years of co-operative goodwill work by trying to take over the job of patrolling the color line. Working-class support of the Klan would not only potentially lead to a rise in vigilante violence but undermine elite paternalists' (like himself) assumed duty of managing both racial and class order. Hoping to prevent future advertisements promoting the Klan, the Richmond Advertisers' Club released a resolution attacking the organization. The group condemned "activities tending toward a revival of the Ku Klux Klan or any other premeditated action on the part of the individuals or group of individuals which tends to excite racial animosities and to bring the community or the state into disrepute."[94] The Richmond Advertisers' Club along with the *Richmond Times-Dispatch* and the *Richmond News Leader* hoped their public stands against the Klan would weaken whatever appeal the Klan might have with the white working class within the capital city.

Not surprisingly, among white Virginians the strongest opponents of the rise of the second Ku Klux Klan were the paternalistic activists who had been involved for years in interracial cooperation efforts. The Klan's methods and rhetoric were diametrically opposed to their own expressed goals. For years, white Virginians had recognized these individuals, like Munford, Cocke, and Mastin, as influential community leaders who provided the valued civic service of helping to maintain racial harmony. The Klan, however, threatened their agenda. First, the KKK argued that a severe "Negro Problem" existed, which paternalists claimed they effectively had under control. Second, the KKK promoted mob vigilantism as a solution to any threats against white supremacy. White interracial activists found this policy repugnant not only because it challenged their faith in the state's justice system but also because it undermined their authority as self-appointed spokesmen for black Virginians.

Dr. Walter Russell Bowie, rector of St. Paul's Protestant Episcopal Church in Richmond and nephew of Mary Munford, took the lead on behalf of white paternalists in publicly denouncing the new Ku Klux Klan. Soon after the December 1920 Klan march and mass meeting, Bowie spoke from the pulpit on the matter. He vehemently condemned the KKK for its "appeal to the mob passion and to the spirit of lynch law," explaining that while the first Klan "had the relative justification of terrible emergency" (that is, the "horrors" of Reconstruction), the new organization was "an insult to the forces of orderly government."[95] He encouraged the city's Christian ministers to, like himself, use their positions to teach "the right approach" toward "race relations." If elite whites, both clergy and non-clergy, failed to lead by example, then he feared that there was a real danger that the Klan's subversive influence could "embitter the relationship between the white and colored peoples, and that short cuts of lawlessness should take the place of a patient search for Christian co-operation which is the only way by which a solution of any human problem can be found."[96]

Rooted in the paternalistic interracial tradition, Bowie argued that it was in the best interests of white Virginians to work with African Americans, accept blacks' presence in this country, and recognize whites' own Christian duty to work for the uplift of their darker-skinned neighbors. Although careful not to directly criticize the tradition of segregation, the minister believed earnestly that practicality and morality demanded interracial communication with African American leaders. "Equally unmistakable," Bowie declared, "should be the determination that the negro is part of the civilization which involves us all, [and] should be assured of justice, a sympathy and a co-operation in his legitimate desires for improvement which no violence, and no secret organization, shall engender."[97] He argued that individuals like himself, not the Ku Klux Klan, were properly qualified to manage Virginia's racial order.

Reverend Bowie's sermon was widely reported upon throughout the city. Richmond newspapers carried detailed accounts. The *Richmond Times-Dispatch,* for example, quoted the long speech nearly verbatim and featured an editorial praising Bowie for his courage in speaking against the Klan and taking a stand for the "right" kind of white supremacy.[98] The *Richmond Planet* also covered the speech in elaborate detail.[99] The African American paper declared that Bowie "has the courage of his convictions. He is a valuable asset to any community and he represents a type of Southerner whose ranks are being largely augmented."[100] At a time when the Ku Klux Klan was rapidly gaining popularity throughout the nation, many elite whites throughout Virginia were unified in their opposition to the secret vigilante organization and unwilling to cede their exclusive control over the state's racial policies.[101]

Given this prevailing mind-set among elite whites, it was not surprising when the United Daughters of the Confederacy (UDC), the major proponent of Lost Cause values, joined the fight against the KKK. The ladies of this organization rooted in Confederate lore were angered by the second manifestation of the KKK's use of the Ku Klux Klan name. They praised the elite white men who formed the original Klan during the 1860s as heroes who sought to protect white women and save the South from "scalawags" and "carpetbaggers" during the remembered "dark" days of Reconstruction. The UDC protested that "it was a name and an order of such men as General Nathan B. Forrest, chief of the Klan, and among its members were the very bravest and noblest of Southern heroes." Thus, the Richmond chapter of the UDC petitioned the General Assembly in early December 1920 "to prohibit the use of this name made sacred by the men who bore it in years gone by."[102]

Although staunch segregationists typically confident in their assumptions about African American inferiority, Virginian members of the UDC spoke out against the 1920s vigilante secret organization. They agreed with the second Klan's goals of unchallenged white supremacy but believed, like paternalistic activists, that the new group's tactics could only tarnish the Old Dominion's (self) image.[103]

While the Klan did become a persistent presence within the state during the 1920s, the group never yielded the same political power or influence common in other states. Opposition was always vocal. Various local governments spoke out against the Klan. Richmond's Common Council was so disturbed by the display of secrecy at the September 1921 march that they banned any future parades of masked men.[104] White clergy in Roanoke convinced their city council to go on record officially against the organization.[105] In Richmond, where paternalistic white leaders were especially vocal in their denunciation of the Klan, the local KKK branch disbanded and disavowed any connection with the national organization. The Klan received greater support in the Tidewater area (the center of new industrial jobs in the state) than in Virginia's capital. Yet, even there opposition was ever-present. In the words of Louis Jaffe, the white editor of the *Norfolk Virginian-Pilot*, the Ku Klux Klan had "no place in a free country."[106]

In 1920, the Norfolk newcomer Jaffe was still developing a name for himself, having just moved to the city the year before. He had yet to become known as perhaps the state's most liberal white journalist who chose to take on the Ku Klux Klan despite the many threats it would bring to both himself and his family. His hatred of social injustice and mob violence was rooted in part in his Jewish roots, although Jaffe joined the Episcopalian Church several years after moving to Norfolk. Taking a more direct approach and attack than particularly the white Richmond editors, Jaffe rejected any depictions of the KKK as a harmless social club and argued instead that "from the moment it sprang like Minerva, full panoplied, from the head of Emperor Simmons," the organization followed "a celebrated mission of hate."[107] He even criticized his fellow white editors for not doing enough in resorting to "editorial reticence alternating with gentle wrist-slappings."[108] Jaffe's path, which had just begun in 1920, differed considerably — in methods, if not always motives — from that of the more entrenched paternalist white editors.

Black Virginian leaders generally praised whites' public condemnations of the Ku Klux Klan without backing Jaffe's criticism of certain white editors. John Mitchell Jr., for example, heralded the white dailies the *Richmond Times-Dispatch* and the *Richmond News Leader* for the positions they took against the Klan. Following the *Richmond News Leader*'s decision not to print any further KKK recruitment ads, Mitchell pronounced: "We are glad that the better class of white and colored people are of one mind relative to this sinister organization. It cannot do other than cause trouble between the races."[109] In Norfolk, P. B. Young followed a path similar to Mitchell's, speaking against the Klan in his paper as well as working through his position as president and founder of the city's chapter of the NAACP. As for his fellow Norfolk editor, Young found himself over the years at times aligned with Louis Jaffe and other times not. Divided by race, Jaffe and Young's professional relationship, however, never had the contentious personal rivalry of Young and Mitchell's.[110]

When the Klan began its recruitment drive in Richmond, Mitchell used his newspaper as a forum to inform African Americans of the danger they faced and spur them into active protest. Whites' condemnations of the secret organization were widely reported, but the editor wanted black Virginians to act for themselves and not rely solely on the work of whites. Speaking to black and, hopefully, white readers, Mitchell emphasized that "many colored people are prepared to join with the white people in upholding law and order and in defending themselves."[111] In December, Mitchell again attempted to rally black Virginians by reminding them that "the crusade against the Ku Klux Klan has just begun, so far as the white people of this community are concerned. It is now in order for the colored ministers to take up the slogan and by their conservative utterances and positive assertion to allay the feeling of unrest that has been aroused by these unusual displays by certain elements among the white people, who in their thoughtlessness have done so much to injure one of the humblest and most loyal races of people upon the face of the globe."[112] He encouraged black ministers to take the lead in the fight against the Klan, believing their influence could best prevent a potential race war. Yet, Mitchell also believed that self-protection against vigilante action was necessary. Although it has not been documented, stories abounded of Pythian soldiers (from the Knights of Pythias, a fraternal order headed by Mitchell) patrolling Jackson Ward in the early 1920s to be on guard against potential Klan action.[113]

This emphasis on black agency, however, did not indicate a refusal to accept the assistance of whites when beneficial, especially when it opened new opportunities for African Americans. "It behooves all law abiding colored citizens, regardless of sex," Mitchell acquiesced, "to co-operate with these leaders amongst the white people and to do what we can to control the dissolute, lawless classes in our midst."[114] Reflecting class division among black Virginians and speaking from an elitist position (a viewpoint shared by most of Richmond's black leaders) to the "better class" of African Americans, Mitchell explained that it was their duty to control the black masses that he partially blamed for the rise of white vigilantism. "Many of our own people," he informed his readers, "are as dangerous to our own welfare as are mad dogs or infectious diseases."[115] He believed that careful monitoring of the actions of working-class blacks, whose needs he understood little better than did his white counterparts, would not only stem racial violence but demonstrate to white activists the advantages and efficiency of allowing "better class" blacks to control their own. This contribution, he hoped, would serve to make interracial initiatives less paternalistically one-sided and more equal. "By a co-operative effort along the lines marked out and emphasized by these press and ministerial leaders," Mitchell predicted, "a mutual understanding will follow and all will work valiantly together for the triumph of those ideals which will make our beloved South-land one of the brightest and safest spots on the globe."[116]

At the same time as the Fulton rape and its aftermath as well as the KKK recruitment drives, members of Richmond's Chamber of Commerce were in the midst of a survey of African American living conditions in the city. Rather than abandoning their study in the face of racial tension, the white businessmen issued public denouncements of the lack of adequate housing for blacks, poor street conditions, and general dismal city maintenance in African American sections.[117] In part, this action was taken out of embarrassment over some nationally publicized criticism the city received about its treatment of its black population. "Not so many months ago," explained the editor of the *Richmond Times-Dispatch*, "a writer in a widely read magazine published in a Northern city called [the] attention of the world at large to the miserable housing conditions in which the Negroes of Richmond were compelled to exist. Whereupon most of us waxed righteously indignant at the alleged injustice he had put upon this city."[118] These accusations forced city leaders, however, to conduct a review of African American sections, primarily Jackson Ward. In turn, the report of the Chamber of Commerce admitted that the situation was "not only deplorable but 'such as to invite pestilence.'"[119]

   In response, a number of white city leaders as well as the daily newspapers called for Progressive reforms, praising individuals such as Janet Henderson Randolph (the wife of Norman V. Randolph), who had been crusading for improvements for years. Rather than a liberal threat to segregation, the white press praised Mrs. Randolph's interracial efforts as benevolent and an example of the true supremacy of the white race. Randolph herself was considered the epitome of the proper southern lady, founding the first Richmond chapter of the United Daughters of the Confederacy in 1896 and serving as its president for thirty-one years.[120] Whites like Randolph felt that it was both their duty and obligation to improve Jackson Ward not because they cared about blacks' rights as citizens but because they were concerned about upholding their state's reputation (in their own eyes) of paternalistic gentility as well as fulfilling a Christian and Progressive duty to help those they deemed less fortunate. In this same vein, white reformers had a stake in proving that blacks had not committed the Fulton crime because evidence to the contrary would have cast doubt on their claims of control over the black race. Many of these white Virginians believed that it was their moral obligation as the "superior" race to help a less fortunate race put under their protection by the providence of God's will. "The Negroes," argued the *Richmond Times-Dispatch*, "deserve well at the hands of Richmond far better than they have received. Industrious, thrifty and law-abiding, they have earned their place here."[121] Instead of blaming African Americans for the recent racial tension, the editor of the *Richmond Times-Dispatch* praised black Richmonders for their conduct throughout the ordeal:

> Never has this been more vividly realized than during the recent troublous days when inflamed minds [were] incited to race antagonisms. Throughout that time of uncertainty the Negroes listened to the wise and calm counsel of their recognized leaders and it was due largely to their exemplary behavior that Richmond's reputation as respecter of the law was maintained. That is but an instance, but it is indicative of the general good feeling between the white and colored citizens of this city. To preserve and promote that feeling and in common justice to the Negroes and as a safeguard to the health of the city itself Richmond should delay no longer in housing them decently and comfortably.[122]

Simply, the editor condescendingly concluded that blacks should be rewarded for good behavior; specifically with municipal services that whites already took for granted.

Despite these proclamations and public approval of interracial cooperation efforts, the conditions African Americans faced improved only marginally. Efforts were made to fill potholes and clean streets when white outrage demanded action, but conditions reverted when the white politicians forgot about the issues, assuming them to have been simply fixed without considering the long-term financial commitments necessary for change. But the root of the problem remained Jim Crow, and most whites still refused to recognize segregation as the underlying cause of the chronic housing shortage, increased poverty, and one of the highest African American death rates in the country. Separate could never be equal. As a result, in the post–World War I era, African Americans realized more clearly than ever that real change to the dilapidated African American neighborhoods would not come until the right of the franchise had been restored to the black masses. White advocates of blacks' concerns proved a poor substitute for direct representation.

6

Contested Authority

If the Negro leaders in the South are wise, they will see in this action of the
Republican Party the hand of Providence. It will enable the white men of the
South, when this fear of the Negro in politics as a race is removed, to so create an
atmosphere of friendliness toward the Negro, that many of the things that he, the
Negro, has hoped to gain by politics in the way of better housing, better schools,
better facilities for traveling, economic justice, justice in the courts, etc. *will be his
by right of justice and public opinion.*
—Anonymous white Virginian concerning the exclusion of African American
delegates from the Republican state convention, 1921

POST-WORLD WAR I Virginia witnessed a new sense of disillusionment
and frustration among black leaders. Despite efforts to follow the rules
of paternalist cooperation, segregation was becoming increasingly restrictive, and racial violence was becoming more widespread. Even during the
war, in 1917, John Mitchell Jr. asked his readers, "What are we to receive in the
way of recognition in return for this loyalty?" He lamented bitterly: "We have
been promised improved housing conditions. Have we secured these conditions?
We have been promised a park. Have we been able to say just where the location
is? We have been promised a new high school building. Has the money been
appropriated for the erection of the structure?" He concluded that even though
many whites had "dealt justly with us," those whites did not have "the controlling
power."[1] Promises meant little if they were not followed by results, and the paternalist generation was beginning to lose its influence as white politicians began to
reject the ideals of paternalism.

In the first two decades of the twentieth century, interracial cooperation in
Virginia had worked successfully to mediate racial tensions; paternalistic whites
offered money and influence to African American uplift projects, if the work fit
within the segregationist framework, in exchange for blacks allowing these whites
to act as their political representatives and liaisons to state and local government.

Although some blacks still voted and maintained a dialogue with elected officials, Mary Munford, Joseph Mastin, Jackson Davis, and similar whites spoke with authority that they were best qualified to assess the needs of black Virginians. This silent deal reinforced these whites' paternalistic mind-sets, offering them not only the self-satisfaction of their benevolence but increased control over black space. These whites were indeed respected for their social status and family connections, yet the degree they were listened to by elected officials able to effect change varied by circumstance, causing their influence to begin to wane as formerly private charitable endeavors were increasingly governmentalized. And, in fact, that loss of control of those reforms was a result of their own Progressive successes.

The debate over the franchise was an old one. Black men gained the right to vote with the passage of the Fifteenth Amendment in 1870, and, although whites attempted various illegal tactics to manipulate the African American electorate, blacks in Virginia took advantage of their new right and became a substantial electoral force. Some white Democrats tried to make paternalistic appeals for blacks to place their faith in and vote for their former masters, but most African Americans became staunch supporters of the Republican Party that they credited with their emancipation.[2] By the 1880s, African Americans were expanding their political rights by seeking elected offices. They even received some real cooperation and support from the white power structure within the state when William Mahone, a powerful political demagogue associated with the Readjuster movement in the early 1880s, experimented with building political coalitions across racial lines.[3] Yet, the situation deteriorated in the 1890s, when increased racial tension sparked in part by economic depression led a number of southern states to rewrite their constitutions to disenfranchise blacks. Virginia whites followed suit in 1901. The new constitution adopted following the 1901–2 constitutional convention effectively disfranchised the majority of African Americans as well as a substantial number of poor whites through poll taxes, literacy tests, and other seemingly unconstitutional methods.[4]

Not surprisingly, whites justified their actions through paternalistic rhetoric. In 1918, Richard L. Morton, a white University of Virginia graduate student, summed up white Virginians' interpretation of these developments in his dissertation titled "The Negro in Virginia Politics, 1865–1902." Morton argued that disfranchisement was necessary to ensure the bonds of friendship between the races. "Improved conditions and the increasing harmony existing between the two races," he explained, "could only have come through the removal of the negro from sectionalism and politics."[5] He believed it had been necessary to protect inexperienced and unprepared freedmen and -women from the burden of voting. The white delegates to the 1901–2 constitutional convention, Morton asserted, should be praised for saving their darker-skinned neighbors from the burden of being forced into the franchise by "the unscrupulous leaders of the negroes [who] endeavored to keep them united by vilifying the whites and by stirring up racial prejudice and passions."[6] Morton conveniently forgot to address the continuance of electoral fraud even after the disfranchisement.

African Americans strongly disagreed with this poor assessment of their fitness to vote, and, in fact, before the 1901–2 convention many blacks in the state were convinced their electoral rights were in no immediate danger. Responding in 1899 to growing momentum across the state in support of disfranchisement, the *Richmond Planet* proclaimed: "If two hundred and fifty years of unrequited toil, and the shedding of our blood for this nation in the Revolutionary War, in the War of 1812, and in the War of the Rebellion did not entitle us to freedom, what would have entitled us to it? Freedom without the right of franchise would be a mockery. . . . But why discuss this matter? . . . We have the right to vote and we intend to retain the right. The nation knows our services and from its past record it has never gone back on any of its saviours."[7] African Americans, hoping this would be an opportunity for whites to prove their claims of paternalism, did not think that their years of loyalty would be so easily dismissed. Yet, despite their efforts to protest and speak out against the new constitution, most black Virginians lost the right to vote. They did not account for the twisted logic of paternalism that justified disfranchisement as a needed protection for the black race.

Thousands of African Americans within the state overcame the restrictions and continued to vote, but the hope of creating a powerful political force with which whites would be forced to contend was, at least temporarily, abandoned.[8] These middle-class or elite blacks who could afford to pay the poll tax and succeeded in registering could be found throughout the state but were centered particularly in urban areas that offered greater opportunities for prosperous African American businessmen. Whites were aware of these voters but generally paid little attention to their actions and dismissed them as too few in number to influence elections and handicapped by their unwavering support of the Republican Party in a solidly Democratic state. The ballot, they reasoned, held little real power when retained only by a few blacks who had virtually no voice within the dominant political parties or state and local governments.

White reformers quietly ignored the fact that most of the African American leaders with whom they worked still voted, because the persistence of black voters contradicted whites' assertions that African Americans accepted the white political order. These voters undermined white reformers self-proclaimed position as spokesmen for black Virginians. Yet, white reformers continued to claim these roles for themselves. Although this arrangement benefited whites, black leaders worked to use these whites' willingness to speak on behalf of African American causes to garner governmental or white public support for their reform agendas. They played this game because they knew it worked. By appealing to whites to live up to their promise of separate but equal, white activists helped black reformers accomplish a variety of projects. When Thomas Walker became concerned about the plight of children convicted of minor crimes and placed in jails with hardened criminals, his efforts to revise Virginia's laws handling these juveniles were ignored until the white reformer Dr. Joseph Mastin joined forces with Walker and presented the initiative before the General Assembly.[9] Similarly, Janie Porter Barrett turned to Mary Munford and other whites to lobby the General Assembly for the needed financial support to open and operate her Virginia Industrial School for Colored Girls. In return for blacks' downplaying their political voice, whites promised to reward African Americans with better living conditions, greater educational opportunities, separate but equal traveling conditions, economic prosperity, and a fairer court system. Good behavior would supposedly be rewarded by the generosity and gratitude of the white populace. White activists viewed African American disfranchisement to be a golden opportunity to prove the effectiveness of paternalism. They concluded that African Americans had no need of direct political access when whites, like themselves, could better assess and represent the needs of black communities throughout Virginia.

African American leaders, however, never believed so naively in the justice of public opinion. Instead, they understood that the 1901–2 state constitutional convention had only marked the beginning of an ongoing campaign to limit their civil liberties. They fought to hold on to their limited remaining rights. Although many leaders including Thomas Walker, John Mitchell Jr., Maggie Lena Walker, Mary Burwell, Janie Porter Barrett, Lillian Payne, and Ora Stokes courted the aid of white activists and cultivated influential white "friends" who would lobby white politicians on their behalf, they were also keenly interested and well informed about the intricacies of national, state, and local politics and refused to cede the right of such knowledge to whites. By the second decade of the twentieth century, thousands of blacks within the state still voted. These numbers increased in 1920 when black women gained the franchise with the passage of the Nineteenth Amendment. Most of these middle-class and professional African Americans voters remained active in the Republican Party.

Foremost, these individuals cared about the deteriorating living conditions among their race, particularly in large cities like Richmond where African Americans were overcrowded as a result of residential segregation laws into overpriced, yet dilapidated housing. By the outbreak of World War I, overcrowding had reached troubling proportions. These issues were of paramount importance to black leaders because residential segregation laws hurt well-to-do and poor alike,

forcing both the black elites and the disfranchised black masses to live in dilapidated neighborhoods. While previous segregationist policies like that of public
transportation could be avoided by those with the funds to do so—for example,
by buying private cars—the Vonderlehr statute offered no loopholes for class privilege. Thus, black elites in Virginia began to feel strongly the effects of their race's
large-scale disfranchisement. From the pages of the *Richmond Planet,* John Mitchell Jr. cautioned his readers that "grading streets and laying new side-walks cannot
be done in the section where colored people live for the reason that they are voteless, so to speak, and the white folks in other sections are 'vote-full.'"[10] Mitchell
and others could and did vote, but they realized their efforts had little impact when
the majority of the race was disfranchised. White paternalists talked incessantly
of the need to improve conditions, but the situation changed little. Committees
conducted studies, individuals lobbied city and town councils, but little practical
progress was made. As time passed, black activists increasingly doubted the ability
of their white "friends" to lobby persuasively on their behalf.

The passage of the Nineteenth Amendment in August 1920 marked the fruition
of a movement that for years had raised difficult racial questions within Virginia.
Although Tennessee assured the success of the amendment as the thirty-sixth
state to ratify, southern states in general were against giving women the franchise. Confronted with the radical idea of women voting, white southerners once
again played the race card, worried not only about their pure white women being
sullied by having to visit polling places but also the potential effect of the new
law in enfranchising African American women. Mississippi had briefly considered extending woman suffrage as a method to ensure white supremacy during
their 1890 constitutional convention, the event that marked the beginning of the
disfranchisement movement. Yet, after 1890, most white southerners concluded
that woman suffrage would only mean the potential for black women to vote,
and thus determined to limit the electorate to [privileged] white men when at all
possible. A strong woman suffrage movement, however, arose in Virginia with
the formation of the Equal Suffrage League of Virginia (all white and primarily
female) in 1909, which became the League of Women Voters after ratification. A
similar organization of African American women was never formed in the state.
A number of black women's clubs expressed interest in and support for "votes
for women," but no African American Virginian woman actively campaigned in
favor of the initiative because they knew to do so would only aid the antisuffrage
movement within the state.

    In comparison with states in the Lower South, like Louisiana and Mississippi,
the Equal Suffrage League of Virginia attempted to avoid the race issue whenever

possible. Although most were whites who accepted segregation, these women were schooled in the tradition of genteel paternalism and believed that the proper way to handle "race relations" was through white-dictated benevolence. Some whites paid no credence to the customary professions of friendship and were quite comfortable in their blatant racism, but others like Mary Munford, Mary Johnston, Lila Valentine, Adele Clark, Lucy Randolph Mason, and Nora Houston were uneasy playing the race card, feeling it was crass, unnecessary, and even immoral. These women, headed by Valentine, were the leaders of the organization and, not surprisingly, supporters of interracial cooperation. Most of these women accepted white superiority but ridiculed any "uncivilized" suggestions that African Americans were a threat to the white populace.[11]

Virginia suffrage leaders, despite their best efforts, could never entirely escape what they referred to as the "Negro Question." The more radical racists throughout the South set the tone for the suffrage movement in the region. In particular, Kate Gordon of Louisiana established herself as one of the most blatant racists in the nation by using every opportunity available to speak and write about her fears of black domination. While some white Virginia suffragists wholeheartedly agreed with and supported Gordon and her regional organization, the Southern States Woman Suffrage Conference, others, particularly those paternalists also interested in interracial cooperation efforts, were appalled by Gordon's unapologetic racism. Mary Johnston, the nationally renowned novelist and one of the Equal Suffrage League's most popular speakers, ultimately curtailed her activism in the movement because she found it increasingly difficult to work with Gordon. In 1915, Johnston wrote her friend Lila Valentine, president of the Equal Suffrage League of Virginia: "I, no more than you, like the matter or the tone of Kate Gordon's utterance. . . . In many instances they were so opposed to my own moral and mental convictions, silent and expressed, that, standing to the outsider as they must do for the opinion of the conference as a whole, I am coming to feel that I cannot much longer leave my name upon its letter heads, even as an honorary vice-president. Apparently, she sees the universal situation through the window pane of Louisiana politics."[12] Johnston responded like a typical Virginian white paternalist. Although perhaps more aware of the problems of discrimination and the debilitating blight of segregation in her home state than some of her counterparts, Johnston did not believe that Virginia had a "race problem" like Louisiana. She earnestly viewed "race relations" in the Old Dominion to be smoother and considered Gordon's forthright racism to be crass and unbecoming. Accordingly, Johnston renounced her post as an honorary vice president of the Southern States Woman Suffrage Conference and, the following year, formally resigned from the organization.

But the general white populace was not as confident about the security of white supremacy as these paternalists, and their fears intensified with the passage of the Nineteenth Amendment in 1920. Some white politicians worried about reports of massive numbers of black women lining up to register. White newspapers fed this fear by speculating daily whether the white power structure was in danger.[13] Although relatively silent during the struggle for ratification, black women in Virginia, most prominently Maggie Lena Walker and Ora B. Stokes in Richmond, took charge of organizing registration campaigns for African American women.[14] In the end, however, whites' concerns were groundless. Walker and Stokes, among others throughout the state, did make tremendous efforts in encouraging significant numbers of black women to attempt to register, but relatively few actually succeeded. Some black women were able to register but only in similar proportions to black men. In Richmond, white officials hindered the attempts of black women to register by forcing them to apply in a separate office from white women, inconveniently located in the basement. The registrars employed all sorts of tricks, such as changing and shortening hours without notice. Some white suffragists, now less afraid of expressing their support of African Americans after the amendment had been passed, protested to the electoral board on behalf of black women. In the end, these white women, who included Adele Clark and Nora Houston, received assurances from the electoral board that the black women would receive the same registrar's office hours as whites.[15] Yet, this concession did not prove enough. The disfranchisement methods established by the 1901–2 state constitutional convention successfully prevented most black women as well as black men from exercising their political rights.

Despite these displays of cooperation including white women patrolling African American polls on Election Day to stem violence, the Equal Suffrage League and its successor, the League of Women Voters, excluded black women. Clark later admitted that the white suffragists "never had the nerve to enroll the Negro women" because of fear of public backlash.[16] These white women were raised on the tenets of white supremacy and worked within the constraints of segregation but felt no threat in the ability of a limited number of "qualified" African Americans to vote. They believed that protecting Virginia's contemporary reputation for racial harmony was far more important in maintaining the racial status quo. Thus, the status of blacks' political rights within Virginia continued to deteriorate despite the new black women voters.

Nor were black men entirely supportive of women voting. Despite the work of black women like Walker and Stokes, African American men frequently associated "manhood" with the obtainment or reobtainment (in the case of the franchise) of full citizenship rights. "This is a critical period in the race's history," John Mitchell Jr. warned, "and only cool headed, conservative, manly leaders should

The Virginia League of Women Voters in 1923. Adele Clark
is standing second from the left. Clark's friend and longtime
companion, Nora Houston, is in the back, near the center, fifth
from the right. (Courtesy of Virginia Historical Society)

be permitted to speak for us"; a group in which Mitchell undoubtedly included
himself.[17] These men repeatedly stressed the "manliness" of protesting segregation
without regard for the fact that some of the most prominent African American
reformers were women, including not only the nationally renowned Walker but
also Janie Porter Barrett and Ora B. Stokes, among others. Although he never
discouraged black women's activism directly, Mitchell downplayed their work and
gave little publicity to their achievements in his newspaper. Mitchell and other
African American male leaders like him never considered the importance of fighting for gender as well as racial equality. In particular, Mitchell was always rather
wary of Maggie Lena Walker. This stemmed in part from the fact that they were
presidents of competing banks and that Walker's bank, the St. Luke Penny Savings Bank, was more successful than Mitchell's Mechanics Savings Bank. When
Mitchell's institution experienced a near run in November 1912, he was effusive in

his praise of two local white banks that offered help if needed but expressed only an obligatory "thank you" for Walker's offer of assistance. Mitchell's bank failed in the early 1920s, but Walker's prospered throughout the era.[18]

The political situation worsened further in the early 1920s, when the Republican Party, of which most remaining African American voters were faithful followers, began to distance itself from that loyal base. Whites' efforts to push blacks out of the party in the South were not new, but in 1920–21 the "lily-white movement" reappeared with renewed vigor and threatened to obliterate the remaining vestiges of African Americans' political rights.[19] The first major indicator occurred in mid-1920 at the Republican National Convention when the lily-white faction of the party in Virginia maneuvered to have all their delegates seated and all elected black delegates refused admittance.[20] Angered by the event, black Virginians held their own party meetings to discuss their next course of action. These gatherings primarily provided opportunities to vent frustration.[21] The African American faction, however, ran one candidate for United States Senate, the lawyer J. R. Pollard. Although the party knew Pollard had no realistic chance of winning the election, African Americans across the state were heartened when their candidate polled 17,576 votes—a sign of the lingering commitment of blacks to hold on to their electoral rights.[22]

Rather than pulling the race together, these early lily-black sentiments brought division within black communities throughout the state. P. B. Young, editor of the *Norfolk Journal and Guide*, accused John Mitchell Jr. of not being supportive of the new race efforts despite his own conservative accommodationist stance. Mitchell retorted that he supported the black Republicans but questioned whether the initiative was well planned.[23] "Now is the time for reason and friendly conversation," Mitchell retorted to Young in a heated exchange between their two papers; "We are standing on the brink of a political abyss, so far as the present Republican Party is concerned and the way in an opposite direction must be sought to the end that the political labor of well-nigh half a century may not be needlessly thrown away."[24] Mitchell feared that publicized political activism would hurt black leaders' relationships with their white "friends" and break up old interracial alliances. Some African Americans resented Mitchell's tentative stance. Dr. D. A. Ferguson of Richmond accused the editor of making pronouncements that sounded eerily similar to the "editorials which ofttimes appear in our daily papers with comments favorable to our Racial achievements or efforts, but conclude with a gentle reminder that we are 'good niggers.'"[25] While Mitchell saw his position as practical, Ferguson suggested he was motivated instead by cowardly self-preservation.

Mitchell employed an accommodationist stance with whites because he believed it was the best route for African Americans in Virginia to regain widespread access to the ballot. He adhered to the rules of racial decorum, sought to make friends among whites, and utilized the system of interracial cooperation. Mitchell's actions and declarations always angered some people on both sides of the color line. But, despite qualms about his sometimes arrogant personal manner, the majority of black Virginians respected his accomplishments. He was, at heart, a realist who cared deeply about stemming discrimination and expanding the rights of his race. He spoke more candidly and openly about the status and nature of Virginia's race problems than most other black leaders within the state and believed that no amount of outside pressure from the North or other sections of the country could force the South to amend its racial ways.

Mitchell insisted that change had to occur from within. When the United States Congress in January 1921 began to question whether disfranchisement practices should alter states' allotted representation, he laughed at the attempts of some southern congressmen to pretend that African Americans were not barred from voting. "No honorable Southerner will deny that the Negro electorate has been denied the right of suffrage," Mitchell declared mockingly; "Senator Ben Tillman did not deny it and Senator James K. Vardaman, with all of his faults was never guilty of contradicting a fact that is known in all of this land."[26] The crux of this particular tirade was that black Virginians, realistically, could expect little help from the national government. The administration in Washington knew and tacitly supported the violations against the Fifteenth Amendment happening throughout the South. "As the matter now stands," Mitchell reasoned, "colored people in 'this neck of the woods' are not looking to Washington any more for help. They are looking to the white men, with whom they have lived to see to it that their rights and privileges are accorded to them. We have expressed the opinion time and again that the time will come when the right of franchise for the colored people will be accorded to them by the South, even should it be opposed by the white people of the North."[27] Mitchell believed that the only possibility of regaining lost rights was to stay in the South and play the system they had been raised to understand. He proposed that blacks use the professed paternalism of whites to their own advantage whenever and however possible. In short, he declared: "Colored men must be manly, God-fearing, polite and obliging, but they must insist upon their citizenship rights and combine with the better class of white people in the South to secure them. Outside help is beneficial but inside results are to be secured right here."[28] Black Virginians, he concluded, needed white Virginians' help if they ever hoped to obtain greater citizenship rights.

By 1921, however, many black reformers no longer believed that their white "friends" would ever help restore their political rights regardless of how often they proved themselves worthy. The increasing strictures of segregation proved to these black leaders that white paternalists were incapable of acting effectively as their political advocates and that this system of "indirect influence" was no substitute for direct political power. Even Mitchell reevaluated the need for an all-black political movement. Racial tensions had seemingly improved during World War I with newly enlisted black soldiers heading off to training camps being cheered and praised alongside their white counterparts. Cooperation efforts during the war abounded as Virginians, black and white, raced to prove their patriotism. Yet, the advent of world peace only increased racial tension at home. Some African Americans were embittered by this betrayal of their loyalty, bravery, and patriotism. "When the war was going on and we were all members of the Red Cross," one reader wrote the *Richmond Planet,* "the white people met us in our school houses and shook loving hands and said that we were all brothers and sisters. Since the war has ended, where are they now?" In response, John Mitchell Jr. quipped bitterly: "When another war comes on, these same conditions will exist again. All you have to do is wait for another war."[29]

These feelings of discontent came to a head in July 1921, when Virginia's white Republican Party officials, for the first time, refused to seat the black delegates at the state convention in Norfolk. Although black Virginians feared attempts to exclude their representatives to the scheduled July 14 meeting, they were stunned by the totality of the success of the lily-whites. African American delegates were not simply discouraged from attending but physically barred entrance by white policemen stationed at the doors.[30] All talk of trying to "storm the citadel" that Bastille Day came to naught, as those turned away had no choice but to retreat and nurse their wounded pride in private.[31] Whites within the Republican Party did not unanimously agree on the new "closed door" policy, but, to the dismay of black party members, internal dissent among whites virtually ceased once the official decision was made. Years of dedicated service to the party had been met with betrayal.[32] These select African Americans had retained the right to vote, despite enormous obstacles. Yet, the actions of the lily-whites stripped this access to the ballot of its power. Without a party that at least paid lip service to their concerns, Mitchell, Pollard, Young, and other elite black Virginians were as effectively disfranchised as the less fortunate black masses.

For solace and explanation of the events in Norfolk, Janie Porter Barrett, then superintendent of the Virginia Industrial School for Colored Girls, turned to Annie Schmelz, the white reformer who worked so closely with Barrett on a number of projects but particularly as longtime chairman of the board of managers at Barrett's school. Barrett and Schmelz had perhaps one of the closest professional relationships between any two black and white women in the state at that time. Barrett desired answers to the Republican Party's renewed devotion to "lily-whitism," but Schmelz responded only with justifications. Barrett's inquiry appealed to Schmelz's sense of paternalism. Viewing the request as a plea for enlightenment from an intellectual inferior, Schmelz agonized over how to respond, believing it was her responsibility to educate not only Barrett but all the women Barrett represented from the Virginia State Federation of Colored Women's Clubs as to the necessity and justice of the current political situation. "I shall do the best for you and all the splendid women you represent," Schmelz promised; "I believe you know I have always tried to do my best for you." While Barrett sought a white ally to fight against the racial injustice, she received only a detailed treatise, totaling eight typed pages, on why the action was necessary. "I do not believe that anything I ever undertook," Schmelz confessed, "seemed quite so difficult as what I am now attempting to do."[33]

Schmelz found her correspondence with Barrett concerning the Norfolk convention to be a laborious effort, but one that filled her with self-satisfaction and inflated her sense of purpose as an advocate for African American concerns. When Barrett asked her, "Won't you make it clear to me [so] that I may make it clear to my women," Schmelz used the opportunity to justify the need for the lily-white movement and encourage black compliance.[34] She refused to speak in abstractions and generalities as one of her white friends suggested and instead wrote in a frank, unapologetic manner, plainly laying her argument before Barrett. The honesty in her response to Barrett's concerns make these letters rare testaments to the multifaceted and complex relationships between white and black reformers, particularly women who tried to connect not only on a professional level but on a personal one as mothers and wives.

Schmelz chose not to turn to her friend Henry W. Anderson, the white Republican candidate, for answers, believing that he was too close to the incident and that African Americans, like Barrett, would not see him to be "*the friend I know him to be*" of the colored race." Instead, she determined to "think out the 'why'" for herself. However, she did recount a recent brief encounter with Anderson in which he told her that he had been too "absorbed with the task of planning the platform which would be just to both races and remove the race question from political agitation" and that he "knew nothing of what happened to the delegates" until after the meeting was over.[35] Schmelz admitted to being initially surprised and confused by the white Republican's actions, but she chose sides long before she committed herself on paper. She relied on the tenets of white supremacy and paternalism to reconcile the seeming incongruity of the recent events and her own commitment to the fair treatment of African Americans under a policy of separate but equal. Exceptions, she determined, had to be made in the interest of

Annie Schmelz, 1916. (Courtesy of the Hampton History Museum, Hampton, Virginia, Cheyne Studio Collection, 2009.15.2199 (1104))

racial harmony. She concluded that discrimination was a necessary evil that whites must occasionally employ in order to protect and aid black interests. Although not a Republican herself, Schmelz fully supported the lily-white policy and trusted Anderson's judgment.

Schmelz claimed that in order to understand the recent events it was necessary to examine the background of the issue, namely the history of African Americans and the franchise over the past one hundred years. She placed blame on the Republican administration that freed slaves through the Civil War with "blood which need never have been shed, had the North given the South a little more time to work out her plans." She concluded that "from *that* day until the action of the convention in Norfolk, your people have been little less than *exploited* by the Republican party."[36] Expecting argument from Barrett as to her interpretation that the North forced bloodshed on a South dedicated to the freedom of slaves, Schmelz declared that her "statement was not a *conjecture*, it is a fact" established by the Daughters of Confederacy, an organization dedicated not only to the remembrance of the Lost Cause but to proving its validity. Schmelz believed devoutly in Lost Cause interpretations of Reconstruction and blamed the Republican Party for exploiting blacks and destroying the supposed bonds between slaves and their masters by giving freedmen the vote. The party, she contended, "shattered the confidence of the Negro in his best friend—the best Southern white people, and no matter how much the Southern white man did for the negro, *and all that he has done will never be* known, no matter how much help was given, no matter how great was the burden of the two races which the South carried, *help was given*, and the burden [was] carried in face of the fact that the *Southern white man knew that every Negro who went to the polls would vote against him*."[37] Schmelz believed that only through interracial cooperation work, in which she was actively involved, could this bond between southern whites and blacks be truly healed. Interracialism had to work to prove that paternalism was not a lie.

In Schmelz's view, Republicans severely damaged not only racial harmony within the South but also retarded the development of the black race by alienating African Americans from their white allies. The childlike race, she argued, needed white supervision. Unlike radical white southerners like John Powell, Thomas Dixon, and Benjamin Tillman, Schmelz believed in the ability of the African American race to progress and evolve. Although she was glad of the demise of slavery, she felt the institution had helped civilize its chattel rather than stunt their growth. "You are here," Schmelz told Barrett, "and I thank God for it, for I believe it was his plan, even by slavery, to bring you from that dark continent, here, to the light and knowledge of our Blessed Lord and Savior, Jesus the Christ." Schmelz condemned the irresponsible actions of Republicans who gave the ballot

to blacks when they were "yet children." She compared the action to Barrett placing the Virginia Industrial School of Colored Girls into the hands of one of her
students, saying, "I shall put this institution into your hands for *you* to manage."
Schmelz concluded that the passage of the Fifteenth Amendment, giving African
Americans the right of franchise, was "like putting firebrands into the hands of
munition [*sic*] workers."[38]

Schmelz chose her analogies her carefully. She did not blame blacks for their
reckless behavior but presented them as being used by others: freed when they
were unprepared, urged to vote when they were ignorant of that responsibility,
and used as pawns by a Republican administration determined to destroy the
South by eliminating the friendship between the races. Thus, Schmelz, in her
critique of African Americans' electoral history, was careful not to hold blacks responsible for past corruption. Instead, she stressed that blacks were simply ill-used
and in the wrong place at the wrong time. In doing so, she dismissed all possibility
of black political agency. She concluded that the question was not whether African
Americans could act on their own behalf but rather which group of whites should
serve as their political representatives. Not surprisingly, Schmelz argued that native white Virginians such as herself instead of white northerners were the proper
guardians of African American concerns. Apart from the unspoken benefits and
privileges of white supremacy, Schmelz believed that it was her moral responsibility to repay past "debts" and revive the gospel of paternalism.

Schmelz claimed that the Republican Party needed to purge blacks from their
ranks in order to regain the credibility and respect necessary to revive a healthy
two-party system in the state. Like other elite Virginians, Schmelz was deeply
concerned with the reputation of the Old Dominion. She feared that Democratic
dominance within the state was stunting its growth and hindering reformist zeal.
But Schmelz stressed to Janie Barrett that she did not hold African Americans
responsible for this deficiency. "While I blame no one," she confided, "I declare
to you most emphatically that Virginia, who gave birth to the American Republic,
a State that by right of age, opportunity, prestige, and background should lead
every other State in the nation, I tell you, we are trailing along *in the dust of many
other States!*" She did not believe that politics was the only way to solve the problems
of the state but also stressed other "forces far greater than politics with which we
may work and which in the end will bring politics to that high plane of unselfish
service, where justice and righteousness to all people, white and black, rich and
poor, will be administered."[39] She considered the newly formed Commission on
Interracial Cooperation to be the most important of these efforts. Without concern
for the contradictions in her conclusions, she advised Barrett that the only way to
achieve this "justice and righteousness to all people" was for African Americans

to continue to work with whites in interracial reform, distance themselves from politics, and allow for the resurgence of a two-party system.

Schmelz did not necessarily discourage voting. In fact, she hoped the actions of the Republican Party would act as an electric shock to the black voter and convince him or her of the advantages of voting independently. Yet, Schmelz encouraged blacks to abandon all hope of political leadership in a society in which they were so vastly outnumbered by whites, noting that "it is self-evident that God has not planned it to be that way, and those of your leaders who are trying to put such impossible ideas and ideals into the mass mind of your people, are doing them not only an injustice, but to my mind a great injury." Instead, she defined blacks' roles as voters very narrowly. African Americans, she argued, could and should vote for the candidates they believed best represented their interests. Schmelz assumed that these candidates would always be white and considered elections as opportunities for blacks to demonstrate their faith in their white friends. Simply, she wanted a continuation of the indirect influence system on which interracial cooperation was based and dismissed any reason for blacks needing more direct political participation. Quoting Ora B. Stokes from a recent Virginia State Federation of Colored Women's Clubs meeting, Schmelz summarized: "Pay your poll tax, study your city, county, state and national government. Study each candidate's record, plank and platform, then vote for the best man and the best measures, regardless of whether the party be Republican or Democrat."[40]

Schmelz stressed to Barrett that African Americans had to be constantly aware of and in tune with the fluctuations of public opinion, primarily that of white Virginians. That endeavor, she argued, offered more opportunities for improving racial tensions than did politics. "Mrs. Barrett," she lectured, "this thing of public opinion is a power the extent of which few of us realize. It is far greater than politics for it can sway the control of politics. When we establish the right sort of public opinion the Day is Won."[41] Barrett, however, saw the fallacies of Schmelz's reasoning. Schmelz, like most of the state's paternalists, only viewed the issue through a white perspective. Blacks, Schmelz believed, should live their lives in accordance with white wishes. She interpreted that "concern with public opinion" meant African Americans needed to stay perpetually in tune with the whims of whites' passions. Dismissal of political concerns and acceptance of indirect political representation by whites meant the continuance of a discriminatory Jim Crow culture. Schmelz considered the ultimate goal of interracial cooperation efforts to be the insurance of race harmony *through* the smooth maintenance of segregation. Schmelz and her white colleagues failed to understand that the black leaders with whom they worked did not share their conviction that segregation was beneficial to both races. In the aftermath of World War I, when their patriotism was rewarded with further restrictions of their civil rights, African Americans could no longer pretend that separate could possibly be equal.

Annie Schmelz ardently believed in the righteousness of segregation, but she feared more than anything the threats of black Republicans to form their own party. Accordingly, she used her letter to warn Barrett against such an action. She cautioned Barrett at length: "To my mind the organization of the Colored Republican Party in Virginia can result in but one thing—a blocking of the way for the realization of the very thing the Negro is fighting to gain. They are creating the wrong kind of public opinion and they do not seem to realize that in seeking to organize themselves into a separate party, they are not only defeating the desires of their white friends to serve them, but *they are segregating the Negroes of this State into a class, a group, by themselves, standing in declared antagonism to the white people of all parties.*"[42] Schmelz, failing to see the hypocrisy in her own advice, underscored whites' understanding of segregation as a system dictated and managed by whites, despite promises of separate but equal. Whites had the freedom to segregate, but African Americans could only be segregated.

The threat of black Virginians to form their own political party endangered paternalist whites' base of power by publicizing the truth that blacks were not happy to play the role of second-class citizens. This act threatened to unravel interracial cooperation networks and undermine the basic justifications for paternalism as well as the culture of segregation. These whites considered blacks to be, by necessity, under their guidance and understood their "enlightened" wisdom and segregation as a convenient means to protect their own racial interests. The conception of two spheres, white and black, in Jim Crow Virginia was always an illusion. Not only did races mix every day on streets, businesses, and white homes, but also black space was always open to white invasion. While whites could shut off areas of white space, blacks could never prevent white intervention or interference. The black "world" was simply a poorly protected enclave within the larger (white) society. The work of white interracialists depended on this reality. While outwardly expressing support of the doctrine of "separate but equal," they used inherent contradictions of the Jim Crow culture to justify the assumption of their positions as paternalistic guardians of black Virginians. White paternalists believed that they, like masters of old, could "protect" worthy African Americans.

Interracial cooperation was based on these seemingly incongruent ideals. But whites glossed over these inconsistencies because of their unquestioning belief in the righteousness of white supremacy. Thus, Schmelz never understood the hypocrisy of her condemnation of an all-black party. Instead (perhaps correctly) she only saw danger to the continuation of interracial activism. "They are deliberately cutting themselves off from their friends," Schmelz exclaimed, "seeking that which they clearly [can] never gain and endangering all progress so far attained. . . . This party is not only not needed—you asked me if the third party were needed—but it will be a positive handicap to your race." She concluded, rather than "emphasizing '*political rights*' it will be far greater and finer to emphasize 'Opportunity and Responsibility as a Citizen'!"[43] She failed to add that these "opportunities and responsibilities" were entirely subject to the changeable whims of the white public.

Janie Porter Barrett contested this arbitrary distinction of "proper segregation," leading Schmelz, in a second letter, to plead, "Mrs. Barrett, I do not blame you for being hurt and upset, but what I am trying to do for your people is to *take* the results of this action and to keep you from turning these results into *disaster* for your race!" She reiterated her fear that a third party would destroy the progress made in racial understanding and noted that many white Democrats with whom she consulted concerning Barrett's inquiry agreed with her assessment. In the words of one unnamed friend: "If the Negroes of Virginia desire to effectively neutralize all the efforts of their white friends who have been working towards bettering their condition, I know of no more effectual way to do it than to put a negro ticket in the field. They can set themselves back fifty years by such actions."[44] White paternalists were desperately concerned about the entrance of an all-black party onto the state's political scene but not for the obvious reasons. Schmelz and her counterparts knew there was absolutely no possibility of a lily-black faction achieving electoral success. If anything, a black political party would almost assuredly guarantee white political dominance by working to remove, even more effectively than the lily-white initiatives, blacks from the two white-controlled major parties. Yet, such a movement challenged white supremacy on an ideological level and that of perceived paternalistic attachment.

The formation of a lily-black Republican Party threatened to destroy the very basis of paternalistic interracial cooperation. An all-black slate of candidates translated into a public admission by African Americans that they did not trust whites to be their political representatives. Blacks had long understood the limitations of this concept of indirect access to political power, but whites, like Schmelz, had complete faith in the system. Accordingly, they were surprised and appalled by news of the formation of a black Republican Party. Not recognizing the hypocrisy of her words, Schmelz lamented: "Now, for your leaders to organize a third party and to go up and down and over this state, as they will go from now until November, speaking to *thousands* of our colored people, going with anger and revenge in their hearts, inciting these thousands of the negro race against this large group of the white race composing the Republican party, it will react upon your people in the most disastrous manner. . . . Nothing in the world would so retard, and maybe defeat the object of Inter racial work."[45] She did not question whether interracial work was also being hurt by the white Republican and Democratic candidates who crossed the state in frantic campaigns, each trying to prove that he was the most dedicated white supremacist.

The correspondence between Annie Schmelz and Janie Porter Barrett is significant in both its frank discussion of racial concerns and its rare insight into the relationship between two dedicated activists separated by the color line. As women, their friendship was proper in the eyes of white society because it replicated the relationship between mistresses and maids long established in white homes. That they were acting in the public rather than the private realm, however, moved their work out of that traditional paradigm. Barrett and Schmelz came together from positions of power as appointed spokesman for their race and gender, and, although Barrett was careful not to overstep her prescribed racial role, she was too proud and accomplished to ever pretend to be subservient. Yet, Schmelz never considered Barrett to be her equal. She recognized that Barrett could not be treated as she would her housemaid, but she also never offered her the same respect that she would a white woman of similar standing. Although Barrett was a sophisticated, educated, respected, well-to-do woman with a more illustrious social welfare career than Schmelz, the white woman patronizingly viewed herself as a mentor to Barrett. Moreover, Schmelz idealized her profound connection with Barrett, assuming, like the old bonds between the races that were part of Lost Cause lore, that the African American woman felt the same way. "When you come to think about it," Schmelz mused, "there are, in proportion to the numbers of people in both races, an amazingly small number who come together in just the splendid way that you and I do. . . . There are not a great number of contacts such as you and I have. And the greatest work I shall ever do for your people lies just ahead of me in this Inter racial work, the object of which is to establish among great numbers of *both* races everywhere, *just* such contacts as you and I have."[46] Schmelz counted on the work to bring not only racial harmony but also to fulfill her Christian duty.

Despite her professions of a profound connection, Schmelz entirely misunderstood Barrett's reasoning for writing. Barrett did not desire a lecture or instruction on why the Republican's new discriminatory policy was a godsend to blacks; rather, she was seeking support from a white "friend" of African Americans. She gave Schmelz the opportunity to show that she could indeed act as a representative of the black race to the white establishment by protesting the blatant discrimination. Schmelz instead demonstrated, in a lengthy manner, how little she understood the real problems at the root of racial tensions. When Barrett disagreed with Schmelz's assessment of Reconstruction and Republican exploitation of African Americans, Schmelz dismissed her concerns and told her to "*reread* my paper, and you will see that I do not refer to the background of your people, but to the background of the Republican party!" Barrett realized that the carefully drawn distinctions Schmelz made were in reality useless in fighting prejudice. Schmelz could not see outside the Lost Cause framework in which she was raised. She also rejected Barrett's objections to her interpretation of slavery as an idyllic era of racial harmony. "My dear Mrs. Barrett," Schmelz chided, "speaking of the background for your people, why should they object to discuss a past that has been the stepping stone which has placed the Negroes in America head and shoulders above the Negroes in any other part of the world, for that is how you now stand." She never considered that it was her interpretation rather than her subject matter that bothered Barrett. After restating her case as if Barrett were a child unable to understand the complexity of her reasoning, Schmelz threatened, "Should my motive be misunderstood by your people, you could never misunderstand me, of course I would have to withdraw my activity from your race."[47] Instead, she reasoned, she could turn her attention to problems among working-class whites as many of her white friends encouraged. To Barrett and other African American leaders, this was a serious consideration. Schmelz, despite her condescension, was one of the leading white advocates of African American interests in Virginia.

Although not afraid to test boundaries, Barrett had no desire to thwart Schmelz's activism. Schmelz had collaborated closely with Barrett for years in her longtime role as chairman of the Board of the Virginia Industrial School for Colored Girls as well as in their work together on the Commission on Interracial Cooperation.[48] Speaking that same fall of 1921 before the Virginia State Federation of Colored Women's Clubs annual meeting held that year in Lexington, Barrett reported: "The inter-racial movement being launched in different States is most important. There will never be a time when good will between the races will be more needed than now." Reflecting on her experiences with whites and the need to recognize genuine attempts at goodwill, she reminded her audience that:

> You and I have learned from experience how much can be accomplished by white and colored people trusting each other and working together. The Virginia Industrial School is an example. Neither the white nor the colored women could have done that piece of work alone. . . . You and I are in a position to speak for the sincerity and the loyalty of some of the white men and women who are as anxious as we are to right wrongs, for we have tested them. We can never stand by and hear white people denounced as a whole because of the wrongdoings of some, without telling of those we know in the North and the South who are working unceasingly for justice and fair play for all.[49]

Despite Schmelz's limited understanding of the African American perspective, she had still passed Barrett's test of being committed to the interracial cause.

In defiance of these private warnings along with more public accusations of the white press, African American leaders in Virginia decided to form their own party and nominate a slate of candidates for the 1921 state election. This act of protest evidenced a gradual transition in the interracial cooperation movement in Virginia, as black Virginians publicly questioned the utility and efficacy of paternalism. On September 5, 1921, assorted black leaders, many of the same individuals who were active in reform and community cooperation efforts with whites, held a separate Republican convention in Richmond, drawing more than six hundred black Virginians from across the state. Although against any racial exclusion, all those present were African American. The group nominated a slate of African Americans to run for state election. The ticket was headed by John Mitchell Jr. for governor, Theodore Nash for lieutenant governor, J. Thomas Newsome for attorney general, and Maggie Lena Walker for superintendent of public instruction.[50] Candidate Newsome declared that their actions were necessary because "enemies have captured the organization of the Grand Old Party in Virginia. . . . This barefaced outlawry is not republicanism and the time is ripe for revolt."[51]

The lily-black party, a name they did not embrace because of its racial distinction, claimed to be the true Republican Party based upon the ideals—as they believed them—of the party that had freed their forefathers. In the election platform, they proclaimed their desire to be treated as equal citizens: "We condemn as utterly evasive and willfully misleading the attempt to confuse the participation of any group of people in politics with a desire to change the social understanding always existing between the races in this State and while we respectfully and unreservedly demand to be treated as other citizens with all the rights, privileges, and immunities as accorded them, including the rights to vote and to be voted for still we resent the insinuation that we desire or intend in anywise to disturb the very cordial relations existing between the best of both races in Virginia."[52] These African American candidates did not dare to call for social equality. In fact, they specifically denounced such suggestions. Yet, they did claim "unreservedly" their full rights and privileges as law-abiding residents of the state. Mitchell, Nash, Newsome, and Walker charged that "race relations" had been severely damaged, not by any actions of their own but by the lily-whites breaking the agreed-upon racial practices and customs. They were no longer content to wait on white paternalists for reform and declared publicly their belief that direct political representation was their right as Virginia citizens.

Mitchell had previously been against the idea of a black Republican faction, but he changed his mind in the summer of 1921, when the lily-whites took drastic action by barring black delegates from the state convention. He accepted the nomination as the gubernatorial candidate both because the offer appealed to

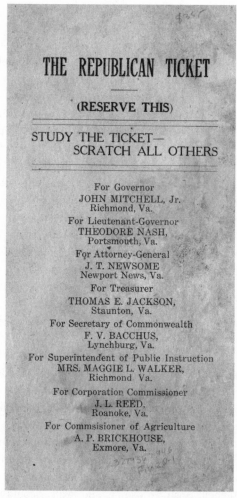

THE REPUBLICAN TICKET

(RESERVE THIS)

STUDY THE TICKET—
SCRATCH ALL OTHERS

For Governor
JOHN MITCHELL, Jr.
Richmond, Va.

For Lieutenant-Governor
THEODORE NASH,
Portsmouth, Va.

For Attorney-General
J. T. NEWSOME
Newport News, Va.

For Treasurer
THOMAS E. JACKSON,
Staunton, Va.

For Secretary of Commonwealth
F. V. BACCHUS,
Lynchburg, Va.

For Superintendent of Public Instruction
MRS. MAGGIE L. WALKER,
Richmond Va.

For Corporation Commissioner
J. L. REED,
Roanoke, Va.

For Commsisioner of Agriculture
A. P. BRICKHOUSE,
Exmore, Va.

Virginia Republican Party flyer, 1921, advertising the all–African
American protest ticket. (Ms2008–058, Courtesy of Special
Collections, University Libraries, Virginia Tech, Blacksburg)

his pride and also because he felt it to be the only socially responsible course of
action. Interestingly, P. B. Young also changed positions and became the most
outspoken African American critic of the lily-black movement in the state. The
Norfolk editor was motivated in part by his hurt at being cast aside as a candidate
in favor of Mitchell, but he also saw the movement as very dangerous to the efforts
of black leaders, like himself (and Mitchell) to build positive race relations. Young

saw the strategy, in the words of his biographer Henry Lewis Suggs, to be "political suicide."[53] Many black Virginians agreed with Young and were against the all-black ticket.[54] These individuals argued that the action made African Americans no better than the whites who had forced them out of the Republican Party. Yet, supporters of the movement felt black Virginians had no choice but to publicly demonstrate their resentment of the ever-increasing racial inequity. They believed, in the words of a handbill advertising one protest meeting, that "If colored people cannot be allowed to enter a courthouse to attend a republican meeting, but can be forced to bear arms — What can we expect next?"[55] Their patriotism and sacrifice in the war had only been rewarded with rebuke. Although some black Virginians continued to argue that the campaign was a mistake that would lead to worse treatment at the hands of whites, many African Americans viewed their exclusion from the Republican convention to be an unacceptable insult that could not be ignored and a dismal harbinger of future discrimination. The white populace, in general, watched the race with interest but not considerable alarm. The lily-black campaign was reported on but, perhaps surprisingly, evoked little ire or fear.[56] Southwestern Virginia's *Clinch Valley News* surmised that the "the politicians are puzzled over the negro vote which will be cast this fall. The question presented is whether vengeance, party regularity, or race consciousness will be the factor to determine which way this vote will go."[57]

Black supporters of the protest campaign included many black leaders involved in interracial cooperation efforts. Not only Walker and Mitchell but others like Janie Porter Barrett were convinced that the movement was necessary to racial integrity. They saw no conflict between their support for paternalistic interracialism and an all-black ticket for the 1921 state election. Rejecting the label "lily-black," they argued that their convention had denounced racial exclusion and, in fact, had courted the support of whites. While no whites actually accepted the offer to attend, the invitation had at least been extended. Thus, even while heading an all-black ticket, Mitchell, Nash, Newsome, and Walker could rightfully claim to be against racial segregation and political exclusion. These values coincided with, rather than contradicted, their belief in the necessity and utility of interracialism.

But even blacks in favor of the lily-black campaign recognized the bitter irony of the whole course of events. The lily-whites, Mitchell declared, forced "colored people to do what they really did not want to do. If they had participated in the Republican convention at Norfolk, they would have nominated white men only for elective positions."[58] He still hoped to cultivate a relationship with whites, especially from an elitist class position. Mitchell declared: "There is really no antagonism between the better class of white people and the better class of colored people. They are friends and their desire is to remain so." On a certain level, he found the campaign to be a "ludicrous" process because he held "no hope, no prospect of its success."[59] Yet, he believed the point was to advertise the "unjust conditions" and needed reforms facing African Americans throughout Virginia.

Ironically, one of these needed reforms—the abolition of the poll tax—was part of the main platform of the new lily-white Republican Party. The gubernatorial nominee Henry Anderson argued that the 1901–2 constitutional convention that had disfranchised large portions of the Virginia electorate did not have the legal authority to declare the new document as law without first submitting it to the people.[60] Yet, Mitchell and his counterparts had lost faith in whites' assurances and stated intentions. They were tired of compromises that ultimately denied their political and civil rights. Moreover, from a purely classist position, they were not deeply concerned with the poll tax, which they saw as a relatively minor obstacle to voting. Newsome, for example, publicly laughed at the suggestion that any African American voter would "sacrifice his political freedom and endanger the future of his children" by not voting in order to save "the pitiful sum of one dollar and fifty cents!"[61] Black Republicans who supported the abolition of the poll tax were not moved by this single issue to vote for Henry Anderson. Instead, they decided to strike out on their own, knowing that their third-party campaign would destroy any meager hopes the Republican Party had of winning in Virginia. Frustrated by their inability to make any positive changes to the political climate, African Americans decided to use their lingering political access (the vote) to impact the election by ensuring a Republican loss. They did not believe Democrats would treat them substantially better but respected the fact that at least white Democrats were straightforward and honest (however racist) in their dealings with African Americans.

The bleak prospect of electoral success did not stem enthusiasm for the African American candidates in black communities across the state. Many voters argued that the integrity of their race depended on African Americans standing together and symbolically refusing to submit to white control. Fred Newman, of Harrisonburg, asked, "Will you accept the unmanly part and yet give your full strength, your one vote, to Hon. Henry W. Anderson and show to the people of the State, that we are satisfied with what "Marse Chas" hands us?"[62] Although they knew they had no chance of winning the state election, some of the black candidates, including Nash, Newsome, and Walker, conducted a vigorous campaign and traveled throughout the state making speeches. Mitchell, on the other hand, largely dismissed the need to campaign and went on a three-week trip to California to attend a banking conference. As Election Day neared, however, Mitchell returned and joined others in appearances across the state, including enthusiastic speeches in Danville, Staunton, and Newport News.[63] On the eve of the election, the candidates staged a large rally in Richmond. Showing up a white Republican rally the previous evening that had only one band and eight hundred people, five thousand black Richmonders came out to watch the black candidates' rally and parade featuring five bands.[64] Walker and Mitchell were the main attractions as they rode through Jackson Ward in their impressive automobiles.[65]

Whites also watched the race with interest, questioning the extent of black Virginians' support for the lily-black movement. The *Richmond News Leader* sent the reporter R. L. C. Barrett out in the field to talk to blacks throughout the state to investigate "whether a new race consciousness would lead him [the African American voter] to the support of John Mitchell Jr., Negro candidate for governor," or whether party loyalties would result in votes for Anderson. Barrett found the project harder than expected because "the average Negro does not care to discuss politics with a white man."[66] In Louisa, however, he found one man willing to discuss the election. Barrett assured his readers of the African American man's "qualifications," stating that he had "always been the friend of the white man and his business is entirely supported by [the] white race."[67] The unnamed individual declared support for Mitchell and his running mates. "I intend to vote for the Mitchell ticket and all of my friends all [will] vote the same way," the man professed; "It may be that some of the old-time Negroes, out in the sticks, will vote for Mr. Anderson, because they do not understand the situation but news, 'by grapevine' travels mighty fast among the Negroes and there will be few of them who will not know the facts on election day."[68] Barrett heard similar professions from black Virginians when visiting Petersburg.

The extent to which this support translated into results on Election Day became a matter of debate. The conclusion of the November 8, 1921, election played out as expected, and the Democratic gubernatorial nominee, E. Lee Trinkle, won by a 70,000-vote majority over the white Republican candidate, Anderson. Early reports suggested Mitchell received nearly 20,000 votes, but the final official results credited him with only 5,230 votes. The validity of these early estimates was questionable. Evidence showed that some degree of vote tampering resulted in the misrepresentation of African American voting strength. In Richmond alone, officials credited Mitchell with only 1,402 votes after discarding an additional 1,324 ballots with the excuse that they were not marked according to regulation. As a result of Mitchell's influential critic, P. B. Young, Mitchell only received 90 votes out of the 1,600 registered African Americans in Norfolk.[69] Soon after the election, the black Republican Party dissipated.[70]

In retrospect, the final tally and the quick demise of the third party meant little in terms of the overall significance of the events. African Americans within Virginia believed the election to be a great success "to those who have been endeav-

oring wholly and solely to register a protest against the present party management."[71] They achieved their purpose by announcing in a grand gesture their
dissatisfaction with the political status quo. In Richmond, blacks celebrated with a
parade featuring the Elks Brass Band and, as before, Maggie Walker and Mitchell in their automobiles. Pollard, Walker, and Mitchell spoke at a mass meeting
held afterward. Mitchell praised black Virginians for their courageous protest. He
spoke of "the work done by the colored people, of their loyalty to the Government,
of their valor upon the battlefield of France . . . bleeding and dying and facing the
German's poison . . . [on] the front line," comparing that with the experience of
Henry W. Anderson, who had been "in charge of the Red Cross camps behind
the lines, over which were flown the Red Cross sign, which means 'Don't shoot
here.'"[72] The African American candidates did not win the election, but pride in
their efforts strengthened resolve to defy white demands. Although they did not
gain any elected offices, they did help destroy any potential electoral success of
their lily-white foes. Black Virginians knew that, at least in the near future, whites
would continue to rule state and local government, but they refused to see their
situation as one without options. The movement proved to many African Americans that they still retained the dignity to refuse to take the crumbs offered to them
by white society.

Soon after the election, both John Mitchell Jr. and Thomas Newsome wrote
governor-elect E. Lee Trinkle, offering their support and congratulations. They
acted both out of decorum and also the practical desire to build bridges with those
in power. Trinkle responded politely, pledging that "the colored race will get fair
treatment at my hands. I shall be glad to do all I can at any time to promote their
happiness, contentment, and prosperity. I have a very kindly feeling towards the
colored race, and sincerely desire their advancement in all lines of life."[73] Mitchell
believed Trinkle would live up to his word because "he represents, that liberal type
of Southerners, who do not 'play to the galleries' and who say just what they will
do and who will do just what they say. All the colored people of the Grand Old
Commonwealth ask is to be treated fairly and squarely."[74] Trinkle was supportive
of interracial work and did attempt to at least listen to the concerns of black Virginians throughout his term of office.

African Americans remained as involved with interracial cooperation after the
election of 1921 as before, but subtle changes occurred. They spoke out with increasing frequency about the rights they *deserved* as citizens of the Old Dominion.
A *Richmond Planet* reporter explained: "All the colored folks in Virginia want their
civil and political rights. They want to be given an equal chance in the courts of
law and they want all talk of race and colored left out in dealing with official matters. They are ready to pay their proportion of taxes and they want the right to do

their proportion of voting."[75] The meaning of interracial cooperation shifted. As black and white activists gathered in meetings of the newly formed Commission on Interracial Cooperation, African Americans began to speak more of rights and the underlying inequity of segregation rather than simply of practical material benefits. No longer willing to suppress their criticism of Jim Crow out of deference to their white friends, black activists worked to transform interracial projects into opportunities to push for change in the racial order. The events of 1921 articulated a new, more defiant voice among African American leaders, who knew that white support could not be entirely trusted no matter how reliable the source appeared. However, throughout this protest the "polite" discourse of racial interaction in Virginia continued. Where contested elections in Florida in 1920 led to bloody conflict, Virginia saw no bloodshed.[76]

Mitchell and his fellow candidates knew, from the beginning, that they had no chance of winning state office, but they chose to run as a protest not only against the lily-white efforts of the Republican Party but also in defiance of their proclaimed white "friends" with whom they had worked in the past on numerous cooperative efforts. They used the election of 1921 to publicize their frustration with a system of paternalistic indirect influence that typically ignored the underlying racial inequities in the state. The events brought to the forefront of interracial activism blacks' demands for self-representation. These African Americans could no longer pretend to believe that separate could one day be equal. Interracial cooperation did prevent large-scale outbreaks of racial violence in the state. But, apart from this success, broken promises following World War I, amplified race-baiting with the passage of the Nineteenth Amendment, and the ever-increasing strictures of segregation were black activists' only reward for trying to work within the Jim Crow framework.

African American leaders, however, did not abandon the concept of working with whites. "By a co-operative effort," the *Richmond Planet* proclaimed, "a mutual understanding will follow and *all will work valiantly together for the triumph of those ideals* which will make our beloved South-land one of brightest and safest spots of the globe."[77] A new emphasis was placed on defining exactly what those ideals were. While prominent black Virginians continued to join and promote interracial initiatives, they were no longer content to let whites act as their primary representatives to the white government. Realizing that segregation restrictions and racial inequality were increasing, they used interracial forums such as the newly formed Commission on Interracial Cooperation, the Richmond Urban League, and the Richmond Community House for Colored People to discuss their need for equal rights as citizens rather than simply the allotment of public resources as they had done in the past. Restoration of the franchise to the African American masses and greater political access were at the forefront of their concerns. Although forced, to some degree, to continue to accept the opportunities presented to them by white interracial activists who had not altered their paternalistic mind-sets, black leaders became increasingly resentful of whites' pressures to accept a system of indirect political influence and were no longer cautious or reticent in their criticism of seg-regation. The lily-black party failed in electoral terms, but the movement marked a beginning of a new trend in the racial history of the state, where interracial meetings focused less on illusions of separate but equal and more on debates of basic citizenship rights.

7

Rethinking Alliances

I do not consider segregation and co-operation as opposed alternatives. Of course, the race problem could not only be ameliorated but made non-existent by amalgamation. This would mean getting rid of the race problem by getting rid of the races. *I consider segregation the sanest form of cooperation.*
—John Powell, 1925

IN THE 1920S, paternalistic reform efforts transformed with the waning of the personal nature of reform work as it became more institutionalized. In some cases, this was a result of the activists' Progressive successes. A number of the reforms of the uplift and cooperation generation were taken on (although not always well) by the state government. In other cases, organizations simply grew over time and became less dependent on the same core of activists. New, larger groups formed, like the Commission on Interracial Cooperation, providing a more organizational and less ad hoc approach to interracial cooperation. These factors along with age caused some of the older members of the early interracial generation to gradually begin to narrow their activism. Mary Munford stopped serving on the board of managers of the Virginia Industrial School for Colored Girls once it was taken over by the state and the responsibilities of the board narrowed. Even Maggie Lena Walker, the most nationally well-known of these Virginia reformers, began to limit her involvement in some organizations.

For example, in January 1925, Jesse O. Thomas, the African American field secretary of the National Urban League, wrote Maggie Lena Walker to express his concern about the poor attendance of blacks (and her in particular) at the board meetings of the Richmond Urban League (RUL), a clearinghouse organization for directing and overseeing social service and welfare work for African Americans.[1] "The danger," he warned, was that her absence would "serve to discourage your chairman and other white members of your Board, whose enthusiasm and interet [*sic*] will be dampened and the race's welfare will lose a very much active concern." Thomas reminded Walker that while the RUL was "inter-racial in character, it is regarded as a Negro organization," thus the African American board members should have the responsibility of sustaining interest in the group.[2] Walker, never one to mince words, was annoyed by Thomas's insinuations of her negligence. She explained her absence as the result of a busy schedule and illness, adding that since the RUL was now in the Community Chest and fund raising was no longer necessary, "the secretary will be in a position to create interest enough among the citizens of our race to give the white officers encouragement."[3] Walker was irritated that Thomas expected her to appease whites and act the role of grateful black recipient when her considerable professional skills (that is, fund raising) were no longer of much use. In response, Thomas encouraged Walker not to resign because her "name and [the] influence that goes with it cannot be overestimated." Instead, he suggested that Walker and the other black board members choose some individual who "would be sufficiently active so as not to discourage white members."[4] In a twist upon traditional (white) southern ideology, black leaders believed whites would be appeased and kept happily about their task by a representative African American willing to enact the racialized role expected of him or her by white society. On a certain level, some interracial organizations became as much about blacks "managing" whites' activism as about white activists "managing" racial order.

Maggie Lena Walker was not one to cave to anyone. Like many of her colleagues, black and white, Walker grew up in the aftermath of the Civil War. She was born in 1864 in Richmond, which was then still enduring the ravages of war, in the home of Elizabeth Van Lew, a famous Union spy and also avid abolitionist. Elizabeth Draper, Walker's mother, was a former slave who worked for Van Lew as a cook. Walker's father was a white man, Eccles Cuthbert, although her parents never married. Despite this extraordinary background, Walker did not have a privileged childhood. Draper married William Mitchell, a butler, soon after Maggie's birth, yet his suspicious death by drowning in February 1876 brought poverty to the family. Maggie aided her mother in running a small laundry to make ends meet.[5]

Walker had an untiring work ethic that pushed her to succeed despite her race and sex. Her commitment to African American self-improvement and uplift eventually led her to become the first African American woman to found a bank with her establishment of the St. Luke Penny Savings Bank in November 1903.[6] This bank encapsulated her ideal of African American progress through self-help. Walker became an active participant of the interracial generation, playing an active role in myriad reforms. Apart from the paternalist projects, Walker helped found a local chapter of the NAACP in Richmond in 1917 and served for years as vice president and as a member of the national executive board. Yet, she refused the office of president of the local NAACP in 1925 because she feared it might

Maggie Lena Walker with Richmond neighborhood children. (Courtesy
of Maggie L. Walker National Historic Site, National Park Service)

weaken her standing among whites.[7] She knew that she needed to walk a fine line
between defiance and accommodation to be in a position to effect change.

Indeed, change was a constant in the 1920s, but it was not always for the better.
Rather than a decade of racial impasse and stability, the 1920s marked a new era in
the racial history of the state. As some white Virginians sought to extend segregation,
they met unexpected opposition. While influential white interracialists continued
in their paternalistic policies and developed more formal avenues to further their
social welfare projects and concerns through organizations like the Commission
on Interracial Cooperation and the National Urban League, a more radical sect
of white extremists gained popularity in the state led by the charismatic musician
John Powell. As a result, these new interracial organizations were increasingly
perceived as a threat, especially as support for paternalism waned within the state.
     Not only did public perceptions of interracial cooperation change in the 1920s,
but the nature of the work changed as well, restructuring along organizational
lines. Earlier, these efforts were conducted in a relatively ad hoc manner, driven
primarily by individual initiative rather than associational affiliation but often
drawing from the same group of interracial reformers. In some cases, projects
were based on whites' evaluations of what African Americans most needed. While
blacks sometimes initiated the work and played an active role in shaping the practical details, the success of the work often depended on the commitment of white
activists. There were exceptions to this rule, such as Janie Porter Barrett's skill-
ful promotion of the Virginia Industrial School for Colored Girls. Yet, too often
these initiatives became whites' efforts to manage and control black space as they

deemed necessary. Rather than suggesting equality, "interracial cooperation" typically involved whites' efforts to aid black uplift and encourage African Americans to peacefully conform to the culture of segregation. Most white activists never imagined that African Americans ever had anything substantial to offer in improving the white side of the color line. This structure began to change in the 1920s. Although whites continued to determine primarily the direction of interracial initiatives, African Americans gained a greater voice as the work became more formally structured through a variety of organizations, including the Commission on Interracial Cooperation, the Young Women's Christian Association, the National Urban League, and the Community House for Negro People.

A few white southerners, headed by Will W. Alexander, along with several African American leaders founded the Commission on Interracial Cooperation (CIC) in Atlanta on April 9, 1919, in the hope of ameliorating post–World War I racial violence.[8] Like earlier informal interracial efforts, the organization did not seek any radical overthrow of the relatively newly embraced "southern way of life," that is, segregation. The group worked only to reduce racial tensions rather than questioning the root of the problem — assumptions of white supremacy. Through county, state, and national committees, white and black southerners, as recorded in the minutes, worked to "build up and maintain right relations between the races" through education and recruiting the assistance of interested religious and benevolent organizations.[9] Over the years, the CIC did make significant gains in reducing lynchings with the help of groups like Jessie Daniel Ames's Association of Southern Women for the Prevention of Lynching (founded in 1930).[10] The organization also fought to expose the illegal practices of the Ku Klux Klan as well as address another fundamental blight of southern society, that of economic inequality. Although the NAACP was initially wary of the CIC, Joel R. Spingarn, then president, endorsed the group in 1920.[11] The CIC extended the ideas of interracial cooperation long developed in Virginia, to promote racial peace and also to attempt to rehabilitate the South's image as a lawless and uncivilized region.

The organization soon sought membership not only across the color line but across the gender line as well. White women (and later African American women) became active members soon after it was founded, working to boost interest in the group by promoting the CIC within their own local, state, and national women's groups. Wide-scale female involvement first began in July 1920, when the white Women's Missionary Council of the Southern Methodist Church sent delegates to the national convention of the Colored Woman's Clubs held that year in Tuskegee, Alabama.[12] Drawn to the event out of the concern that it was their Christian duty to become involved in interracial work, the women later reported to their larger organization that "they realized that in that group of colored women was massed a potential power — a power of womanhood and motherhood — which was mobilizing in a desperate effort to lift the race to a plane where it should walk among the nations of the earth — unashamed and unafraid." They also recognized that the African American women they termed "a great national asset" were suspicious of "their white sisters."[13] After this experience, the white delegates advocated that southern white women needed to recognize their "own strategic place" in uplifting African Americans. They encouraged interested white women to educate themselves on housing and sanitation conditions, address the concerns of African American women and children, and also promote awareness of the "Negro's contribution to American life" in literature, poetry, music, and art.[14] They believed that, as women, their innate maternal compassion would enable them to better understand the needs of black women and the black race as a whole.

To mobilize, these activists organized a meeting in Memphis held in early October 1920 that brought together white leaders representing a variety of women's groups across the South.[15] Carrie Parks Johnson of Georgia, later to become one of the leading white female directors in the national CIC office, helped plan what became known as the Memphis Conference, inviting several African American women including Margaret Washington, Jennie Moton, Elizabeth Haynes, and Charlotte Hawkins Brown to speak on "what it means to be a Negro."[16] For some of the white women present, this was the first time they listened to black women expressing their troubles, concerns, and hopes.[17] A few individuals, like Johnson, brought together from across the region found the conference to be an eye-opening, life-changing experience where they began to glimpse "the pulsing desire of the colored woman and mother for the better things of life for herself, her home and her race . . . legitimate aspirations of womanhood and motherhood."[18] Johnson and other white women viewed the experience in terms of a religious revelation, embracing African American uplift as their new "cause."[19]

In October 1922, African American women officially became part of the Commission on Interracial Cooperation as well. At that time, seven African American women were appointed to the Women's General Committee representing a variety of respected organizations: Mary McLeod Bethune (African Methodist Episcopal Church), Lugenia Burns Hope (Baptist Church), Minnie Lou Crosthwait (Congregational Church), Marion Wilkinson (Episcopal Church), Mary McCrorey (Presbyterian Church), Margaret Washington (Woman's Clubs), and Charlotte H. Brown (YWCA). All of these women were well-established and respected reformers, and the majority were wives or widows of prominent African American leaders, including John Hope, Henry Lawrence McCrorey, and Booker T. Washington. The women were encouraged to "work slowly and constructively, always bearing in mind that it is *all* the women and *all* the homes of both races which must be reached."[20]

Despite these somewhat cautious professions of camaraderie and limited recognition of the so-called "bonds of womanhood," these interracial interactions, like earlier initiatives, did not threaten the color line or the culture of segregation. Although some white women began to recognize commonalities with African American women, most of these still accepted assumptions of white superiority and African American inferiority. They were, however, now willing to formally invite black women into their interracial organizations. The majority of white women of the CIC never saw their black counterparts as equals but rather as little sisters whom they felt a sense of responsibility to watch over. But this new formalized format of interracial cooperation did offer African American women more opportunities to share their concerns and suggest potential reforms. These CIC women ran their meetings with careful attention to proper procedure in accordance with their agreed-upon constitution. This structure created a forum where black women could speak out with relative assurance that their opinions would not be dismissed. These were controlled environments where the delicate rules of social etiquette were not ignored but were at times secondary to organizational order. In this environment, African American women were given the courtesy titles of Mrs. or Miss that would have been awkward in more informal settings.[21] These advancements offered new opportunities for African Americans to more freely express their concerns about life under segregation but did not alter the innate prejudice of most white activists or convince them of the faulty logic of white supremacy.

Although only small advances were made in terms of greater inclusion and better treatment of African American activists, many white southerners were worried about the seemingly radical nature of this new organization. The CIC was criticized by much of the white press across the South as a potential threat to white supremacy. Alexander and most of the other white members did not speak against segregation. In fact, they generally supported Jim Crow, but some white southerners and a new generation of white politicians saw dangers in the work, believing this new cooperation might be the first step toward racial and social equality.[22] White southerners questioned the utility of cooperative work and began to label the white paternalists of the early interracial generation as being "soft" and old-fashioned on the race issue. Even in Virginia with its long history of paternalistic interracial cooperation, the Commission on Interracial Cooperation was viewed as suspect. While smaller-scale, more private initiatives had been seen as essential to making segregation work, this new organizational approach was believed by many to be not only unwise but potentially dangerous.

Despite these criticisms, around the same time as the founding of the national

CIC a similar organization was founded in Virginia. Although these initial inter-racial committees in several states were exclusively comprised of white men, or-ganizers in Virginia, drawing upon years of experience with similar work, sought support across both racial and gender lines. Shortly after Will Alexander's official founding of the Commission on Interracial Cooperation in Georgia, a group of ten Virginians formed their own "Committee on Inter-racial Understanding and Co-operation" to "create better understanding and cooperation between the races and to encourage and cooperate with all agencies created for similar purposes."[23] Al-though several prominent white males were present including Jackson Davis, the meeting was presided over by a white woman, Mary Munford, and attended by at least one African American woman, Rosa D. Bowser. Bowser was not appointed as an officer of the new organization, but Munford became a vice chairman. A white man, Dr. Robert Emory Blackwell, president of Randolph Macon College from 1902 to 1938, was elected chairman. The purpose of the organization was to promote the study of African American problems in such areas as housing, sanita-tion, legal aid, educational and recreational facilities, and bettering economic con-ditions.[24] These were familiar and well-established areas of reform for white pater-nalists in Virginia. While similar groups in other states excluded women from these endeavors, Virginians sought to utilize Munford's, Bowser's, and other women's considerable experience in addressing these matters.[25] For years, these Virginian women had proven their effectiveness in similar initiatives and, thus, they assumed without question leadership roles in the new interracial organization.

Drawing on this past work, Virginians quickly mobilized to join the Commission on Interracial Cooperation. In accordance with the organization's guidelines, the initial members were all male. Women, however, stayed involved in the process. Four white women from across the state attended the 1920 Memphis meeting. These included Lula Vanderslice Britt (Suffolk), Annie Moore Potts (Richmond), Annie Schmelz (Hampton), and Mary F. Powers (Bayard).[26] Mary Munford was asked to speak at the conference and, although unable to attend, was actively involved in the founding of the Women's General Committee of the CIC.[27] African Amer-ican women including Janie Porter Barrett also played a key role in incorporating black women into the national CIC.[28] As one of the first black women to become involved, Barrett helped to convince white women from across the South of the utility of interracial cooperation and argued for African Americans' full inclusion in the organization. In the midst of this activism, women soon became influential members of the Virginia CIC. Both Barrett and her fellow Virginian Maggie Lena Walker held positions on the Women's General Committee based in Atlanta.[29]

An all-white group women (including Annie Schmelz, Mary Munford, Kate Langley Bosher, Adele Clark, Martha McNeill, Nora Houston, and Clara Louise McConnell) officially constituted the Women's Section of the Virginia State Committee on Inter-Racial Cooperation in Richmond on November 16, 1921. In stating their commitment to improving relations with black Virginians, they professed their abhorrence of "any conditions in our midst that tend to widen the breach between peoples whom circumstances have thrown together and whose destinies are inevitably interwoven in our own and coming generations. We believe righteousness, justice, peace and good will can be established between races of different colors."[30] This declaration, however, did not go as far as denouncing Jim Crow. The majority of these white Virginians still did not identify segregation as one of those conditions causing a breach between the races but rather as a civil modern solution for blacks and whites to live together in peace. Instead, the group stressed instead the need to promote greater interracial understanding.

The Women's Section of the Virginia CIC called for in-depth study of African American life to raise whites' awareness of their responsibilities toward their black neighbors. In addition, they petitioned the press to emphasize racial positives rather than negatives, spoke against vigilantism, and worked to cultivate "public sentiment" to be more receptive toward reform. Believing that "no community is stronger than its weakest link," these women stressed the need for "a single standard of morals, for the protection of all womanhood and equal punishment for all offenders against the same."[31] Although left unspoken, protection of black womanhood largely meant discouraging illicit and often forced sexual relations between African American women and white men — a problem of great personal interest to many white women. With these stated agenda points, the new association placed itself closely in line with the ideals and goals of the national Women's General Committee based in Georgia. Although the majority of new members (twenty-one of the thirty) came from Richmond, the women's sections of the Virginia CIC drew a number of individuals from across the state, including Annie Schmelz from Hampton and Clara Louise McConnell from Radford (wife of the first president of the then-named State Teachers College at Radford).[32] They saw themselves as representatives of the state organization to their own local civic and religious groups.

These women were the core of the generation of interracial reformers who embraced paternalism between 1900 and 1930. They hoped to use their individual reform experiences to develop new strategies to encourage other groups to become interested in interracial endeavors. For example, soon after the founding of the Virginia CIC, Mary Munford released a detailed work plan for white women's missionary societies wishing to inform themselves on the conditions of African American educational opportunities and facilities.[33] Like many Progressive activists, Munford believed education was essential to eventual reform. Her plan consisted of three steps. First, she encouraged each group to visit a local black school to witness for themselves present conditions. Second, she suggested that the white women request a white county supervisor or principal to deliver a lecture before one their meetings on the current status and potential problems of the institution. In addition, Munford believed some "representative negro" should be invited to offer "the point of view of parents with children in the school." As the final step, Munford advised that state supervisors of African American schools, "who are always white men," and black county demonstration agents as well as visiting industrial teachers "would appreciate the opportunity of presenting this work" to local white women's groups.[34]

Elite white women, like Munford, saw themselves as experts on the black race. For years, they had been involved in paternalistic cooperation and were known not only in Virginia but across the country for their activism and experience. The formation of a national Commission on Interracial Cooperation gave Munford, Cocke, Schmelz, and others the opportunity to demonstrate their "expertise," which they believed to be their right and duty as Virginians. Thus, Munford wrote her guidelines to help teach others how to conduct interracial work and, in particular, encourage more white women to become interested in African American education. She first developed this plan of action for the national board of the YWCA and then sent a copy to Carrie Johnson of the CIC national office in Atlanta to distribute among assorted local and state CIC women's groups. Munford professed her assurance that the work would not only have "a most encouraging effect upon the negroes themselves" but would "hold up the hands of the officials who are doing their best to give negroes good schools and help to encourage any other officials that might be less active in promoting this branch of our educational work."[35] Mary Munford and the other white women of the Virginia CIC saw themselves not as members of a single organization but rather as representatives of the white race seeking to educate and uplift the general populace. They viewed joining the new interracial organization as building upon their history of reform activism, not as a separate and unrelated cause.

The Women's Section of the Virginia State Committee on Inter-Racial Cooperation was founded by whites, but African American women soon became involved. Only months after the group's genesis, Ora B. Stokes attended the May 1922 meeting. Stokes informed those present that the Virginia State Federation of Colored Women's Clubs and the national Federation of Colored Women's Clubs would hold their conferences in Richmond that upcoming August. Stokes requested the committee's "cooperation with her in securing the help of the city in securing funds and the use of the city Auditorium for these conventions."[36] The group agreed, realizing that the assistance of whites would ease considerably the potential red tape Stokes faced in dealing with the city government, and appointed two white women, Myrtle Helsabeck (wife of the minister of Third Christian Church) and Antoinette Thomas (wife of the principal of Richmond High School), to work directly with Stokes. But Stokes did not merely appear before the committee as a petitioner. She used her organizational skills not only to plan the upcoming Federation of Colored Women's Clubs gatherings but also to negotiate with Dr. John M. Gandy, the African American president of the Virginia Normal and Industrial Institute, to hold the summer 1923 CIC conference on the Petersburg campus.[37] Although not officially members of the Virginia CIC, African American women took active roles in the organization from its onset.

The CIC was, in accordance with its name and mission, interracial, but the exact status of African Americans within the Virginia organization remained somewhat ambiguous for several years. African American women such as Ora B. Stokes and men such as Thomas C. Walker frequently attended meetings with whites but were considered more parallel than equal members. At the October 1922 meeting of the women's section, Carrie Johnson of the national office advised the whites present that "some states had added two or three outstanding Negro women to their committees, while others had formed parallel colored women's committees that there might be cooperative work."[38] In the latter case, she suggested that a joint executive committee then be appointed, comprised of six members representing both white and black women. The national office also suggested including black women on projects that pertained to African American life, such as public welfare concerns.[39] Although many of the white women present had been working with these same African American women on a one-on-one basis for years, they chose the parallel option. Two years later, however, the issue remained a hot topic of discussion. Janie Porter Barrett again "opened the question of colored (women) members of the Inter-Racial Committee."[40] Lengthy discussion ensued, but the solution remained unclear. The fact that the exact nature of their membership in the Virginia CIC was ambiguous throughout the first half of the decade did not deter African American activism. It did, however, demonstrate white paternalists' increasing reluctance to even appear to challenge the racial status quo and also why black activists questioned trusting whites, as well as the changing structure of interracial activism.

In spite of this confusion, African American participants in the Virginia CIC were listed on the organization's official letterhead as early as late 1923. The names were divided by male and female, but, in a break from Jim Crow decorum, there was no distinction between "black" and "white." In defiance of the southern "tradition" of refusing to grant African Americans courtesy titles, all women, black and white, were listed formally as "Mrs." or "Miss." White women tended to be identified more often than black women under their husband's names (for example,

Mrs. B. B. Munford rather than Mrs. Mary Munford), with several exceptions. In contrast, none of the men were designated as "Mr.," and only the more specific courtesy titles of "Rev.," "Hon.," or "Dr." were used. White and black men alike with no additional titles were listed simply by their name (examples — Jackson Davis and Thomas C. Walker).[41] While these whites feared breaking a widely agreed-upon racial taboo by honoring African American men with "Mr.," a title that could imply social equality, the group found it easier to bend the rules when dealing with black women. White paternalists did not believe black women to be as great a social, economic, or even sexual threat as black men, thus offering them courtesy titles seemed to pose little risk to the racial order. On this front of social change, the privileges of gender quietly won out over racial etiquette.

In November 1924, R. W. Miles, secretary of the Virginia, North Carolina, and South Carolina divisions of the CIC, declared after a meeting of the Virginia General Committee in Richmond that "while visible results of this movement come slowly, there is reason to believe situations have been met, conditions ameliorated, and in some instances outbreaks averted."[42] The group was working toward many practical improvements, such as securing better library privileges for African Americans. Dr. Mastin, the white secretary of the state Board of Charities and Corrections, pressed the need for more probation officers and juvenile courts. Ora Stokes made a "plea for consideration of Negroes on street cars and other public carriers." Thomas Walker pushed a plan for appointing a committee to work with the State Board of Welfare and appear before the General Assembly concerning the ever-present housing issue.[43] The local newspapers, black and white, followed these meetings closely, announcing new endeavors like a planned new bill in October 1924 to submit to the legislature that would "tend to better housing conditions for the negroes of the State."[44] Yet, details, as was a continuing problem with the organization, were somewhat vague. With these expanded areas of interest, the organization grew. By May 1926, the Virginia State Committee on Inter-Racial Cooperation had ninety-one members. Although whites (R. E. Blackwell and Annie Schmelz) held the chairman positions of both the general committee and women's section, there were a number of African American participants. Many individuals (forty-five) were Richmond residents, but a significant number represented other regions of the state.[45] Interracial cooperation was still mainly viewed as an urban concern, but interest spread to rural areas as well.

Although the CIC attracted growing numbers of new members, the organization also faced increasing opposition. For years, these whites' interracial work had earned them praise from both white and black Virginians, but, by the mid-1920s, they found themselves embattled. White interracialists faced criticism from some white Virginians and white politicians, who worried that these paternalists were inadvertently (or perhaps covertly) undermining the culture of segregation. From the other side, black activists were continually pushing for the expansion of African American rights. While white paternalists had once been seen unquestionably as leaders in managing the state's "race relations," both black activists as well as other whites now questioned their authority. Despite these critiques, the members of the Virginia CIC were proud of the progress they had made and declared in their 1930 annual report: "We believe that for the present our work in promoting better race relations must continue to be done quietly. We must rely on the tactful approach of interested friends in this movement and keep the Commission as an organization in the background until the masses of our people are educated to an appreciation of personal responsibility wherever injustice is done to any member of any race."[46] Although pleased with their progress, the members believed that their work should be "done quietly" and out of the public eye in order to avoid further condemnations of their work. While earlier paternalists were not at all silent about their mission, some of these individuals became more reticent in the 1920s. They realized that the upheavals following World War I and racial hysteria (through the rise of the Ku Klux Klan and Anglo-Saxon Clubs) had eroded white Virginians' sense of paternalism.

Munford and others of the paternalistic reform generation were still respected as genteel Virginian aristocracy, but a number of white Virginians began to debate whether paternalism itself was outdated and no longer a viable solution for the modern world. Nonelite whites tired of elite whites' dominance of not just African Americans but other whites. Moreover, many of the white elite "aristocracy" and elected leaders of Virginia were no longer largely supportive of the doctrine of paternalism. Older activists like Munford were being replaced by a younger generation who still respected the older paternalists but saw them as increasingly out of touch. These new, more conservative white elites largely opposed the doctrines of paternalism and resented assumptions that whites like Cocke, Davis, Bowie, Bryan, and Munford were really best qualified to dictate the state's racial policies. Thus, whites across the state and especially white political leaders began to question the authority of white paternalists to manage "race relations." White interracial activists, however, viewing their work to be practical and without any radical implications, found it difficult to understand why anyone would consider interracial initiatives to be anything other than the fulfillment of benevolent southern traditions. They believed, in the words of Munford, that "all right thinking people desire to see conditions such that will tend to the best development of both races."[47] They had not changed, but the perceptions of their work had.

As cross-racial activism became more structured in the 1920s through not only the Commission on Interracial Cooperation but also numerous other organizations including the YWCA and Interracial Conference of Church Women, more whites (prompted by the white press) worried that these "efforts to better race relations" were becoming potential opportunities to promote social equality.[48] The interracial initiatives of the CIC received widespread publicity, largely unfavorable. Helping individual African Americans was seen as acceptable acts of benevolence, but large-scale organizational initiatives seemed to some more like racial concessions than demonstrations of paternalism because they moved beyond the personal and dealt with issues of the African American race as a whole. A number of white politicians believed that the new structure opened doors of opportunity for blacks, who were increasingly adept (as symbolized by the 1921 lily-black movement) at speaking for themselves rather than through white representatives. For the first time in years, white Virginians debated which whites were best suited to monitor the color line.

Although most white paternalists had no intention of disrupting the racial status quo, the increasingly formal nature of interracial endeavors in the 1920s created new opportunities for African Americans to express their social concerns. In the past, this work stemmed from informal communications between blacks and whites. Those interactions often occurred on whites' terms and were subject to strict rules of racial etiquette. The emergence of new structured interracial organizations, however, offered African Americans a more secure footing to assert their opinions and advance their agendas. For example, the Community House for Colored People, a Richmond association founded by black and white activists to encourage social work within black neighborhoods, distributed positions of power across the color line. Whites and blacks alike filled numerous elected offices. Two whites, Judge J. Ricks and Father Charles H. Hannigan, were president and chairman of the committee-in-charge respectively, but Lillian Payne, a black woman with a long career of activism through the Independent Order of St. Luke, acted as executive secretary and managed the daily running of the organization.[49] Payne had also served as the first editor of the *St. Luke Herald*. Mary Munford and Maggie Lena Walker both served as vice presidents.[50] Payne, Walker, and other black leaders helped shaped the agenda of the Community House, including the content of the outreach programs aimed at educating African Americans as to the importance and techniques of social welfare initiatives.[51] As officers, they could assert their opinions and affect the direction of the organization without endangering themselves by outwardly defying racial boundaries.

Although the tangible results of interracial cooperation changed little in the post–World War I era, the world had changed. White Virginians were not immune to the racial hysteria and 100 percent Americanism campaigns of the early 1920s, despite the limited reception that the Ku Klux Klan received in the state. Considering themselves above any crude vigilante tactics, many whites preferred to keep the Old Dominion's "tradition" of polite racism. Thus, many whites were attracted to the Anglo-Saxon Clubs of America founded by the renowned concert pianist and composer John Powell in September of 1922. Powell promoted his new organization as a genteel alternative to the KKK that dealt in scholarly eugenic facts rather than virulent racial passions. With this "civilized" appeal, the Anglo-Saxon Clubs received enthusiastic support, peaking in 1935 with thirty-one posts in Virginia and a scattering of groups outside the state. The Women's Racial Integrity Club of Richmond alone had forty members. Powell feared that whites were becoming increasingly lackadaisical in their commitment to racial integrity and suggested that new interracial cooperation organizations were part of the problem.[52] He argued that the whites involved in these "efforts to better race relations" were naïve and blind to the impending threat of racial amalgamation. John Powell embraced tenets of eugenics.[53] Yet, Powell was not alone in his interest in this pseudoscience that built upon the theories of scientific racism.

In the 1920s and 1930s, eugenics was considered a viable scientific field and became popular across the United States. In Virginia, this obsession with "pure blood" and scientific ordering would eventually lead to the sterilization of more than eight thousand Virginians declared feeble-minded or somehow defective between the 1920s and the 1930s. Many of those sterilized in the state were African Americans, particularly black women. Virginia was not alone in this practice. Across the nation, more than seventy thousand Americans were sterilized in this period.[54] In *Sexuality, Politics, and Social Control in Virginia,* the historian Pippa Holloway effectively showed how these sterilization efforts were new attempts in the state to control and manage both African Americans and working-class whites.[55] As paternalism waned, new radical means of handling the so-called race problem emerged. Supporters of these drastic means justified them as yet another needed extension of the state, a practice ironically encouraged by the Progressive paternalists themselves as they sought greater governmental aid in social reforms. Beginning in the 1920s, the regulation of sexuality became increasingly popular in the state in the drastic form of sterilization but also in seemingly less obtrusive ways like censorship of films and books. As a result, Holloway concluded, "sexual regulation both reflected and sustained the relationships of power operating in Virginia."[56] Unlike older paternalistic methods of social reform that encouraged interracial conferencing, this new tactic cut not only African Americans out of the conversation but largely working-class whites and women as well.

This dark era of eugenics in Virginia, however, was just beginning in the early 1920s, and John Powell played a large role in popularizing these ideas. In July

John Powell. (Courtesy of Library of Congress, Prints & Photographs Division)

1923, he laid his argument before the state in a long essay in the *Richmond Times-Dispatch* entitled "Is White America to Become a Negroid Nation?" In it, he drew upon Mendel's law of heredity to justify white dominance, arguing that "in crossing two varieties, the more primitive, the less highly specialized variety, always dominates." This, he declared, was "why every race that has crossed blood with the Negro has failed to maintain its civilization and culture." Powell did not see himself as a radical racist but instead as a dispassionate realist who considered it a "national tragedy [for] the Negro problem, which should be always considered calmly and without prejudice. . . [to] be thrown into the cockpit of party politics."[57] He appointed himself as a messenger of reason to help white Americans open their eyes and understand that their race was in risk of extinction. Powell shared with dismay that after standing on the corner of Second and Broad in Richmond for forty-five minutes, he had counted "200 Negroes, of whom only five were black."[58] Rather than considering the long-standing tradition of white men's exploitative affairs with African American women as one of the major reasons for miscegenation, Powell blamed the breakdown of social and caste lines for the darkening of the white race.[59] He drew attention, in particular, to "the use of the forms of address of social equality by whites collaborating with Negroes on welfare committees and training schools." In deference to the fact that those whites whom he criticized were among the elites of the state, he explained that their actions were "undoubtedly actuated by the noblest motives," insisting that he mentioned "the matter merely to show the advance of social equality under existing conditions."[60] White paternalists involved in interracial endeavors now faced open criticism for the work they considered homage to their "benevolent" aristocratic heritage. They began to be categorized as sadly out of touch with modern times.

The Anglo-Saxon Clubs were not against all forms of cooperation across the color line. Powell, for example, was an enthusiastic supporter of Marcus Garvey and his "Africa for Africans" movement.[61] He corresponded with Garvey and some of Garvey's African American followers. Powell even accepted an offer to speak before Garvey's Universal Negro Improvement Association.[62] He saw no hypocrisy in working with black leaders as long as their beliefs meshed with his. While Garvey never accepted Powell's theories about white supremacy, both shared concerns that the blood of their respective races was being diluted by miscegenation. Thus, the Universal Negro Improvement Association's plan to encourage African Americans to recolonize to Africa fit perfectly with Powell's vision of saving white America from becoming a "Negroid Nation."[63] Unlike white paternalists, like Mary Munford and her nephew Reverend Walter Bowie, who believed it was their God-given and inherited responsibility to uplift the African American race, Powell saw no promising future for blacks in America. He claimed not to blame

African Americans for the "Negro Problem." He even, like paternalists, praised "the Negro" for "his docility and fidelity under slavery, especially during the War of Secession" and also for "his brawn and muscle [that] enabled us [whites] to accomplish in decades that which otherwise would have taken centuries." Although he stated that those past sacrifices required blacks to be treated with "meticulous fairness" and "large generosity," Powell argued that failure to preserve the color line was "no kindness to the Negro."[64] He challenged paternalists' positions as racial experts, arguing that Munford, Bowie, Schmelz, and like individuals were mistaken about what African Americans needed. Powell believed that cooperation should entail working together to create truly separate racial spaces rather than white interracialists' efforts to oversee and direct African American life.

Accordingly, Powell developed his own theory concerning interracial cooperation. In explaining his position to one young black scholar, Thomas Dabney, Powell confided: "I do not consider segregation and co-operation as opposed alternatives. Of course, the race problem could not only be ameliorated but made non-existent by amalgamation. This would mean getting rid of the race problem by getting rid of the races. *I consider segregation the sanest form of cooperation.*" Powell concluded that "geographical separation is the only possible means of preserving racial integrity."[65] Thus, his vision of segregation entailed two mutually exclusive white and black worlds, ideally located in physically separate regions. This ideal promoted by the Anglo-Saxon Clubs differed drastically from the Jim Crow culture envisioned by Virginia's elite white paternalists, who saw social control, not inflexible separation, to be the ultimate goal. White interracialists understood African Americans as essential components of the state's economy, especially in the menial positions of domestic service and industrial labor. Thus, their efforts toward cross-racial reforms had two goals: to secure racial peace under white control and also to promote a contented and healthy workforce. Powell and his followers, on the contrary, desired to make Virginia white, seeing no benefits to promoting African American communities within the state. True cooperation, Powell argued, meant the races working together to become as separate as possible.[66]

The Anglo-Saxon Clubs believed that the first step to making the state white was new legislation that would ensure the pure blood of future Virginians. In 1923, John Powell along with Ernest Cox (author of *White America*, 1923) and W. A. Plecker, state registrar of vital statistics, began to lobby the General Assembly for a racial integrity bill that would redefine white and nonwhite, require mandatory registration with the Bureau of Vital Statistics as to race, and make it unlawful for whites to marry anyone but whites.[67] Laws against intermarriage were not new in the state. The first of these statutes dated back to the 1600s. Yet, Powell, Cox, and Plecker believed current legislation had failed to stem the rising number of mixed-race Virginians. They argued that the most recent law (passed in 1910) defining blacks as any person possessing ⅟₁₆ black blood (altered from the ¼ standard set in the years following the Civil War) resulted in too many African Americans passing as white and ultimately marrying whites. Accordingly, the Anglo Saxon Clubs campaigned to have "white" redefined as an individual having no drop of nonwhite blood, with the single exception of ⅟₆₄th of American Indian blood to appease those Virginia elites who prided themselves on being descendants of Pocahontas.[68] Although Powell asserted that there was nothing "defamatory or derogatory to the Negro" in the assertion that "one drop of Negro blood makes the Negro," he saw no hypocrisy in his simultaneous claims that "no race even slightly tainted with Negro blood has failed to decay culturally."[69] In response to the Anglo-Saxon Clubs' vigorous campaigning and popular white support statewide, the General Assembly passed the bill in March 1924 after amending only the impractical provision requiring the retroactive registration of all Virginians born before 1924 and raising the percentage of "allowed" Indian blood from ⅟₆₄ to ⅟₁₆ in order to avoid any potential embarrassment to some of the state's "best" white families who claimed relation to Pocahontas.[70]

Anglo-Saxon Clubs members blamed interracial cooperation, both the new organizations (such as the CIC) as well as the older tradition of cross-racial reforms across the state, for the rise in miscegenation. John Powell argued that this work had ruined the old racial balance and gave African Americans hope that social equality was a tangible possibility. He believed paternalists were naïve and old-fashioned, supporting black uplift causes without the foresight to recognize the potential threats to white supremacy. Powell considered reform work like improving higher education facilities for blacks to be dangerous. He feared the opportunities that blacks received at places like Hampton Institute, which had for years depended in part on the goodwill of elite whites in fund raising and on their board of trustees to promote and sustain the school. He worried about the message this support sent to black Virginians. Powell encouraged Anglo-Saxon Club devotees to be cautious of institutions like Hampton becoming sites of racial equality.

Powell and the Anglo-Saxon Clubs sharply focused their attention on Hampton Institute in early 1925. The controversy began quietly one evening when Grace Copeland, a white woman, arrived late to a performance at Hampton's Ogden Hall of the Denishawn Dancers—a famous modern dance troupe out of Los Angeles. For convenience and because of the crowd, Copeland was seated next to African Americans. Copeland knew ahead of time that Hampton had a loose policy in terms of interracial seating before she attended, yet she was shocked to be actually placed beside blacks and later related the embarrassing incident to her husband. Walter Scott Copeland, editor of the *Newport News Daily Press*, was scandalized by the incident. He had for a while been concerned about Hampton's willingness to bend white rules of racial etiquette in order to please the school's students. Copeland determined to make an example of his wife's experience and educate the state about the supposed subversive practices of the institution. On March 20, 1925, he printed his first scathing editorial accusing the institution and its white principal, James E. Gregg, of teaching social equality.[71]

The Anglo-Saxon Clubs quickly took up Copeland's crusade. Hoping to shame white paternalists into withdrawing their support for the school, members of the white supremacist group attempted to use their influence with Governor E. Lee Trinkle and other prominent white members of the Southern Advisory Committee to stall Hampton Institute's ongoing fund drive.[72] Although the fund drive itself was ultimately successful, whites across the state responded to Copeland's and the Anglo-Saxon Clubs' claims about the "true" nature of the school. As such, a number of white Virginians began to publicly protest the "outrages" of Hampton. Powell built upon the 1920s climate of racial distrust to create a witch-hunt. In November 1925, at a meeting in Hampton, Anglo-Saxon Club members encouraged their local delegate, George Alvin Massenburg, to present a bill to the state legislature requiring segregated seating at all public assemblages held in Virginia.[73]

After its official introduction in January, the Massenburg bill met considerable opposition. Several white daily newspapers including the *Norfolk Virginian-Pilot* and the *Richmond News Leader* spoke against the measure, arguing that it was unnecessary. The board of directors of the Richmond Chamber of Commerce also denounced the proposed law.[74] While these whites did not promote racial intermixing, they believed that it was unnecessary and even uncivil to pass a law on something that had always been managed by tradition. They did not publicly protest segregation as a means to maintain white racial order, yet they argued that paternalism was also effective in protecting white supremacy and that de facto segregation was sometimes more efficient than de jure segregation. These paternalists admitted that aberrations occasionally happened at places like Hampton but stressed that these were isolated incidents that the Anglo-Saxon Clubs had blown out of proportion. On a personal level, they worried the proposed law would destroy the gains they had made in interracial communication and cooperation.

Disregarding the appeals of white paternalists across Virginia, the Massenburg bill gained widespread support among whites. Addressing the public, Powell challenged his critics: "If the charges brought by the Newport News Daily Press are unfounded, the superintendent and board of the Institute should definitely so state. If on the other hand these charges are true, the American public which is being asked to support the Institute has a right to be thoroughly informed as to the situation . . . [I am] impelled by no animus against the negro nor against Hampton Institute, but springs from a desire to clarify a situation injurious to negro education and dangerous to the whole country."[75] Indirectly, to avoid any direct confrontation, Powell accused white paternalists of concealing the "true" nature of their interracial work and telling half-truths to the white public. Powell's apocalyptic claims that the current path of benevolent race management would only lead to the mongrelization of the white race resonated with Virginians, who feared their privileges of whiteness were endangered in the tumultuous postwar era. A number of whites became convinced by the Anglo-Saxon Clubs' pronouncements that whites, as members of a superior race, deserved to be shielded from efforts to assert racial equality. The Anglo-Saxon Clubs appealed to all classes of whites from the middle and working classes, who feared any blurring of the color line could compromise their social and economic footholds. Powell, whose musical career had made him a wealthy man, cared deeply about preserving the state's aristocracy. Supporters of the white supremacist organization banded together in their belief that paternalism was no longer an effective strategy for the twentieth century.[76]

As a result of these changes, many white Virginians became wary of the ability of elite white paternalists, like Munford, Bowie, and Flannagan, to act competently as managers of white supremacy and criticized their participation in the new interracial associations. They paid less attention to the generations-old appeal of the paternalistic responsibility whites owed the descendants of their family's "beloved" slaves and became increasingly worried that African Americans might threaten whites' future economic and social security. With the sight of young black men in uniform proclaiming their manhood during World War I and the 1921 lily-black movement foreshadowing a future push for African Americans' civil and political rights fresh in their memories, many whites decided that the liberalism of the CIC was dangerous. Although they largely believed that older white members of the CIC and other interracial organizations had no intention of endangering segregation, these concerned whites and a new generation of white politicians feared that white paternalist leaders, despite being well-meaning and of impeccable family standing, were out of touch with modern times and were being manipulated into making racial concessions, like the extension of courtesy titles to some black leaders. This led to a shift in attitude among a younger generation of whites, who believed racial issues were best settled by the law and government rather than private and informal endeavors. Powell claimed that the Massenburg bill would not "inflict any hardship" on African Americans because "no self-respecting person of either race desires the races to be mixed at public entertainments," but his real concern was the preservation of white supremacy and not the effects of the law on black Virginians.[77]

While Powell and his followers argued that the new measure would only legislate present custom, white paternalists knew that Powell cared less about racial

harmony than about racial integrity. These critics of the Massenburg bill challenged the Anglo-Saxon Clubs to explain why they felt it was necessary to codify
what was already standard practice. White paternalists still believed that interracial cooperation work was achieving unprecedented success in bettering the lives
of all Virginians and suppressing outbreaks of violence in the state. They saw no
practical explanation for why Virginia, which they claimed to be a paragon of
racial harmony, to become the first state to pass a public assemblages Jim Crow
statute that would define segregation until the passage of the Civil Rights Act of
1964.[78] Paternalists, like Munford, thought the whole controversy to be embarrassing and unworthy of Virginians. They believed their current and past methods of
social management were entirely successful in bringing about a relatively peaceful situation. Statistical data showing fewer lynchings and mass racial violence in
Virginia offered validity to their claims, although these facts did not account for
racial bias in the legal system. White interracial reformers saw the Massenburg
bill to be unnecessary as well as dangerous to the delicate equilibrium of understanding within the state. Early in the controversy, these activists began to protest
the reactionary condemnations of Hampton Institute. Jackson Davis, a lifelong
Virginian and promoter of African American education as the field agent for the
General Education Board, met in April 1925 with Governor Trinkle to encourage him to "be tolerant" of President Gregg, who had to act, to a certain extent,
"in accordance with the wishes of Northern people & Negroes."[79] Davis and his
counterparts believed small concessions to African Americans were necessary to
maintain a beneficial communication between the races and were not harmful if
contained within black spaces. They argued that isolated incidents such as Copeland's experience while visiting Hampton Institute were no threat to the white
racial order or the continuance of segregation.

    Black Virginians saw the situation more clearly than the white populace of the
state, realizing that the issue had less to do with tradition than whites' fears that
the sanctity of Anglo-Saxon dominance was threatened by the economic and intellectual progress of the African American race. They knew it was not a coincidence
that the controversy began at a black university well known for its commitment
to racial uplift. Hampton Institute was renowned as the school where Booker T.
Washington was educated and formulated his ideology of accommodation, but
white radicals like Powell worried about any higher education of the black race
even under the justification that it provided practical industrial training.[80] Although the debate centered outwardly on segregation at public gatherings, many
whites viewed the philosophy and teachings of the school to be the real root of
the "problem." P. B. Young, the editor of the African American *Journal and Guide,*
questioned rhetorically if the hullabaloo was "because Hampton Negroes are

treated as human beings and at the other places they are treated as inferior human beings?"[81] Powell and the Anglo-Saxon Club members feared any institutions like Hampton or organizations like the Commission on Interracial Cooperation that even suggested African Americans had the potential to become more than second-class citizens.

Unused to controversy, some white members of the Hampton's board of trustees, northern and southern, were uncertain how to respond. They were supportive of the school's policies but were concerned that their defense of the institution could be misinterpreted as approval of racial equality. They were uncomfortable when thrust into the spotlight, unsure of whether action on their part would help or hinder the cause. Led by the president of the board, William Howard Taft (chief justice of the Supreme Court and former president of the United States), the trustees appointed a committee to carefully consider and prepare a written protest of the Anglo-Saxon Clubs' attack. Yet, in early March 1926, when the time came to take a public stand on the issue, they voted (only days before the passage of the Massenburg Law) to refrain from making any official statement.[82] Although white paternalists spoke out against the public assemblages measure, their protests were largely behind the scenes and reserved in contrast with the fervent lobbying of white extremists.[83] This was a distinct departure from their earlier public practices before the 1920s, when they proudly and publicly proclaimed their work. As interracial cooperation efforts became less accepted by the general white populace in the 1920s, these paternalists lost their position of influence.

John Powell believed white paternalists' protests of the Massenburg bill were misguided and a sign of those individuals' poor grasp on reality and skewed understanding of racial as well as gender boundaries. Unlike the interracial organizations in Virginia where women held important organizational positions, the Anglo-Saxon Clubs of America was a white male association concerned, like the Ku Klux Klan, with the maintenance of proper gender roles. Thus, John Powell noted with some contempt that a woman, Mary Munford, was the "mainspring of the anti-Massenburg lobby" and deplored her feminine tactics such as holding a dinner party to "entice" legislators potentially "amenable to the seductions of her 'liberal' philosophy."[84] With these words, he very subtly implied that Munford was improperly using her sexuality as influence — a bold insult to her extensive expertise. Condescendingly, Powell decided to write Munford directly to bring to her "attention certain grave aspects of the case" that he was sure she had "overlooked."[85]

Wishing to spare her "bitter regret," Powell explained to Munford that the last few years had witnessed extensive lawlessness and violence that should not be ignored out of temerity to take positive legal action. Although he acquiesced that proponents of the bill were not advocating mixed racial seating at public events, Powell insisted that whites' "opposition will be so understood by the negroes, within and without the state, & will serve as an incitement to further attacks on the color line."[86] He viewed Munford and other paternalists as out-of-touch liberals who unwittingly "spoiled" the African American population of the state by supporting interracial cooperation efforts. While Munford's assessment of racial interaction within the state occasionally bordered on idyllic, Powell's vision neared apocryphal dimensions. "In all seriousness," he confided to Munford, "I warn you the defeat of this bill may bring tragedy and horror upon the oldest English-speaking community in America."[87] Powell condescendingly hoped his unsolicited instruction would help Munford, merely a woman, to see the "truth." Munford, however, with decades more experience in social activism than the musician, remained convinced, even after the bill was passed into law, that the new segregation measure was, at best, extraneous and, at worst, damaging to her own work and the interracial balance she had helped to build.

A groundswell backlash influenced an increasing number of delegates and senators to favor the legislation despite the opposition of these paternalistic whites across the state. In March 1926, the bill passed the General Assembly. Feeling pressure from both sides of the issue, Governor Harry F. Byrd resisted taking any position for or against the measure, refusing to either veto or sign the bill. Thus, the Massenburg public assemblages statute became law without the governor's signature. Soon after, Byrd quietly confided to President Gregg of Hampton that he found the whole controversy "extremely regrettable."[88] The overt racism in passing what the historian J. Douglas Smith has called "the broadest and most restrictive measure of its kind in the United States" seemed unseemly to both Byrd and Gregg and against Virginia's tradition of "polite racism."[89]

Two years later, the state moved forward in a more positive direction toward stemming racial passions with the Anti-Lynching Law of 1928. White paternalists in the state, along with black leaders, had decried lynching as barbaric for years and inconsistent with the supposedly smooth race relations in Virginia. Although vigilante violence in the state remained lower than in other southern states, several particularly brutal lynchings, including the 1925 murder of Raymond Bird in Sussex County, revived the issue. The General Assembly finally took action, primarily because of the fervent crusade of Louis Jaffe in both a series of scathing public editorials in his *Norfolk Virginian-Pilot* and private letters to Governor Harry Byrd. The law went into effect in 1928, making Virginia the first state to define lynching as a state crime. Jaffe's success also illustrated the growing trend of turning to government to carry out reformist ideals that had begun with paternalists outside of government circles. However, with little means within the law to effectively

enforce it, no white was ever actually convicted under the law for lynching an
African American. Even the passage of this promising legislation had little effect
on the deeply embedded racial discrimination in the state.[90]

African Americans joined white interracialists in their condemnations of the racial
integrity bills and public assemblages laws. Soon after the passage of the Massenburg Law in March 1926, Gordon Hancock, an African American professor
at Virginia Union and active participant in many interracial associations, wrote
a letter to the editor of the white daily *Richmond News Leader* to express his relief
that revisions to the Racial Integrity Act of 1924 had been defeated in the General
Assembly.[91] He explained that the bill would have been an insult to the Old Dominion's integrity because it "lacked the essential characteristics of stalwart states-
manship such as has hallowed the name of Virginia wherever students of history
ponder the names of great men." Hancock recognized the declining influence
of paternalism in the state and worried its passing would ultimately hurt African
American progress and uplift. He candidly denounced segregation as making "the
business of being a negro . . . irksome and embarrassing."[92] Black Virginians faced
the daily discriminations of hurtful racial slurs, misrepresentation by the press,
substandard housing and living conditions, the inconvenience of Jim Crow cars,
undeserved moral censure, and inferior educational facilities, but he feared the
situation would grow worse if white Virginians turned away from their claims
of a paternalistic heritage. While Hancock regretted the limitations of the white
paternalists interested in interracial reform, he was more concerned about the
uncompromising nature of white extremists like Powell and a new generation of
conservative white politicians. Thus, he encouraged African Americans to continue trying to work with whites in interracial cooperation efforts.

Hancock, like John Mitchell, Janie Porter Barrett, Thomas Walker, and numerous other black leaders, believed that encroaching segregation required practicality and a willingness to court whites' benevolent interest in uplift initiatives. In
the 1920s, African Americans gained a new foothold in interracial work by taking
formal positions in the new organizations and using these new structured forums
to vocalize their concerns in a more open manner and be treated with greater
courtesy as fellow reformers rather than simply as racial inferiors. Following the
experiences of World War I, its aftermath, and the election of 1921, black Virginians were less willing to meekly acquiesce to white demands. But many African
Americans in the state still believed that although the situation was bad, it would
be much worse if they lost the condescending interest of white paternalists. Thus,
Hancock, in 1926, called for "the negroes of Virginia [to] again reaffirm their faith
in white friends of humanity and reconsecrate their supremest [*sic*] endeavors to

the common weal to the end that mutually the races will work for a mutual integrity that does not need legislation as a guarantee of its perpetuation."[93] Hancock decided that even though the white paternalists with whom he worked often did not question the efficacy of segregation, they were better than the alternative. As such, Hancock and other black leaders hoped paternalism would prevail even while many white Virginians lost faith in its utility. He concluded that communication across the color line was African Americans' only chance to prevent further legislation designed to keep the black race in their "place." Hancock refused to be treated "as a means to an end, rather than as a sharer in the civic development of his community, and above all . . . as a social menace."[94]

Other African Americans took a harsher tone against white paternalists and accommodating black leaders. T. J. J. Mosby, writing the *Richmond Planet*, protested: "It is very often said on public occasions when the interest of the race is being considered, that there is no friction between the good white folks and the best colored people. This milk and honey speech you frequently hear in these parts by . . . most of our leaders [implies] that the good white folks do not work against the best interest of the colored people. I am wondering do the speakers really believe what they say."[95] Mosby spoke for many nameless black Virginians when he questioned the frequent proclamations of racial goodwill as racial inequity became increasingly visible throughout the state. Apart from residential segregation laws that stymied the economic growth of black neighborhoods, Jim Crow laws were continually extended and modified during this era. Segregation pervaded many aspects of black Virginians' lives. African Americans could no longer enjoy many of the city parks, were forced into overcrowded housing, and had little means to fight the high death rate among their race. They made strides in gaining wider access to higher education but found few employment opportunities upon graduation, apart from the traditional jobs of manual labor and domestic service.

By 1930, public perceptions of interracial cooperation efforts had changed dramatically in Virginia. Generally, the white public was increasingly critical of these formerly accepted initiatives in the wake of national racial tumult and the unmistakable signs that African Americans were wary of their second-class citizenship. Although many of Virginia's leaders still employed paternalism as a tested strategy for public relations and service, the business of managing racial order became primarily a publicly legislated endeavor rather than face-to-face negotiations across the color line. White interracialists' seemingly minor concessions to black reformers suggested the limitations of paternalism. As such, a number of white Virginians began to fear that interracial cooperation would ultimately undermine their enjoyed privileges of whiteness and could eventually become the death knell of white supremacy.

CONCLUSION

New Strategies in a Changed World

I trust that at no very distant date such co-operation will be so much a matter of course that no one will think of mentioning it. When that time comes I hope the word "interracial" will be dropped as without meaning. This word is not used when enough racial representatives work together but only to emphasize a supposed difference between Negroes and whites as members of some movement. But until that transition is completed, the term is, perhaps, evidence of advance, although it is just the first spade-work for co-operation.
— Thomas Calhoun Walker

D
URING HIS LONG career as a lawyer, civil rights crusader, and child welfare advocate, Thomas Walker became very skilled at handling whites. He knew that one of the best ways to reach "well-meaning" whites was by appealing to their sentimentality. Thus, he later recalled in his memoirs that "in discussing co-operation as a necessity in correcting wrong race relations, whether we like to co-operate or not, I used to tell white audiences the story of two messengers in the Civil War."[1] These soldiers, who Walker judicially avoided identifying as Confederate or Union, headed toward the front lines of a battle to deliver their important missives. As they neared their destination, both met with misfortune. Bullets struck one messenger in his eyes, leaving him blinded. The second found himself lame after he received a serious injury to his legs. Both rendered individually helpless, they were forced to work together to carry out their orders. With dramatic imagery, Walker concluded, "the one who had lost the use of his legs managed to crawl into the arms of the one who had been blinded. He became eyes for the blind man and the blind man became legs for him so that, by joining what was left of each of them, both of them reached their destination." He explained to his white listeners that ignorance had in the past deprived the black man of the "legs nature gave him" and that whites likewise had been blinded to the "fact that an intelligent Negro is legally a citizen and can be vital help in time of need—which is, in my observation, always."[2] Through this analogy, Walker

hoped to convince whites that only together could white and black Virginians
"build a stable enlightened citizenship."[3]

Although rather over-the-top and perhaps a veiled mocking of whites' Lost
Cause romanticism, strategies such as Walker's appeal for leaders across racial
lines to work together to solve issues of racial strife as well as implement Progressive reforms were highly effective in the early twentieth century. This form
of interracial activism, prevalent from 1900 to 1930, offers new insight into the
defining and reworking of segregation in Virginia. A study of the experiences of a
unique generation of interracial activists—Thomas Walker, Maggie Lena Walker,
Mary Munford, Annie Schmelz, John Mitchell Jr., Joseph Mastin, and Janie Porter Barrett, among others—reveals not only the complexity of the relationships
between Virginia elites but also a different perspective on the meaning of the term
"interracial cooperation." Rather than attempts to overthrow the South's culture
of segregation as associated with the later civil rights movement, most whites in
Virginia, at least before 1921, generally accepted interracial work as necessary to
racial harmony.[4] Instead of challenging racial discrimination, "efforts to better
race relations" in these early years attempted, in the words of John Mitchell, to
"make more palatable the various species of injustice dealt out to the Negro in
America, and particularly in the South, by the dominant white race."[5]

These often overlooked interactions reveal a fresh perspective on the building of
segregation, where interracial communication was necessary to maintaining social
peace and order. Cross-racial initiatives did not generally result in grand gestures
or become opportunities for African Americans to relate the emotional distress of
discrimination. Instead, the work focused on the mundane, practical aspects of ap-
proaching Progressive reforms and expanding municipal services in a society that
supposedly had separate black and white worlds, though in reality those worlds
were always intricately connected. Rather than threatening the culture of segregation, interracial cooperation in pre–World War I Virginia functioned as a system
of negotiation through which Jim Crow was created and legitimized.

This began to change in the 1920s as interracial approaches transformed and
paternalism was challenged. African Americans' increased militancy in their denunciations of Jim Crow, the popularity of the Anglo-Saxon Clubs and their
critique of interracial initiatives, the development of a new formally structured
interracial movement, the usurpation of some reforms by the state government,
and in-fighting among whites over proper racial management and the continuing
utility of paternalism all led to a dramatic change in public opinion concerning
interracial cooperation among whites in the state. Forgetting earlier acceptance
of such initiatives as necessary to making segregation "work," many white Virginians decided these cross-racial efforts epitomized by the new Commission on

Interracial Cooperation were a threat to the region's white supremacist racial hierarchy. The white majority began to question the motivations of whites involved in the seemingly heretical organization. Interracial work received increasingly bad press, and whites feared African American leaders' protestations of the inequities of segregation. Simply, whites worried they were losing control over both African American lives and black space. They debated whether Virginia's long tradition of paternalism had run its course and was no longer useful in dealing with the state's "race problem." John Powell and his Anglo-Saxon Club followers worked to separate these white reformers from one source of their power—their paternalistic representation of African Americans. Doubts emerged about whether white paternalists were still to be trusted as experts at "handling" black Virginians. Frightened whites spread rumors replete with sexual innuendos, including a persistent story that Munford kept a cherished picture of Booker T. Washington clandestinely hidden in her bureau.[6] These fears led to a decline in influence of a generation of reformers who were once outspoken and proud of their work.

Despite this gradual shift in white public opinion, however, most of these white activists continued to believe in the righteousness of their work and the efficacy of paternalism. Individuals like Munford, Davis, Flannagan, Schmelz, and Cocke still expressed that their Lost Cause heritage entitled them both to know what was best for the African American race and also to instruct the white Virginian masses on how to most effectively deal with their black neighbors. Although they objected to what they saw to be crass tactics of the white radicals of the Anglo-Saxon Clubs to expand legalized Jim Crow into areas of life already segregated by tradition, these white paternalists were hesitant to publicly question the morality of Jim Crow or its utility in ensuring white supremacy. They were aware of the growing dissatisfaction of African Americans with segregation but considered this yet another reason to stay on their present course and blamed the clamoring on the insensitive reactionary rhetoric of men like John Powell.

Like Annie Schmelz, the white head of the Women's Section of the Virginia CIC, white paternalists worried that the vocalized discontent of African American leaders would only turn more whites against the interracial organizations. Rather than viewing the poor conditions in Virginia as a reason for black protest, Schmelz argued that deteriorating conditions were precisely why blacks needed to trust their white "protectors" (herself included). Schmelz spoke for many when she pondered, "How can they [African Americans] hope to secure political leadership in a country where they are twelve million against one hundred million and where their race during the past decade increased at the rate of only six and five[-]tenths per cent as against sixteen per cent of the white race?"[7] Most of these whites never wavered in their belief that blacks still benefited from their white benevolence. Yet, the influence of these individuals began to wane in the late 1920s. By that time, many of the activists like Munford, who died on July 3, 1938, were reaching the end of their careers. Munford's passing did not go unnoticed but was marked by an extensive front-page article in the *Richmond Times-Dispatch*. She was praised for her charitable works, particularly in education and interracial cooperation. Her obituary placed her activism firmly within the paternalistic tradition of the Lost Cause: "Having been brought up with well-loved Negro servants, the bettering of race relations became naturally a question of keen interest with her." And, Munford, in the words of an unnamed friend, was "a grand fighter and she never gave up."[8] With the passing of these somewhat legendary white reformers who had dominated cooperation activism in the state between 1900 and 1930, paternalism in Virginia faltered.[9] As a new generation took hold, racial issues were increasingly addressed by law and expanding Progressive government services, leaving the older Social Gospel reformers with less of a role to play.

Although Munford, Schmelz, and others continued to espouse the value of paternalistic interracial cooperation throughout their lives, African American activists were well aware of the limitations of paternalism. These black leaders daily witnessed the problems of poor housing, widespread disease, high death rates, and lack of educational and employment opportunities that began years before the advent of the Great Depression in October 1929. Cooperative efforts had kept racial violence to a minimal level in the state but failed to stem the deteriorating conditions facing black Virginians or addressed the inequitable legal system. Living conditions steadily worsened.

National criticism forced white Richmonders to acknowledge the concerns of the city's black residents. In 1921, the *Richmond Times-Dispatch* reflected that when "a writer in a widely read magazine published in a Northern city called the attention of the world at large to the miserable housing conditions in which the Negroes of Richmond were compelled to exist . . . [most whites] waxed righteously indignant at the alleged injustice he had put upon this city." Soon after, however, a study conducted by the Richmond Chamber of Commerce found that the situation in black neighborhoods was "not only deplorable, but such as to invite pestilence."[10] The white daily noted:

> The Negroes deserve well at the hands of Richmond, far better than they have received. Industrious, thrifty and law-abiding, they have earned their place here. Never has this been more vividly realized than during the recent troublous days when inflamed minds incited to race antagonisms. Throughout that time of uncertainty the Negroes listened to the wise and calm counsel of their recognized leaders and it was due largely to their exemplary behavior that Richmond's rep-

utation as respecter of the law was maintained. That is but an instance, but it is indicative of the general good feeling between the white and colored citizens of this city. To preserve and promote that feeling and in common justice to the Negroes and as a safeguard to the health of the city itself Richmond should delay no longer in housing them decently and comfortably.[11]

Despite this professed goodwill of whites in addition to numerous individual and organizational interracial initiatives, the editor of the *Richmond Times-Dispatch* admitted that "so far little [had] been done."[12] Progress was always minimal because white paternalists rarely acknowledged segregation as the root of the problem rather than the solution.

In June 1928, the Richmond Council of Social Agencies appointed a Negro Welfare Survey Committee to further assess the status of black Richmonders. This biracial group of twelve who included frequent interracial reformers such as Lucy Randolph Mason, Jackson Davis, and Gordon Hancock organized and conducted one of the largest and most comprehensive studies of African American life in Richmond. These twelve appointed individuals recruited more than seventy "socially informed white and colored persons" to serve on assorted subcommittees addressing such issues as economic status and dependency, health and housing, recreation, education, and behavior problems.[13] Through questionnaires sent to black Richmonders and also their white employers as well as door-to-door canvassing of black neighborhoods, the Negro Welfare Survey Committee compiled an enormous amount of data.

As liberal-minded reformers, the whites involved in the study believed African Americans were capable of progress, and, although many were still unwilling to acknowledge the detrimental impact of segregation on African Americans, they sought to understand the economic and environmental factors affecting black Virginians. The committee set out to ask, "Eliminating from consideration all biological and anthropological factors, are the medical, education, recreational, economic, and social opportunities of the Richmonder adequate to his needs?"[14] While never openly admitting the flaws of white supremacy, white researchers (encouraged by their African American colleagues) tried to, at least theoretically, take biological notions of inferiority out of the equation. Their findings as to the situation facing black Virginians were not optimistic. Statistics argued quite irrefutably that African Americans were not prospering under the auspices of paternalistic segregation.

According to July 1927 census figures, an estimated 194,444 people lived in Richmond: 138,525 whites and 55,919 African Americans.[15] However, although blacks only represented 29 percent of the city's population, African Americans contracted diseases at a disproportionate rate and had a higher risk of dying at an early age. The death rate among black residents of the city (20.43 per 1,000 people) was nearly double that of whites (11.54 per 1,000 people), and the average age of death for blacks (37.2) was nearly fifteen years younger than for whites (52.1). Black children were particularly vulnerable. Out of every 1,000 African American infants, 113 died in comparison with 59 out of every 1,000 white babies. African Americans consistently had an infant mortality rate nearly double that of whites despite having a slightly higher birth rate.[16] Their death rate from tuberculosis was nearly triple that of whites.[17] Black children under fifteen were dying from tuberculosis at one of the highest rates in the country (160.7 deaths per every 100,000 residents). In New Orleans, a city known for its poverty and poor health conditions among African Americans, the rate was almost half that of Richmond (76.9/100,000). Chicago, in comparison, had only 35.3 out every 100,000 black children die of tuberculosis.[18] The death rates of African Americans in Richmond were not only above state averages but were among the highest in the nation.

Despite the long-established cooperation and uplift efforts of reformers to address the deteriorating health conditions facing black Richmonders, the situation was both deplorable and a nationally embarrassing contradiction to white Virginians' claims of racial harmony. Although tuberculosis rates had dropped slightly in the past decade, in part, through cross-racial initiatives including the founding of a sanatorium for black patients and numerous educational campaigns, the disease continued to ravage the African American population of the city.[19] Through the influence of whites involved in conducting the study, however, results were skewed by the striking absence of any critique of segregation. For example, the final survey report made no mention of the effect of the 1911 Vonderlehr ordinance in creating these wretched health conditions. By physically limiting the parameters of black neighborhoods and preventing expansion, the regulation resulted in desperate overcrowding. This fact, compounded with the city government's refusal to provide basic municipal services including sewage, water, and street cleaning to African American neighborhoods, created an environment where disease epidemics became nearly impossible to control. The survey committee did not address the role of residential segregation in contributing to Richmond's infamous African American mortality rate. Instead, they noted that those blacks surveyed complained much more frequently about housing than about segregation, failing to recognize that housing problems were in fact caused by segregation.[20] This was only one example of how white researchers ignored the detrimental consequences of Jim Crow. Although interracial cooperative endeavors occasionally worked to temporarily improve conditions, such as the building of a black tuberculosis sanatorium, these efforts failed to produce lasting change because whites involved refused to consider (at least publicly) the role of Jim Crow in creating chronic poverty and illness in black neighborhoods.

In addition to health, the black and white committee members found racial inequity in many aspects of Richmond life. For example, a similar proportion of black and white Richmonders were employed, but African Americans overwhelmingly held low-paying laborer jobs, most often in domestic or personal service. Rather than protesting the discriminatory hiring practices, white researchers argued for the need to expand industrial training opportunities among blacks. The committee on "Behavior Problems of the Richmond Negro" found that blacks were much more likely to be arrested than whites. Although African Americans composed only about 29 percent of the city's population, 10,431 blacks were arrested in 1927, only slightly fewer than the 11,080 whites. Black women, in particular, were twice as likely to be incarcerated as white women.[21] The researchers did not question whether these disproportionate numbers resulted, in part, from the discriminatory practices of law enforcement.

In education, African Americans were also treated as second-class citizens. While the city spent $70.72 per every white high school student, black schools were only appropriated $34.06 per child. All principals and nurses, including those at African American schools, were white. Black teachers who did find employment were paid less than their white counterparts; $1,224 in comparison with $1,985 for white high school teachers. In addition to a lower salary, African American educators confronted the challenges of inadequate funding for supplies and also average class sizes that were 42 percent larger. In the 1927–28 school year, the city finally established one kindergarten class for African Americans, although the public schools already offered enough kindergarten classes to cater to nearly a thousand white children.[22] Instead of denouncing these blatantly unequal conditions, the education committee reinforced its belief that more industrial training was needed to ensure a better-prepared work force.

Researchers, however, criticized the Richmond city government for not providing more recreational opportunities for blacks. They believed this to be the root of the race's delinquency problems and disproportionately high arrest rate. Although there were numerous gyms and playgrounds for white children, the city offered few recreational facilities for African American youth. In the entire city, there were no public gyms open to black residents, not even in the public schools. This situation extended to local black colleges as well. The Virginia Union basketball team, for example, had to play their games in a second-floor hall above an undertaker's establishment.[23]

The interracial Negro Welfare Survey Committee found that, despite the decades of work of white and black leaders engaged in paternalistic cooperative and

uplift reform, the conditions of black Richmond neighborhoods remained deplorable and, in fact, were steadily worsening. Housing and health were the most
immediate and overriding concerns, but African Americans also faced inequitable
educational, employment, and recreational opportunities. Reformers had been
discussing the building of a public park for African Americans since the early
1910s, but, as of 1927, no separate park actually existed. Although not officially
barred by law from using the existing public parks, white policemen enforced segregation, making exceptions only for African American chauffeurs accompanying
their white employers and black nurses bringing their young white charges to enjoy some outdoor playtime.[24] These allowances were made for the benefit of whites
and clearly indicated that the true goal of segregation was control and not complete separation. This extensive survey published in 1929 carefully documented
racial discrimination and the failings of Richmond's government to provide for
29 percent of its population.

Despite these striking findings, the Negro Welfare Survey, like the longtime
clamor over the need for an African American park, produced few concrete
changes. White researchers were concerned with the discouraging obviously inequitable conditions, but many were also limited by their continuing belief in efficacy
of segregation. Moreover, while white paternalists became adept at identifying
social and economic problems (apart from that of Jim Crow), they, as they lost influence, had increasing difficulty convincing white governmental officials who controlled the state's budget of the utility of supporting reforms for black Virginians.
Generally, money for any Progressive reform initiative was scarce, particularly if
it was earmarked for African American causes. Thus, the state sometimes took
over Progressive initiatives, like the Virginia Industrial School for Colored Girls,
but then gradually reduced its funding. In face of this difficulty, black committee
members followed the only strategy open to them — educate whites as to the harsh
reality and hope that paternalistic sentiment would translate into more than just
rhetoric. Yet, knowledge was useless if these whites were reluctant to blame segregation and did not have the financial resources to bring about real change even if
they were willing. Although interracial cooperation produced some real successes,
cross-racial initiatives focused too often on studying, rather than solving problems.
White interracialists were handicapped by their vested interest in preserving Lost
Cause paternalism. Even though some of the individuals were beginning to privately question segregation by the late 1920s, very few were willing to voice their
concerns publicly.

This situation began to change in the late 1920s and 1930s as economic, health,
and education conditions worsened. Some white liberals across the South began
to listen more closely to African American concerns. This new younger genera-

tion of white activists included Lucy Randolph Mason, known primarily for her work with the National Consumers League and CIO, as well as southerners like Ralph McGill, Virginia Durr, Lillian Smith, Sarah Patton Boyle, and Katharine Lumpkin. These individuals, in the 1940s, 1950s, and 1960s, openly spoke about the immorality of segregation. Although Mason and others' racial conversions were primarily a later occurrence, African American leaders like Walker, Mitchell, Barrett, and Stokes in the early 1920s began to lay the framework for a redefinition of interracial cooperation by questioning the effectiveness of paternalism to solve modern problems. One of the first public articulations of this dissatisfaction was the 1921 lily-black movement, but the African American struggle against paternalism continued throughout the following decades.

Black leaders used the newly organized interracial organizations like the Commission on Interracial Cooperation to encourage interested whites to actually listen to blacks' concerns. In these more formal settings, black reformers asserted their right to be addressed by the same courtesy titles given whites. They worked over the years to make interracial organizations truly interracial by securing for African Americans equal terms of membership. Over time, they struggled to force white liberals to move past endless studies of "black issues" and start working on real solutions—that is, critical evaluations of the ethical and logistical shortcomings of segregation. The African American professor and activist Gordon Hancock (a man who advocated for years the importance of interracial dialogue and even created the Francis J. Torrence School of Race Relations at Virginia Union) assessed the current status and also history of cooperative work in a 1941 article appearing in the *Norfolk Journal and Guide*.[25] "One of the weaknesses of the old interracial cooperation," Hancock concluded, "was its paternal nature," but now changing times and African American discontent were "calling for another type."[26] Black leaders hoped this new form of interracial cooperation would be based more on concrete efforts to improve conditions across the South rather than benevolently worded justifications for whites trying to control African American lives. At the same time, this new activism was considered radical—distinct from the older generation of mainstream reforms that closely fell in line with the segregated order.

With this transformation, most black leaders began to distance themselves from their former appeals to whites in terms of class alliance and worked instead to build a greater racial unity among black Virginians. Cross-racial reform initiatives in the first two decades of the twentieth century attracted a number of African American classist elites. These individuals, including Thomas Walker, John Mitchell Jr. and Janie Porter Barrett, believed noblesse oblige obligated them to help those deemed socially beneath them. Embracing their own form of paternalism similar to white interracialists' belief in the moral, Christian responsibilities of white supremacy, these black elites felt it was their duty to police the African American race. They were constantly concerned that poor blacks would damage the reputation of the race as a whole. They argued that the "better classes" of blacks had no other choice than to work with white officials and "better class" white reformers to maintain peace. John Mitchell Jr. advised the readers of his *Richmond Planet* that "division should be made upon the basis of right and wrong and that color should form no part of it. A colored man who ruthlessly assaults a white person is an enemy to all of us, endangering our rights and privileges."[27] Yet, over the years, beginning with the 1911 Vonderlehr ordinance in Richmond initiating an era of residential segregation that made no exceptions for the self-identified African American "better classes," black leaders made increasingly frequent appeals for racial unity. African American leaders became more vocal in their wholesale denouncements of Jim Crow and less concerned with their own enactment of paternalism. In November 1921, then in the midst of his campaign for governor on an all-black ticket, Mitchell admonished black Virginians to band together: "Stand up and be men. Colored folks walk upright. Stooping is bad for the kidneys and even worse for your self respect."[28] This group of leaders, however, were aging along with their white counterparts. John Mitchell Jr. died on December 3, 1929, and Maggie Lena Walker in 1934.[29] A new generation was rising that would see the civil rights movement to fruition.

Even in this atmosphere of greater assertion of rights, however, division remained among some black leaders on tactics. While many began to distance themselves from accommodationist policies, others continued to use this as leverage to appeal to white support. Speaking before an interracial (yet segregated) audience at St. Paul's Episcopal Church in Richmond in October 1930, Robert R. Moton, the successor of Booker T. Washington at Tuskegee Institute in Alabama, proclaimed to a receptive crowd: "The 15,000,000 or more Negroes in this country are the most civilized and the most prosperous Negroes in the world. They have reached this state through their contact with Anglo-Saxons in America, and while they were brought here against their will and have no always been able to maintain peace with their white brethren, they should be grateful to God for this contact."[30] Moton was, like Giles Jackson (who died in 1924), of an older generation that relied on paternalism as much as the whites with whom they worked.

Although Janie Porter Barrett continued to be one of the most vocal and active advocates for her race until she died in 1948, she expressed disappointment with the changes her school experienced as it became increasingly a state-run organization and subject to less private direction. On September 1, 1927, the state officially abolished the old board of managers and instead created a smaller five-member board that oversaw the Virginia Industrial School for Colored Girls as well as the state's similar (and less successful) reformatory school for African American boys. At that time, the new chairman became Judge R. H. Cardwell instead of Annie Schmelz (who was not included in the new board).[31] In 1931, Cardwell was replaced by Martha McNeill. The newly appointed five-member board did include one African American, Maggie Lena Walker; however, the board lost much of its interracial balance. After Walker died in 1934, she was replaced by the African American educator Virginia Randolph, well known for her work as the Jeanes Supervising Industrial Teacher in Virginia. This shared and smaller board was less involved.[32] While the annual reports from the first twelve years included long and detailed letters from Schmelz as chairman, the new chairs, particularly Cardwell, preferred brief and impersonal one- or two-paragraph summaries. The school continued to perform well, but Barrett missed the personal connection with her old board members. In 1933, Barrett reminisced about the "sympathetic interest and understanding of our first Board."[33] She especially spoke fondly of Schmelz as "only one of those fine unselfish spirits who gave so freely of their time, energy and money as member of the first Board of Managers" and of Munford and Walker, who served "the institution in countless ways, large and small."[34] Without their help, the school stayed open but was increasingly stressed by lack of funding.

In 1938, the school celebrated a gift of beautiful new gates to mark the entrance to the institution. The gates were not the result of state funding (which was particularly tight in the midst of the Great Depression) but rather were donated by the Virginia State Federation of Colored Women's Clubs.[35] Now seventy-three years old, Barrett had witnessed great changes—positive and negative—in her state and found herself one the last members of the older cooperative and uplift generation that had once been so prominent in the state. John Mitchell Jr., Maggie Lena Walker, and Mary Munford had all passed away. Martha McNeill, Annie Schmelz, T. C. Walker, and Ora Stokes were aged, and like Barrett herself, reaching the end of their activism. Barrett used the celebration to dedicate the new gates as an opportunity to reflect on the past:

> Happy as we are to have this added touch of beauty, a deeper satisfaction comes from the presence of so substantial a means of keeping green the memory of those who gave so much to bring the institution into being: the Negro women with human slavery less than seventy years behind them, and the white women, products of hundreds of years of education and culture, joining hands and working together that the least among them might have their chance. What sacrifice and struggle on the part of the Negro women who had so little to share: what courage in the white women who laid aside custom and inherited traditions to champion a cause so unpopular! I wish that their every encouraging word and helpful act

might be recorded as they burn in my memory, and be preserved as a guide to future generations who may seek to contribute to human betterment.[36]

To Barrett, the gate was a memorial to "brave women, white and black, who forgot their prejudices and overcame their distrust."[37] Two years later, in 1940, Barrett retired. She returned to Hampton, where she lived until her death on August 27, 1948.[38] In 1950, the Virginia Industrial School for Colored Girls was renamed the Janie Porter Barrett School for Girls. She never witnessed the racial integration of her school, which finally occurred in 1965. The institution remained a juvenile correctional facility of the state until closing in 2013.[39]

In early twentieth-century Virginia, interracial cooperation left a legacy of both successes and failures. The work played a central role in the building of segregation in the state by providing a convenient means for whites to declare black space to be merely a subset of the larger white world. Yet these efforts also helped create a system in which the needs and concerns of African Americans were at least studied and often acted upon if the reforms fit within the segregated framework. Looking back on the history of activism in these first decades of the twentieth century, Gordon Hancock reflected in 1944: "Interracialism has not been a total loss, as is so often erroneously supposed by the casual observers who emphasize the many things it has not accomplished rather than the fine things it has, without great failure. The modest methods of the interracialist have obscured many great and substantial achievements in the field of race relations."[40] Interracial cooperation did have significant successes, such as stemming large-scale racial violence and vigilante lynching in Virginia, and even saw the passing of the Virginia Anti-Lynching Law of 1928.[41] Progressive organizations like the Virginia Board of Charities and Corrections ensured that black Virginians were included in the expanding public welfare state. Perhaps most important, cooperative initiatives offered an opening for African American leaders to voice their opinions and eventually agitate for an end to Jim Crow.

Interracial cooperation was essential to the building of Jim Crow Virginia because segregation statutes never created mutually exclusive black and white worlds. Every day the races met on the streets, in businesses, in white homes, and in numerous other venues. Segregationists never implemented absolute racial separation, but the tenets of Jim Crow did provide a language for justifying and glossing over racial discrimination as well as the legal strictures for enforcing white supremacy. Whites never gave up the control that segregation, in theory, demanded. Few white Virginians in the early years of the twentieth century believed blacks capable of surviving in a society equal to yet separate from their influence. Cross-racial activism evolved as one nonviolent method for whites to try to continue to direct African American lives; it encouraged racial discrimination while offering whites the moral satisfaction that these measures were necessary to ensuring racial harmony. Despite white fantasies of an immutable color line, black and white southerners lived in a shared, not parallel, world.

From 1900 to 1930, a unique generation of white and African American elite activists chose to become involved in the imperfect practice of interracial co-operation because they believed it to be the most efficient means available to achieve their individual goals in the biracial world in which they lived. Paternalist whites found a convenient and outwardly benevolent way to patrol the color line and aid in the building of a modern white supremacist culture. African American leaders used the work to obtain needed material concessions in an era of increasing racial discrimination and create a forum to eventually denounce segregation as not only unjust but immoral.

The uplift and cooperation generation helped to determine the extent and intricacies of segregation in Virginia, making Jim Crow "work" in the face of twentieth-century modernity. These reformers worked in an age of paternalism, confident in their work and proud of their successes. Reflecting on his role in those increasingly outdated efforts, Thomas Walker shared his belief that at "no very distant date" "co-operation will be so much a matter of course that no one will think of mentioning it. When that time comes I hope the word 'interracial' will be dropped as without meaning. This word is not used when enough racial rep-resentatives work together but only to emphasize a supposed difference between Negroes and whites as members of some movement. But until that transition is completed, the term is, perhaps, evidence of advance, although it is just the first spade-work for co-operation."[42] African American leaders, like Walker, hoped that one day they could convince whites that notions of racial superiority were inherently flawed. Only then could their cooperation across the color line cease to be a central prop of segregation and become a forum to debate its morality and efficacy. That would be the work of a new generation.

NOTES

Introduction

1. Kollatz, "An Artist's Creation."

2. Broadfoot, Adele Clark interview.

3. Ibid., 21.

4. Ellis, *Race Harmony and Black Progress;* Dykeman and Stokely, *Seeds of Southern Change.*

5. J. Hall, *Revolt against Chivalry.*

6. Gilmore, *Gender and Jim Crow,* 171–78.

7. Ibid., 171.

8. Greenwood, *Bittersweet Legacy;* Dykeman and Stokely, *Seeds of Southern Change.*

9. A. Scott, *The Southern Lady;* J. Hall, *Revolt against Chivalry.*

10. Higginbotham, *Righteous Discontent;* Shaw, *What a Woman Ought to Be and to Do*; Gaines, *Uplifting the Race*; White, *Too Heavy a Load*; Hine, "Black Professionals and Race Consciousness," 1279–94; Hine, *Black Women in White.*

11. Gilmore, *Gender & Jim Crow,* xix.

12. For one collection of essays that explores the wide range of definitions of who are Progressives and what are the differing motivations of these individuals, see Gilmore, ed., *Who Were the Progressives?* For studies of southern Progressives, see Grantham, *Southern Progressivism*; Sallee, *The Whiteness of Child Labor Reform in the New South*; and Link, *The Paradox of Southern Progressivism.*

13. Link, *The Paradox of Southern Progressivism.*

14. These whites were liberals because of their shared belief in Progressive causes with northern reformers, their support for African American uplift, their belief that black progress was possible, and their willingness to consider the environmental factors hurting southern African Americans rather than simply blaming all problems on blacks' supposed innate nature. Regardless, these whites were supporters of segregation. They were both paternalists and liberals. Historians have written on a number of different aspects of white liberalism in the South before the civil rights movement. This work falls into several categories. The first are studies of select individuals like Eagles, *Jonathan Daniels and Race Relations;* and Hobson, *But Now I See.* A second type of this historiography is organizational histories. Examples of these include Egerton, *Speak Now against the Day;* and Sullivan, *Days of Hope.* A third category is the general-overview histories, both contemporary works written during the era before the civil rights movement and later. Generally, these works, by seeking a sweeping synthesis, have tended to be fairly praising accounts of these white liberals as hopeful opponents of white radical racists (see Johnson, *Into the Main Stream;* and Sosna, *Southern Liberals and the Race Issue*).

A final category of literature on white southern liberals includes contemporary autobiographical works by white southerners detailing their "conversions" to liberalism (see Mason, *To Win These Rights;* and Boyle, *The Desegregated Heart*). A wealth of material has been written about African American activism in the South in the early twentieth century before the civil rights movement. For a few examples, see Giddings, *When and Where I Entered;* Gilmore, *Gender & Jim Crow;* and Hunter, *To Joy My Freedom*. For a fuller list, see the bibliography.

15. Peebles-Wilkins, "Janie Porter Barrett and the Virginia Industrial School for Colored Girls," 143–61.

1. Paternalism and Cooperation in the Old Dominion

1. For more on Progressivism and the modernity of segregation, see Link, *The Paradox of Southern Progressivism;* and Ayers, *The Promise of the New South*.

2. George Washington, Thomas Jefferson, James Monroe, James Madison, William Henry Harrison, John Tyler, and Zachary Taylor were all born in Virginia. Woodrow Wilson, the twenty-eighth president, was also from Virginia, born in Staunton on December 28, 1856.

3. See Dunn, *Dominion of Memories*.

4. E. Lewis, *In Their Own Interests: Race, Class, and Power in Twentieth-Century Norfolk, Virginia,* 3.

5. Early twentieth-century southerners, black and white, used this exact term, "cooperation." Although the term "interracial cooperation" has now developed the connotation of liberal (in the twenty-first-century implications of the word) acts undermining the foundations of southern society, segregation in particular, I have chosen to retain the term because it was the language used during the period in question. Contemporary southerners spoke frequently of such acts of "co-operation." My only alteration is to modernize the spelling by removing the hyphen. I use the term "interracialists" to refer to the individuals who frequently participated in these efforts.

6. Mary Munford corresponded with many white Virginia activists concerning racial and nonracial issues. She also kept copies of many Virginia and national Commission on Interracial Cooperation meeting minutes, as well as business concerning the Community House for Colored People and the Richmond Urban League. Thus, her papers are an excellent source for studying white paternalists (Mary Cooke Branch Munford Papers, Accession 28142, Library of Virginia [hereafter Munford Papers]).

7. Bowie, *Sunrise in the South,* 1–39, 46; Munford Papers.

8. "Munford Brilliant Career Brought to Close by Death," *Richmond Times-Dispatch,* June 1, 1910.

9. Saturday Afternoon Club, Richmond, Virginia, Records, 1894–1907, Virginia Historical Society (hereafter SAC Papers); Bowie, *Sunrise in the South,* 28–29, 49–51, 53–74, 103–43; Robert Ogden to Ben Valentine, February 25, 1904, Lila Meade Valentine Papers, Virginia Historical Society (hereafter Valentine Papers); Robert Ogden

to Ben Valentine, n.d., Valentine Papers; Tyler-McGraw, *At the Falls*, 233; Richmond Education Association Papers, Virginia Historical Society. For more information on Munford's involvement in the National Consumers League, see Florence Kelley to Mary Johnston, n.d., Mary Johnston Papers, University of Virginia (hereafter Johnston Papers). Munford also helped to found one of the first YWCA clubs for working (white) women in Richmond.

10. *St. Luke Herald* qtd. in Bowie's *Sunrise in the South*, 171–72.

11. This is a common theme in writings by the whites involved in these interracial efforts (see Hammond, *In Black and White;* and Bowie, *Sunrise in the South*).

12. Morton, "The Negro in Virginia Politics, 1865–1902," 75; Bowie, *Sunrise in the South*, 11–15. For more information on the rise of the Conservatives and post–Civil War politics in Virginia, see Dailey, *Before Jim Crow*.

13. Bowie, *Sunrise in the South*, 13.

14. Ibid., xiii.

15. Beard, *Women's Work in Municipalities*, 211.

16. *Richmond Planet*, February 3, 1912.

17. Ibid. See also Munford Papers.

18. Virginia Historical Society, "A Guide to the Cocke Family Papers, 1794–1981," Virginia Historical Society, 2002, http://ead.lib.virginia.edu/vivaxtf/view?docId=vhs/vi00005.xml;query=;brand=default.

19. Beard, *Women's Work in Municipalities*, 211.

20. Ibid.

21. "Talk Coloure [*sic*] women," June 9, 1911, Mary Johnston Speeches, Johnston Papers, emphasis added.

22. Mary E. Burell to Mary Johnston, June 14, 1911, Johnston Papers.

23. Gilmore, *Gender and Jim Crow;* Greenwood, *Bittersweet Legacy*.

24. Wallenstein, *Cradle of America*, 23–24.

25. Brundage, *Lynching in the New South*.

26. "Stuart Commends Plan of Negro Exposition," *Richmond Times-Dispatch*, June 13, 1915.

27. "I. O. St. Luke Here," *Richmond Planet*, August 25, 1917.

28. Annie Schmelz to Janie Porter Barrett, August 17, 1921, Munford Papers.

29. Alexander, *Race Man*, 72.

30. "Progress of Negro Race," editorial, *Richmond Times-Dispatch*, May 20, 1915.

31. Editorial comment, *Richmond Planet*, March 3, 1906.

32. "An Act of Heroism," *Richmond Planet*, May 18, 1912.

33. "Governor Mann at the Auditorium," *Richmond Planet*, May 11, 1912.

34. Ibid.

35. "Governor Mann Speaks," *Richmond Planet*, August 24, 1912.

36. Editorial comment, *Richmond Planet*, February 7, 1914.

37. James T. Phillips, "Instruments of Race Adjustment," *Richmond Planet*, February 22, 1914.

38. "Gov. Stuart Speaks Plainly," *Richmond Planet*, May 9, 1914.
39. Ibid.
40. Ibid.
41. Ibid.
42. Ibid.
43. Ibid.
44. "Mayor McCarthy's Suggestion," *Richmond Planet*, October 6, 1906.
45. Ibid.
46. Ibid.
47. In her book on Charlotte, Janette Greenwood, like C. Vann Woodward, argues that there was a moment in the 1880s where "race relations" could have been different. She identifies a rise in interracial cooperation efforts in the late nineteenth century on issues like Prohibition and asserts that this work led to the formation of a class alliance among the "better classes" in Charlotte. She shows how this trend fell apart with disfranchisement and segregation at the turn of the century, when whites became no longer willing to forge class alliances that trumped racial lines. Greenwood concludes that even though the chance for things to be different was lost, the work left a "bittersweet legacy" (Greenwood, *Bittersweet Legacy*).
48. Hale, *Making Whiteness*, 43–84. See also Foster, *Ghosts of the Confederacy;* and Brundage, *The Southern Past*.
49. Walter Russell Bowie, "Goodwill and Race Adjustment," draft of speech written for Founder's Day at Hampton Institute 1926, Munford Papers.
50. Ibid.
51. "The Negro. American Adventures — VII," *Richmond Planet*, February 10, 1917.
52. For more about slavery in Virginia, see E. Morgan, *American Slavery, American Freedom;* and P. Morgan, *Slave Counterpoint*.
53. "The Negro. American Adventures — VII," *Richmond Planet*, February 10, 1917.
54. "Gov. Stuart Speaks Plainly," *Richmond Planet*, May 9, 1914. For another example, this one by William T. Dabney, business manager of the Richmond Chamber of Commerce, see "Business Manager Dabney's Great Address," *Richmond Planet*, March 3, 1917. For more about the mammy figure, see Hale, *Making Whiteness*, 92–94, 105.
55. For example, see "A Pathetic Incident," *Richmond Planet*, January 31, 1914.
56. "A White Gentleman's Tribute," *Richmond Planet*, January 10, 1914. Article reprinted from the *Virginia Citizen*.
57. "The Negro. American Adventures — VII," *Richmond Planet*, February 10, 1917.
58. Baker, *Following the Color Line*, 11.
59. For an example of a history of paternalism in the making of another southern city, see Cashin and Eskew, eds., *Paternalism in a Southern City*.
60. Williamson, *Crucible of Race*, 255; J. Smith, *Managing White Supremacy*, 8. Marjorie Wheeler also notes the predominance of elite whites in reform initiatives in her study of the southern suffrage movement (Wheeler, *New Women of the New South*, 38–71).

61. See Tyler-McGraw, *At the Falls;* and Silver, *Twentieth-Century Richmond.*

62. E. D. Caffee, "Colored Richmond," *Crisis,* January 1917, 124–32.

63. For a comprehensive study of pre–Civil War Richmond, see Kimball, *American City, Southern Place.*

64. Lee, "More Than an Image," 3.

65. For more on Jackson Ward and the conditions facing that district, see ibid., 2–11; Tyler-McGraw, *At the Falls,* 227; and Alexander, *Race Man,* 171–77.

66. J. Smith, *Managing White Supremacy,* 31.

67. Caffee, "Colored Richmond," 124–32.

68. Gavins, *The Perils and Prospects of Southern Black Leadership,* 40–41.

69. *Crisis,* September 1913, 218.

70. Ibid., March 1916, 219.

71. "Dr. Freeman Speaks to Y.M.C.A.," *Richmond Planet,* April 11, 1914.

72. "President Wilson's Daughter Speaks," *Richmond Planet,* April 19, 1913.

73. See E. Jordan, "The Impact of the Negro Organization Society on Public Support for Education in Virginia," 8, 24, 30–31.

74. "Great Meeting Here," *Richmond Planet,* November 8, 1913.

75. "Governor Mann and Dr. Washington to Speak," *Richmond Planet,* October 18, 1913; "Great Speakers Here," *Richmond Planet,* November 1, 1913; "Booker T. Washington Coming," *Richmond Planet,* November 1, 1913; "Organization Society to Hold Meeting in Richmond; "Great Meeting Here," *Richmond Planet,* November 8, 1913.

76. "Great Meeting Here," *Richmond Planet,* November 8, 1913.

77. See Culley, "Muted Trumpets: Four Efforts to Better Southern Race Relations."

78. "The Newest South," *Crisis,* July 1913, 131.

79. In *Defying Dixie,* Glenda Gilmore traces the influence of ex-patriot southerners in shaping the work of so-called "northern" organizations like the NAACP and their criticisms of southern segregation.

80. "A Great Conference," *Richmond Planet,* April 5, 1913.

81. Ibid.

82. "The Conference," *Crisis,* June 1913, 87; "Fifth Annual Conference," *Crisis,* May 1913, 37; "A Great Conference," *Richmond Planet,* April 5, 1913. See also Hammond, *In Black and White;* Hammond, *In the Vanguard of a Race;* Hammond, *Race and the South;* McNeal, "James Hardy Dillard: Southern Humanitarian"; and Singal, *The War Within,* 115–52.

83. "The Conference," *Crisis,* June 1913, 87.

84. See Brawley, *Doctor Dillard of the Jeanes;* McNeal, "James Hardy Dillard: Southern Humanitarian"; and Walker, *The Honey-Pod Tree,* 100–103.

85. "James Hardy Dillard," *Journal of Negro History* 25, no. 4 (October 1940): 585–86.

86. Southern white liberals cannot be understood without placing them in the context of the Progressive Era reform of segregation. For one history of American liberalism, see Cohen, *The Reconstruction of American Liberalism, 1865–1914.*

87. *Crisis,* March 1913, 217.

88. Ibid.

89. "The Lucy Mason Testimonial," *Richmond Planet,* July 23, 1932.

2. Encroaching Segregation

1. See Alexander, *Race Man,* 72; and Oliver, "Maggie Lena Walker," 65.

2. Alexander, "Black Protest in the New South," xiii.

3. Ibid.

4. For more on the Readjusters and Mahoneism movement in Virginia, see Dailey, *Before Jim Crow;* and Rachleff, *Black Labor in the South.*

5. Alexander, "Black Protest in the New South," 92–97.

6. See also Alexander, *Race Man.*

7. Editorial comment, *Richmond Planet,* August 25, 1906.

8. Gavins, *The Perils and Prospects of Southern Black Leadership,* 87.

9. "Influence of Southern Sentiment," *Richmond Planet,* December 27, 1913.

10. John Mitchell Jr., editorial comment, *Richmond Planet,* March 10, 1906.

11. "A Little Misunderstanding," *Richmond Planet,* October 17, 1914.

12. Ibid.

13. Ibid.

14. John Mitchell Jr., editorial comment, *Richmond Planet,* November 16, 1912.

15. Dabney, *Virginia,* 435.

16. Woodward, *The Strange Career of Jim Crow.* See Wynes, *Race Relations in Virginia, 1870–1902.*

17. Ayers, *The Promise of the New South.* The first electric streetcar in the country was introduced in Richmond in 1888 (see Oliver, "Maggie Lena Walker," 65).

18. Hale, *Making Whiteness.*

19. For an urban history of how Richmond became segregated in terms of space, see Hoffman, *Race, Class, and Power in the Building of Richmond.*

20. Hale, *Making Whiteness.*

21. Brown, "Womanist Consciousness," 627.

22. Williamson, *The Crucible of Race,* 254–55.

23. J. Smith, *Managing White Supremacy.*

24. J. Smith, "The Campaign for Racial Purity," 95; Sherman, "The Last Stand," 84.

25. Tyler-McGraw, *At the Falls,* 227.

26. E. Lewis, *In Their Own Interests: Race, Class, and Power in Twentieth-Century Norfolk, Virginia,* 47

27. Oliver, "Maggie Lena Walker," 65; Brown, "Womanist Consciousness," 618.

28. Oliver, "Maggie Lena Walker," 65–66.

29. Editorial, *Richmond Planet,* March 17, 1906. See "A Word about Streetcars," *Richmond Planet,* July 21, 1906.

30. "A Word about Streetcars," *Richmond Planet,* July 21, 1906.

31. "Jim Crow Law," *Richmond Planet*, July 7, 1906 quoting *Richmond Times-Dispatch*, July 4, 1906.

32. Ibid.

33. "The Race Question on Railroads," *Richmond Planet*, August 25, 1906.

34. "Trouble on a Streetcar," *Richmond Planet*, August 25, 1906; "Jim Crow Law," *Richmond Planet*, July 7, 1906.

35. "Trouble on a Streetcar," *Richmond Planet*, August 25, 1906.

36. Theodore W. Jones, "What Does It Matter?," letter to the editor, *Richmond Planet*, August 15, 1914.

37. "Will See with Their Own Eyes," *Richmond Planet*, February 3, 1912.

38. *Crisis*, August 1913, 165.

39. "Mayor Ainslie's Comment," *Richmond Planet*, June 7, 1913.

40. Ibid.

41. Ibid.

42. "A Vital Question," *Richmond Planet*, July 12, 1913.

43. Editorial comment, *Richmond Planet*, July 19, 1913.

44. "What Kills the Negro," *Richmond Planet*, July 19, 1913, reprinted from *Richmond Times-Dispatch*, July 13, 1913.

45. Ibid.

46. Editorial, *Richmond News Leader*, November 25, 1913.

47. Ibid.

48. "The News-Leader's Appeal," *Richmond Planet*, December 6, 1913.

49. Another example is the black Richmonders' support for the founding of the new Colored Memorial League Hospital (see "$30,000 to Erect Colored Memorial League Hospital," *Richmond Planet*, May 11, 1912).

50. For more on Booker T. Washington, see Washington, *Up from Slavery;* and Brundage, ed., *Booker T. Washington and Black Progress*.

51. Oliver, "Maggie Lena Walker," 67.

52. Caffee, "Colored Richmond," 127.

53. Oliver, "Maggie Lena Walker," 66–67.

54. Ibid., 68.

55. Caffee, "Colored Richmond," 126. For a detailed study of one African American businessman in Richmond in the early twentieth century, see Michael Plater's biography of R. C. Scott and the history of funeral businesses in the city during Jim Crow (Plater, *African American Entrepreneurship in Richmond, 1890–1940*).

56. Hine, "Black Professionals and Race Consciousness," 1279.

57. *St. Luke Herald*, April 16, 1904.

58. Caffee, "Colored Richmond," 125.

59. "Conditions in Richmond," *Richmond Planet*, March 23, 1912.

60. Ibid.

61. "Another Segregation Bill," *Richmond Planet*, February 3, 1912; "Abusing Race Prejudice," *Richmond Planet*, March 2, 1912.

62. Alexander, *Race Man,* 174; *Crisis,* April 1911, 9.

63. "Segregation Again," *Crisis,* March 1911, 12–13.

64. Beard, *Woman's Work in Municipalities,* 212.

65. Qtd. in *Crisis,* September 1911, 192.

66. Silver, *Twentieth-Century Richmond.* The extent to which race shaped the parameters of Richmond is not unique among southern cities. For example, in *Race in the Shaping of Twentieth-Century Atlanta,* Ronald Bayor offers a thorough urban study of how race influenced nearly every area of Atlanta's development, even convoluting street planning and naming.

67. "May Annex Strip on Brook Road," *Richmond Planet,* January 13, 1912.

68. "The Committee's Invitation," *Richmond Planet,* February 3, 1912.

69. Ibid.

70. Ibid.

71. "Will See with Their Own Eyes," *Richmond Planet,* February 3, 1912; "Colored People Plead for Homes," *Richmond Times-Dispatch,* January 26, 1912.

72. "Will See with Their Own Eyes," *Richmond Planet,* February 3, 1912.

73. Ibid.; "Colored People Plead for Homes," *Richmond Times-Dispatch,* January 26, 1912.

74. "Will See with Their Own Eyes," *Richmond Planet,* February 3, 1912.

75. "Colored People Plead for Homes," *Richmond Times-Dispatch,* January 26, 1912.

76. Ibid.

77. "Fine Home Site for Colored Race," *Richmond Planet,* March 22, 1913. Reprinted from *Richmond Journal.*

78. "Washington Park, Colored Suburb with Future," *Richmond Planet,* August 8, 1914. Reprinted from *Richmond News Leader.*

79. "Mayor Ainslie and the Colored People," *Richmond Planet,* August 2, 1913.

80. Ibid., my emphasis.

81. "Negroes Oppose Separate Parks," *Richmond Planet,* July 26, 1913. Reprinted in entirety from *Richmond Times-Dispatch.*

82. Ibid.

83. "Mayor Ainslie and the Colored People," *Richmond Planet,* August 2, 1913.

84. Ibid.

85. Ibid.

86. "A Colored Park," *Richmond News Leader,* July 26, 1913.

87. "Mayor Ainslie and the Colored People," *Richmond Planet,* August 2, 1913.

88. Ibid.

89. "A Public Park," *Richmond Planet,* August 2, 1913; "A Colored Park," *Richmond News Leader,* July 26, 1913.

90. "A Public Park," *Richmond Planet,* August 2, 1913.

91. "A Word of Advice," *Richmond News Leader,* August 2, 1913, reprinted in *Richmond Planet,* August 9, 1913.

92. Ibid. For a similar editorial, see "Squabble May Be Hurtful to Negroes," *Richmond News Leader,* August 2, 1913.

93. "Plan Negro Park," *Richmond Times-Dispatch,* July 10, 1915.

94. *Crisis,* September 1915, 220.

95. Ibid., October 1913, 271.

96. "Would Block Gate to Colored People," *Richmond Planet,* September 12, 1914.

97. Ibid.

98. "Unbearable Conditions," *Richmond Planet,* September 19, 1914.

99. "Property Rights Involved," editorial, *Richmond Planet,* October 10, 1914.

100. "Votes to Sell Church to Negro Congregation," *Richmond Planet,* November 28, 1914. See also "Negroes May Live in Fifth Street, Court Rules," *Richmond News Leader,* September 16, 1914; "Property Owners Oppose Church Sale to Negroes," *Richmond Times-Dispatch,* September 14, 1914; "Congregation Opposed to Sale of Church," *Richmond Times-Dispatch,* October 13, 1914; "Still Opposing Us," *Richmond Planet,* October 17, 1914; "Mayor Ainslie Signs Ordinance as Amended," *Richmond Times-Dispatch,* October 9, 1914; "Immanuel Baptist Votes to Sell Church," *Richmond Times-Dispatch,* October 19, 1914; "Neighbors Fight Sale of Church to Negroes," *Richmond Times-Dispatch,* November 3, 1914; "Judge Scott Approves Sale of Immanuel Church," *Richmond Planet,* December 12, 1914; and "Still Protesting," *Richmond Planet,* December 19, 1914.

101. "Change Segregation Law," *Richmond Planet,* December 19, 1914.

102. "Immanuel Church Case Is Now before Jury," *Richmond Times-Dispatch,* May 29, 1915.

103. The purchase price is listed as $21,000 in the following article. The cost of changing the entrance is not quoted (see "Judge Scott Approves Sale of Immanuel Church," *Richmond Planet,* December 12, 1914).

104. "Segregation Ordinances Are Invalid," *Richmond Planet,* November 10, 1917.

105. *Nation* article qtd. in *Crisis,* December 1914, 70.

106. "Unbearable Conditions," *Richmond Planet,* September 19, 1914.

107. "Conditions in Richmond," *Richmond Planet,* March 23, 1912. This article was based on a letter to the editor from the general manager of Central Park Water-proof White-washing Company located in New York City and the response by the editor.

108. Theodore W. Jones, "What Does It Matter?," letter to the editor, *Richmond Planet,* August 15, 1914; See also the reprint of this letter in the *Crisis:* "Segregation," *Crisis,* October 1914, 277. I am quoting from the version that was printed in the *Richmond Planet.* The *Crisis* stated the letter also appeared in at least one of the white Richmond dailies.

109. Theodore W. Jones, "What Does It Matter?," letter to the editor, *Richmond Planet,* August 15, 1914.

110. "Colored Quarters," *Richmond Planet,* October 31, 1914. Reprinted in entirety from *Richmond News Leader.*

111. Ibid.

112. See *Richmond Planet,* February 3, 1912. See also Munford Papers, particularly correspondence with or for the YWCA, the Richmond Urban League, Commission on Interracial Cooperation, Woman's Missionary Council, Community House for Colored People, Chamber of Commerce, Virginia War History Commission, and Richmond Council of Churches, among others.

113. "To Test the Law," *Richmond Evening Journal,* May 25, 1912.

114. See "That Segregation Ordinance," *Richmond Planet,* June 1, 1912; and "The Segregation Cases," *Richmond Planet,* May 30, 1914. In Norfolk, Virginia, a residential segregation law was also temporarily overturned (see *Crisis,* March 1914, 222). Black Richmonders watched with interest the legal battles fought in other cities over residential segregation, particularly the struggle in Baltimore against a statute based directly on the Vonderlehr ordinance (see "Segregation Is Defeated," *Baltimore Star,* April 24, 1913; and "Segregation Law Upset," editorial, *Richmond Planet,* May 3, 1913).

115. "Segregation Ordinance Is Held Valid by Court," *Richmond Times-Dispatch,* September 18, 1914.

116. Ibid.

117. "That Segregation Ordinance," *Richmond Planet,* June 1, 1912.

118. "Segregation Law Is Upheld in Kentucky," *Richmond Times-Dispatch,* June 19, 1915; "Expect Segregation Opinion in September," *Richmond Times-Dispatch,* July 18, 1915.

119. "City Attorney Pollard Files His Brief," *Richmond Planet,* February 24, 1917; Oeconomicus, "Side Effects of Segregation in Richmond," *Richmond Planet,* February 24, 1917; "Wage Fight for Equal Justice," *Richmond Planet,* March 24, 1917; excerpt reprinted from Afro-American Page, American Press Association; "Withdraw Objections to the Segregation Brief," *Richmond Planet,* March 31, 1917; "The Segregation Case: Att'y Cohen's Brief," *Richmond Planet,* April 7, 1917.

120. "The Segregation Case: Att'y Cohen's Brief," *Richmond Planet,* April 7, 1917.

121. Segregation Committee Collects Sufficient Funds to Pay All Indebtedness," *Richmond Planet,* May 26, 1917; "Civic League on the Decision," *Richmond Planet,* November 10, 1917.

122. "Fight on Segregation a Mistake," *Richmond Planet,* March 3, 1917. This article contains excerpts from an editorial published in the *Richmond Times-Dispatch* along with commentary by the editor of the *Richmond Planet,* John Mitchell Jr. See also R. S. Johnson, "Mr. Johnson Speaks Again," letter to the editor, *Richmond Planet,* March 10, 1917. In this letter to the editor, R. S. Johnson commends Mitchell for defending African Americans to the white *Richmond Times-Dispatch.*

123. "Fight on Segregation a Mistake," *Richmond Planet,* March 3, 1917.

124. Ibid.

125. "Segregation Ordinances Are Invalid," *Richmond Planet,* November 10, 1917.

126. "The Supreme Court Decision," *Richmond Planet,* November 10, 1917.

127. "The *News-Leader*'s Comment," *Richmond Planet,* November 10, 1917. This article

contains excerpts from an editorial published in the *Richmond News Leader* along with commentary by the editor of the *Richmond Planet*, John Mitchell Jr.

128. Ibid.

129. Ibid.

130. Ibid., my emphasis.

131. "Residential Segregation Law Invalid," *Norfolk Journal and Guide*, May 24, 1930, 1, 15; J. Smith, *Managing White Supremacy*, 204–18.

132. Editorial comments, *Richmond Planet*, August 8, 1914. See Chesson, *Richmond after the War*.

133. Alexander, *Race Man*, 48.

134. "Big Expositions to Show Advance," *Richmond Planet*, December 5, 1914; Gavins, "Hancock, Jackson, and Young.

135. "Tobacco Exhibit Will Be Made Prominent Feature of Great Negro Exposition," *Richmond Times-Dispatch*, May 11, 1915.

136. A White Taxpayer, "Proposed Negro Exposition," *Richmond Times-Dispatch*, February 22, 1914.

137. "Giles Jackson Prepares Executive Proclamation," *Richmond Times-Dispatch*, May 21, 1915.

138. Ibid.

139. "Stuart Commends Plan of Negro Exposition," *Richmond Times-Dispatch*, June 13, 1915.

140. "Negro Exposition Deserves Aid," editorial, *Richmond Times-Dispatch*, June 25, 1915.

141. "Appropriates $5,000 for Big Exposition," *Richmond Times-Dispatch*, May 25, 1915.

142. "President Invited to Visit Richmond," *Richmond Times-Dispatch*, June 8, 1915; "Off to Invite Wilson," *Richmond Times-Dispatch*, June 7, 1915.

143. "President Invited to Visit Richmond," *Richmond Times-Dispatch*, June 8, 1915.

144. "Wilson Commends Plan for Negro Exposition," *Richmond Times-Dispatch*, July 3, 1915.

145. "Negroes Have Right to Be Proud of Their Showing," *Richmond Times-Dispatch*, July 7, 1915.

146. Lee, "Giles B. Jackson (1853–1924)."

147. "Exposition Will Show Progress of Negro Race," *Richmond Times-Dispatch*, June 25, 1915, my emphasis.

148. Ibid.

149. "Negro Exposition Shows Progress Made by Race," *Richmond Times-Dispatch*, July 4, 1915.

150. For an analysis of a similar exhibit, though of dioramas rather than a pantomime, at the 1907 Jamestown Tercentennial Exhibition, see Brundage, "Meta Warrick's 1907 'Negro Tableaux' and (Re) Presenting African American Historical Mem-

ory," 1368–400; see also Jackson and Davis, *The Industrial History of the Negro Race of the United States.*

151. "Board Holds up Money for Negro Exposition," *Richmond Times-Dispatch,* July 14, 1915; "Virginia Day at Negro Historical Exposition," *Richmond Times-Dispatch,* July 16, 1915; "Increased Attendance at Negro Exposition," *Richmond Times-Dispatch,* July 18, 1915; "Increasing Attendance at Negro Exposition," *Richmond Times-Dispatch,* July 20, 1915.

152. "Negro Race Opens Great Exposition," *Richmond Times-Dispatch,* July 5, 1915; "Mayor Opens Big Negro Exposition," *Richmond Times-Dispatch,* July 6, 1915; "Invites White People to Attend Exposition," *Richmond Times-Dispatch,* July 8, 1915; "Gates of Big Exposition Open without Charge," *Richmond Times-Dispatch,* July 10, 1915; "Colored Evangelist Praises Exposition," *Richmond Times-Dispatch,* July 12, 1915; "Gates to Big Negro Fair Wide Open To-day," *Richmond Times-Dispatch,* July 11, 1915; "Pantomime to Show Progress of Negro," *Richmond Times-Dispatch,* July 14, 1915.

153. Philip E. W. Goodwin, letter to the editor, *Richmond Times-Dispatch,* July 18, 1915; Mrs. J. Calvin Stewart, letter to the editor, *Richmond Times-Dispatch,* July 12, 1915.

154. Mrs. J. Calvin Stewart, letter to the editor, *Richmond Times-Dispatch,* July 12, 1915.

155. "Success to Negro Exposition," *Richmond Times-Dispatch,* July 5, 1915.

156. John Mitchell Jr., editorial comment, *Richmond Planet,* October 27, 1906.

3. Public Welfare and the Segregated State

1. A discussion of the development of welfare initiatives over time in Richmond, see Green, *This Business of Relief.*

2. See Walker, *The Honey-Pod Tree.*

3. Ibid., 65.

4. Ibid.

5. Ibid., 66.

6. Ibid.

7. Ibid., 67; A. James, *Virginia's Social Awakening,* 96.

8. Walker, *The Honey-Pod Tree,* 69; A. James, *Virginia's Social Awakening,* 96.

9. Walker, *The Honey-Pod Tree,* 69–70.

10. Ibid., 69.

11. For more on state expansion, see Gordon, *Pitied but Not Entitled;* and Skocpol, *Protecting Soldiers and Mothers.*

12. There are few remaining sources about this organization, so its exact founding date is uncertain. Thomas Walker in his biography, *The Honey-Pod Tree,* discusses at length the Virginia Conference of Social Work's attempts to include African Americans in their reforms. He credits, in particular, the liberal ideals of Dr. Roy Flannagan. Walker states that the group was founded three years before the Board of Charities and Corrections, thus I estimate the Virginia Conference of Social Work was formed in 1905 (Walker, *The Honey-Pod Tree,* 128–33).

13. Ibid., 128.

14. Ibid., 130.

15. Ibid., 129.

16. Ibid., 128–30.

17. Ibid., 130.

18. Ibid. 131.

19. Ibid.

20. Ibid., 132.

21. Ibid., 128–33.

22. Ibid., 133.

23. "Co-operation for Better Health," *Richmond Planet*, April 25, 1914; *Crisis*, January 1914, 111. For more on the NOS, see E. Jordan, "The Impact of the Negro Organization Society on Public Support for Education in Virginia."

24. "The Mayor's Proclamation," *Richmond Times-Dispatch*, May 11, 1915.

25. For a similar example, see Hunter, *To 'Joy My Freedom*.

26. "Richmond's Duty to the Negro and Herself," *Richmond Planet*, November 21, 1914, reprinted from *Richmond Times-Dispatch*. For a study of health campaigns among African American women in Atlanta, see Sarah Judson, "Civil Rights and Civic Health: African American Women's Public Health Work in Early Twentieth-Century Atlanta," *NWSA Journal* 11, no. 3 (1999): 93–111.

27. "Health Conditions," *Richmond Planet*, December 12, 1914.

28. Ibid.; "What Is Tuberculosis?," *Richmond Planet*, April 14, 1917; "The Demon Tuberculosis," *Richmond Planet*, April 27, 1912; "Is Tuberculosis Curable?," *Richmond Planet*, April 21, 1917.

29. "Health Conditions," *Richmond Planet*, December 12, 1914.

30. "Women Launch Appeal for Negro Sanatorium," *Richmond Times-Dispatch*, May 18, 1915.

31. November 8, 1916, Board of Charities and Corrections Minutes, vol. 1, Board of Charities and Corrections Papers, Accession 28142, Library of Virginia (hereafter Board Papers).

32. "What Is Tuberculosis?," *Richmond Planet*, April 14, 1917. For a national study on the work of African American clubwomen in fighting for health reforms among their race, see S. Smith, *Sick and Tired of Being Sick and Tired*.

33. Richard Sucre, "The Great White Plague: The Culture of Death and the Tuberculosis Sanatorium." There are other local examples of interracial cooperative efforts to form African American tuberculosis sanatoriums. For more about a similar initiative in Emporia, see "White and Colored Leagues Co-Operating," *Richmond Times-Dispatch*, June 20, 1915. For another effort in Norfolk, see *Crisis*, June 1911, 52.

34. A. James, *Virginia's Social Awakening*, 2.

35. Ibid., ix; For more on Progressivism, see Link, *The Paradox of Southern Progressivism*; and Hofstadter, *The Progressive Movement, 1900–1915*.

36. A. James, *Virginia's Social Awakening*, 1.

37. Ibid., ix.

38. Ibid., ix, 2; Board of Charities and Corrections Minutes, Board Papers.

39. Two of these women were Mrs. J. P. McConnell (also later a member of the Virginia Commission on Interracial Cooperation) and Mrs. Eudora R. Richardson (see Board of Charities and Corrections Minutes, Board Papers; and Lee, "More Than an Image,"44).

40. Frequent lists are found in the Board of Charities and Correction minutes listing individuals who head charities, orphanages, and similar organizations across the state. In nearly every incidence, women are in charge of "female-" or "child-" designated institutions (see Board Papers). Lee, "More Than an Image,"44; November 11, 1919 and November 16, 1921, Board of Charities and Corrections Minutes, Board Papers.

41. A. James, *Virginia's Social Awakening*, 8.

42. This reform work in Virginia was part of a much broader focus on public health and welfare issues nationwide, both of which were of utmost importance to many Progressive reformers. For discussion of the national picture, see Patterson, *America's Struggle against Poverty, 1900–1994;* and Trattner, *From Poor Law to Welfare State.*

43. Green, *This Business of Relief*, 110–11.

44. Ibid., 133.

45. Ibid., 103–52.

46. A. James, *Virginia's Social Awakening*, 174.

47. Ibid., ix.

48. Shepherd, *Avenues of Faith*, 148–53.

49. Ibid., 150.

50. J. Smith, "The Campaign for Racial," 65–106.

51. Henry Grady qtd. in Walter Russell Bowie speech draft, "Goodwill and Race Adjustment," written for Founder's Day at Hampton Institute 1926, Munford Papers. For more on "New South" ideology, see Ayers, *The Promise of the New South;* Gaston, *The New South Creed;* and Tindall, *The Emergence of the New South.*

52. November 11, 1919, Board of Charities and Corrections Minutes, vol. 2, Board Papers.

53. Dr. Joseph Mastin to Horace Adams, January 18, 1910, Board of Charities and Corrections Minutes, vol. 1, Board Papers.

54. Report on Convict Camps, May 14, 1919, Board of Charities and Corrections Minutes, vol. 1, Board Papers.

55. A. James, *Virginia's Social Awakening*, 150–52.

56. Ibid., 150–53.

57. "Bad Examples for Us," *Richmond Planet*, May 26, 1906.

58. "The Trouble at Bon Air," *Richmond Planet*, October 11, 1913.

59. A. James, *Virginia's Social Awakening*, 90.

60. August 20, 1913, Board minutes, vol. 1, Board Papers.

61. Ibid.

62. Ibid.

63. Ibid.

64. September 13, 1913, editorial, *Richmond Planet;* "Beverley Banks at Bon Air. Rev. Morris Speaks," *Richmond Planet,* July 19, 1913.

65. For more on Progressive reformers treatment of young girls deemed delinquent, see Odem, *Delinquent Daughters.*

66. "The Trouble at Bon Air," *Richmond Planet,* October 25, 1913.

67. Board of Charities and Corrections Minutes, vols. 1 and 2, Board Papers.

68. A. James, *Virginia's Social Awakening,* 44–45, 57.

69. Ibid., 64.

70. Ibid., 66.

71. April 23, 1926, Board of Charities and Corrections Minutes, vol. 2, Board Papers. For more on Gay Bolling Shepperson and her fascinating career, see Wilkerson-Freeman, "The Creation of a Subversive Feminist Dominion," 132–54.

72. Board of Charities and Corrections Minutes, vols. 1 and 2, Board Papers.

73. See Gordon, *Pitied but Not Entitled;* Odem, *Delinquent Daughters;* and Clapp, *Mothers of All Children.*

74. See Negro Welfare Survey Committee, *The Negro in Richmond, Virginia.*

75. July 9, 1911, Board of Charities and Corrections Minutes, vol. 1, Board Papers.

76. Ibid.

77. A. James, *Virginia's Social Awakening,* 61–63.

78. Walker, *The Honey-Pod Tree,* 121.

79. Ibid., 120–22.

80. Ibid., 125, 161.

81. Ibid., 125.

82. A. James, *Virginia's Social Awakening,* 62.

83. Ibid., 58

84. May 6, 1924, Board of Charities and Corrections Minutes, vol. 2, Board Papers; A. James, *Virginia's Social Awakening,* 66.

85. Miss Gay B. Shepperson, report, April 23, 1926, Board of Charities and Corrections Minutes, vol. 2, Board Papers.

86. A. James, *Virginia's Social Awakening,* 62–63.

87. May 4, 1915, Board of Charities and Corrections Minutes, vol. 1, Board Papers.

88. Walker, *The Honey-Pod Tree,* 135.

89. A. James, *Virginia's Social Awakening,* 57–58.

90. Ibid., 58.

91. H. H. Hart to Joseph T. Mastin, July 26, 1909, Board of Charities and Corrections Minutes, vol. 1, Board Papers.

92. November 1924–November 1925 report, Board of Charities and Corrections Minutes, vol. 2, Board Papers.

93. Ibid.

94. The Board of Charities and Corrections were forced to place children in public detention homes when no private homes for available. They would make arrange-

ments with local governments to pay an agreed amount per child. For example, the board paid fifty cents per child to the City of Richmond for each African American dependent placed by the board in their city-owned detention home (see J. Hoge Ricks to Joseph T. Mastin, November 16, 1915, and February 22, 1917, Board of Charities and Corrections Minutes, vol. 1, Board Papers).

95. January 9, 1917, Board of Charities and Corrections Minutes, vol. 1, Board Papers.

96. Ibid.; February 22, 1917, May 1, 1917, and November 17, 1917, Board of Charities and Corrections Minutes, vol. 1, Board Papers.

97. November 16, 1915, Board of Charities and Corrections Minutes, vol. 1, Board Papers.

98. For information on this case, see November 1918, Board of Charities and Corrections Minutes, vol. 1, Board Papers. The Phipps investigation is detailed extensively. Sometime during the period discussed, the proprietor married, thus changing her name from Crawford to Phipps. As such, both names appear in the records. For simplicity, I use only Phipps.

99. Report of H. D. Coghill, October 16, 1918, Board of Charities and Corrections Minutes, vol. 1, Board Papers.

100. Ora Brown Stokes to Joseph T. Mastin, November 3, 1917, Board of Charities and Corrections Minutes, vol. 1, Board Papers; Joseph T. Mastin to State Corporation Commission, November 12, 1917, Board of Charities and Corrections Minutes, vol. 1, Board Papers.

101. Ora Brown Stokes to Joseph T. Mastin, November 3, 1917, Board of Charities and Corrections Minutes, vol. 1, Board Papers.

102. May 6, 1925, Board of Charities and Corrections Minutes, vol. 2, Board Papers.

103. Ibid.

104. Walker, *The Honey-Pod Tree*, 270.

4. Women and Cooperation

1. For more about the complex and varied natures of the relationships between white women and their domestic servants within white homes during the Jim Crow era, see Tucker, *Southern Women*.

2. These women drew upon "southern lady" stereotypes and ideals as a justification for their activism, embracing, as noted by the historian Anastatia Sims, "the power of their femininity" (Sims, *The Power of Femininity in the New South*).

3. Caldwell, *History of the American Negro and His Institutions*, 136–39; "Ora Brown Stokes 1882–1957," historical marker, Richmond, Virginia; Materson, *For the Freedom of Her Race*, 161–62.

4. Ibid., 136–39.

5. Lee, "More Than an Image," 47.

6. Ibid., 41–47; Board of Charities and Corrections Minutes, vol. 1, Board Papers.

7. For a gendered political history of Virginia, see Holloway, *Sexuality, Politics, and Social Control in Virginia.*

8. Brown, "Womanist Consciousness," 610–33.

9. Examples of this trend are found throughout the Board of Charities and Corrections Minutes, vol. 1. In particular, see May 14, 1919, Report to Westmoreland Davis, Board of Charities and Corrections Minutes, Board Papers. Dabney, *Virginia,* 435.

10. For examples, see Munford Papers; Beard, *Woman's Work in Municipalities,* 170–98, 210–15; Ovington, *Portraits in Color,* 127–34, 181–93; Lee, "More Than an Image"; and Oliver, "Maggie Lena Walker." For more on African American women's activism nationally, see Schechter, *Ida B. Wells.*

11. Joan Marie Johnson studied the Federation of Colored Women's Clubs along with the Federation of Women's Clubs in South Carolina during this same time period. Both clubs were also active in Virginia, although they do not play a large role in this study because the white Federation of Women's Clubs had little interest in racial uplift causes or interracial cooperation (J. Johnson, *Southern Ladies, New Women*).

12. Bowie, *Sunrise in the South,* 1–25, 156–57; Ovington, *Portraits in Color,* 15, 181–93; W. Hall, "Janie Porter Barrett," 9; Munford Papers.

13. See Gilmore, *Gender & Jim Crow;* Hunter, *To Joy My Freedom;* and White, *Too Heavy a Load.*

14. W. Hall, "Janie Porter Barrett," 15–20; Ovington, *Portraits in Color,* 181–93.

15. Hammond, *In the Vanguard of a Race,* 87.

16. W. Hall, "Janie Porter Barrett," 10–15, 183; Ovington, *Portraits in Color,* 183–85; Hammond, *In the Vanguard of a Race,* 84–87.

17. W. Hall, "Janie Porter Barrett," 15–20; Board of Charities and Corrections Minutes, Board Papers; A. James, *Virginia's Social Awakening,* 79–97; Salem, *To Better Our World,* 110; Oliver, "Maggie Lena Walker," 82–82; Lee, 60–62; Ovington, *Portraits in Color,* 127–34; Hammond, *In the Vanguard of a Race,* 115–18.

18. November 5, 1912, Board of Charities and Corrections Minutes, Board Papers.

19. Salem, *To Better Our World,* 110–11; Hammond, *In the Vanguard of a Race,* 88–89, 108–18; A. James, *Virginia's Social Awakening,* 92; Munford Papers; Bowie, *Sunrise in the South,* 156–57.

20. Ovington, *Portraits in Color,* 190.

21. Ibid., 186.

22. Hammond, *In the Vanguard of a Race,* 89–93; Ovington, *Portraits in Color,* 186; W. Hall, "Janie Porter Barrett," 20–24; A. James, *Virginia's Social Awakening,* 90–91; "The Trouble at Bon Air," *Richmond Planet,* October 11, 1913; editorial, *Richmond Planet,* September 13, 1913; "Beverley Banks at Bon Air: Rev. Morris Speaks," *Richmond Planet,* July 19, 1913. Barrett's strategy paralleled that of various other African American women activists, like, for example, Charlotte Hawkins Brown (1883–1961) of North Carolina. Both Brown and Barrett cultivated and perhaps created pasts for themselves (Barrett's youth in a wealthy white home and Brown's relationship with the white educator Alice Freeman Palmer), which they frequently referred to as their motivations

for service. For more information on Charlotte Hawkins Brown, see Gilmore, *Gender & Jim Crow*, 178–95.

23. Ovington, *Portraits in Color*, 181–82, 192–93; W. Hall, "Janie Porter Barrett," 6–7, 13; Hammond, *In the Vanguard of a Race*, 78–82, 84–86; Hammond, *In Black and White*.

24. This feeling of obligation was common among early twentieth-century African American female professional women (see Shaw, *What a Woman Ought to Be and to Do*; and Ovington, *Portraits in Color*, 186–91).

25. For similar evidence of middle- and upper-class black and white women working together on behalf of working-class women in Georgia, see Hickey, *Hope and Danger in the New South City*.

26. Ovington, *Portraits in Color*, 186–90; W. Hall, "Janie Porter Barrett," 21–23.

27. Ovington, *Portraits in Color*, 190.

28. Ibid.

29. Ibid.

30. Ibid.

31. Ibid., 190–91.

32. Ibid.; W. Hall, "Janie Porter Barrett," 19. The Virginia Christian case was a major story throughout 1912 in the *Richmond Planet*.

33. Bowie, *Sunrise in the South*, 156–57.

34. Ovington, *Portraits in Color*, 186.

35. Ibid. For more information about Mary Ovington and her friendship with W. E. B. Du Bois, see D. Lewis, *W. E. B. Du Bois*.

36. Hammond, *In the Vanguard of a Race*, 115–16, For an example of how a similar school was founded through white suffragists' support in exchange for black women's votes for reform candidates in Nashville, see Goodstein, "A Rare Alliance," 219–46.

37. "Mr. Henry L. Schmelz Makes Miss Moomaw His Bride," *Richmond Times-Dispatch*, October 7, 1904; "Mrs. Annie M. Schmelz Dies in New York," *Richmond Times-Dispatch*, March 15, 1946: "Industrial Home School," *Southern Workman* 48 (October 1919): 473–75.

38. L. Daniels, "National Women's History Month: Mary Gorton Darling."

39. Lebsock, "Woman Suffrage and White Supremacy," 88.

40. Sixth Annual Report of the Industrial Home School for Colored Girls Peak's Turnout Hanover County Virginia Founded by the Virginia State Federation of Colored Women's Clubs, 1921, 8–9.

41. Ibid., 23.

42. "Industrial Home School," *Southern Workman* 48 (October 1919): 473–75; Sixth Annual Report of the Industrial Home School for Colored Girls Peak's Turnout Hanover County Virginia Founded by the Virginia State Federation of Colored Women's Clubs, 1921. Similar reports of lobbying by these women are found throughout the annual reports of the school.

43. "Industrial Home School," 473–74.

44. Eighth Annual Report of the Industrial Home School for Colored Girls Peak's

Turnout Hanover County Virginia Founded by the Virginia State Federation of Colored Women's Clubs, 1923, 8.

45. Charles E. Stump, "Charles E. Stump," *Broad Ax* (Chicago), June 12, 1920.

46. There are many excellent studies of this woman's movement. For examples, see Flexner's *Century of Struggle;* and Cott, *The Grounding of Modern Feminism.*

5. Race and War

1. Suggs, "P. B. Young of the *Norfolk Journal and Guide,*" 365–67.

2. "How Not to Check Negro Migration," *Richmond Times-Dispatch,* reprinted in *Richmond Planet,* May 5, 1917.

3. Suggs, "P. B. Young of the *Norfolk Journal and Guide,*" 369.

4. Ibid.

5. Ibid., 368–70.

6. For more on P. B. Young, see Suggs, "P. B. Young and the *Norfolk Journal and Guide,* 36; Henry Lewis Suggs, *P. B. Young, Newspaperman;* and Suggs, "Black Strategy and Ideology in the Segregation Era," 161–90.

7. For example, see, "Proposed Remedy for the Negro Exodus," *Richmond Planet,* May 5, 1917.

8. John Mitchell Jr., "The Migration of Colored Folks," *Richmond Planet,* May 19, 1917.

9. Ibid.

10. Henry P. Lipscomb, "The Negro Exodus to the North," letter to the editor, *Richmond Planet,* January 6, 1917.

11. Ibid.

12. Ibid.

13. John Mitchell Jr., editorial comment, *Richmond Planet,* March 31, 1917.

14. "Negro Loyalty," *Richmond Times-Dispatch,* April 10, 1917.

15. Ibid.

16. "How the Negro Can Prove His Loyalty," *Richmond Evening Journal,* April 9, 1917.

17. "Loyalty to the Flag," *Richmond Planet,* April 4, 1917.

18. See "Colored Men and the Registration," *Richmond Planet,* June 9, 1917. See also *Richmond Times-Dispatch,* June 7, 1917.

19. "The Editor Offers His Service to the State," *Richmond Planet,* June 9, 1917.

20. "The Liberty Loan Meeting," *Richmond Planet,* June 16, 1917.

21. Although many Virginians supported the war, opposition did exist and was heard throughout the state. The draft, in particular, caused some discord. With decisions left up to local draft boards, local prejudices at times prevailed, leading more of the working classes to be drafted, across racial lines (Keith, *Rich Man's War, Poor Man's Fight;* see also Kornweibel, "Investigate Everything"; and Ellis, *Race, War, and Surveillance*).

22. "The Red Cross Parade Here," *Richmond Planet,* June 23, 1917.

23. See Brown, "Womanist Consciousness."

24. "I. O. St. Luke Here," *Richmond Planet*, August 25, 1917.

25. Ibid.

26. "Colored Men and Registration, *Richmond Planet*, June 9, 1917.

27. "Remarkable Demonstration Here," *Richmond Planet*, November 3, 1917.

28. Ibid.

29. "A Change for the Better," *Richmond Planet*, November 3, 1917.

30. Ibid.

31. "No Peace Talks for Colored Folks," *Richmond Planet*, October 13, 1917.

32. "The Negroes Departure," *Richmond News Leader*, October 27, 1917.

33. Ibid., my emphasis.

34. Editorial comment, *Richmond Planet*, November 24, 1917.

35. For more on the Virginia War History Commission, see Munford Papers; and A. Davis, ed., *Publications of the Virginia War History Commission.*

36. For more on the historical writings of the United Daughters of the Confederacy, see Hale, "Some Women Have Never Been Reconstructed,"; and Brundage, "White Women and the Politics of Historical Memory in the New South."

37. Meeting notes, Community House for Negro People, February 2, 1919, Munford Papers.

38. Ibid.

39. "Report of the Executive Committee of Conference to Consider Informally the Contribution of the Colored People of Virginia to the War," February 25, 1919, Munford Papers.

40. Ibid.

41. See E. Jordan, "The Impact of the Negro Organization Society."

42. "Report of the Executive Committee of Conference to Consider Informally the Contribution of the Colored People of Virginia to the War," February 25, 1919, Munford Papers.

43. Ibid.

44. Grinnan, "Mary Newton Stanard," 217–20.

45. Mary Stanard to Mary Munford, March 2, 1919, Munford Papers.

46. Ibid.

47. Ibid., my emphasis.

48. Ibid.

49. J. Davis, "Fertilizing Barren Souls," 469.

50. Report of Meeting, undated [March 11, 1919?], Munford Papers.

51. Ibid.

52. Ibid.

53. "Colored Folks in the Great European War," *Richmond Planet*, April 3, 1920.

54. "The War Record of Virginia Negroes," *Richmond Planet*, May 29, 1920.

55. Litwack, *Trouble in Mind*, 481–96; J. Smith, *Managing White Supremacy*, 42.

56. See Higham, *Stranger in the Land.*

57. Faulkner, *Sartoris*, 68.

58. "For Action on Race Riot Peril," *New York Times*, October 5, 1919.

59. "Richmond Chapter of NAACP Wires Attorney General," *Richmond Planet*, April 9, 1921. The Richmond branch of the NAACP in this era had a variable membership and failed to have much endurance. For more on the Richmond NAACP, see J. Smith, *Managing White Supremacy*, 212–13, 241, 243.

60. Hale, *Making Whiteness*, 171–72; Alexander, *Race Man*, 183–84, 192; J. Smith, *Managing White Supremacy*, 45–48; Marlowe, *A Right Worthy Mission*, 179; MacLean, *Behind the Mask of Chivalry*, 47.

61. Suggs, "Black Strategy and Ideology," 168.

62. See "Colored Man Lynched in Virginia," *Richmond Planet*, August 25, 1917; "Governor Orders Investigation of Lynching," *Richmond Planet*, August 25, 1917; "Gov. Stuart Has No Official Knowledge of a Lynching That Occurred on Night of August 22," *Richmond Planet*, August 25, 1917; "Long Record Broken," *Richmond Planet*, August 25, 1917; and "*Times Dispatch* Regrets Lynching," *Richmond Planet*, August 25, 1917. For detailed statistics on lynching in Virginia, see Brundage, *Lynching in the New South*.

63. For an example, see "Brunswick Lynching," *Richmond News Leader*, reprinted in *Richmond Planet*, August 13, 1921.

64. Equal Justice Initiative, *Lynching in America*. For a diverse collection of essays on a variety of aspects pertaining to lynchings, lynching in folk songs, and a reinterpretation of the Leo Frank case, see Brundage, ed., *Under Sentence of Death*. For more about Virginia lynchings, see J. Smith, *Managing White Supremacy*, 16, 27, 38, 41, 45–46, 121, 156, 178–79; and Alexander, *Race Man*, 33, 37–38, 41–59, 62–64, 67, 89, 98, 100, 135, 147, 150–52, 160–67.

65. Equal Justice Initiative, *Lynching in America*, 15.

66. Brundage, "To Howl Loudly," 325–42; Mark Berman, "Even More Black People Were Lynched in the U.S. Than Previously Thought, *Washington Post*, February 10, 2015; Brundage, "Conclusion: Reflections on Lynching Scholarship," 401–14; Avis Thomas-Lester, "A History Scarred by Lynchings," *Washington Post*, July 7, 2005.

67. "Virginia No State for Mobs," *Richmond Times-Dispatch*, December 7, 1920.

68. For more on the racial dynamics of executions in twentieth-century Virginia, see L. Dorr, "Black on White Rape and Retribution in Twentieth Century Virginia," 711–48; and L. Dorr, *White Women, Rape, and the Power of Race in Virginia*. See Brundage, *Lynching in the New South*. For more information on the legal system in twentieth-century Virginia, see Wallenstein, *Blue Laws and Black Codes*. For an example of white southerners mobilizing to protest lynching, see J. Hall, *Revolt against Chivalry*.

69. Mary Johnston, "Nemesis," *Century*, May 1923, 2–22. For more information, see also Brooks, "Proper Voices, Radical Words."

70. Arthur Spingarn to Mary Johnston, May 7, 1923, Johnston Papers.

71. Walter White to Mary Johnston, June 18, 1923, Johnston Papers.

72. "A Lyncher Is Convicted," editorial, *Richmond Planet*, April 16, 1921.

73. Ibid.

74. Brundage, "To Howl Loudly," 325–42.

75. Leidholdt, *The Life of Louis I. Jaffé*, 19–79; Leidholdt, "Louis I. Jaffé (ca. 1888–1950)."

76. Leidholdt, *The Life of Louis I. Jaffé*, 149.

77. Leidholdt, "Louis I. Jaffé (ca. 1888–1950)."

78. "Crime in Fulton," *Richmond Planet*, March 19, 1921.

79. "The Fulton Outrage," *Richmond Planet*, March 19, 1921.

80. Ibid.

81. "Believes White Men Committed Crime in Fulton," *Richmond News Leader*, March 19, 1921.

82. "The Trouble in Fulton," *Richmond Planet*, March 26, 1921.

83. Ibid.

84. See MacLean, *Behind the Mask of Chivalry*.

85. For an example of an African American newspaper's coverage of this trend, see "Ku Klux Klan Is Resurrected in Nine States of South under Charter from Georgia Court," *Richmond Planet*, October 30, 1920.

86. For an example of this effort in the city of Richmond, see "Ku Klux Klan in Richmond," *Richmond Times-Dispatch*, September 20, 1920.

87. See Buni, *The Negro in Virginia Politics*, 176; J. Smith, "The Campaign for Racial Purity," 68; "Stuart Commends Plan of Negro Exposition," *Richmond Times-Dispatch*, June 13, 1915; "I. O. St. Luke Here: Great Meeting at City Auditorium," *Richmond Planet*, August 25, 1917; and Annie Schmelz to Janie Porter Barrett, August 17, 1921, Munford Papers.

88. J. Smith, *Managing White Supremacy*, 73.

89. "Ku Klux Klan Secret Organization Parade the Streets of Richmond," *Richmond Planet*, December 11, 1920.

90. Thousands Watch Ku Klux Klan March Richmond Streets," *Richmond Planet*, September 24, 1921.

91. "Let It Prove Its Americanism," *Richmond Times-Dispatch*, December 7, 1920.

92. Ibid.

93. "Repudiates Ku Klux Klan," *Richmond Planet*, November 27, 1920. The *Richmond Planet* recounts the *Richmond News Leader*'s denunciation editorial.

94. "Richmond Advertisers Condemn Ku Klux Klan: Deplore Any Action Leading to Excite Racial Animosities in America," *Richmond Planet*, December 25, 1920, reprinted from *Richmond Times-Dispatch*, December 18, 1920.

95. "Ku-Klux Menace Peace of South, Dr. Bowie Charges," *Richmond Times-Dispatch*, December 6, 1920. See Maclean, *Behind the Mask of Chivalry*. For more on Reconstruction, see Foner, *Reconstruction*.

96. "Ku-Klux Menace Peace of South, Dr. Bowie Charges," *Richmond Times-Dispatch*, December 6, 1920.

97. Ibid.

98. "Let It Prove Its Americanism," *Richmond Times-Dispatch*, December 7, 1920.

99. "Dr. Bowie Charges Ku Klux Klan Is Menace to Peace of South," *Richmond Planet*, December 11, 1920.

100. "Dr. Bowie's Deliverances," *Richmond Planet*, October 8, 1921.

101. Samuel Shepherd mentions whites' protests against the Ku Klux Klan in his urban and religious history of Richmond in the early twentieth century. His study covers the Episcopalians, Methodists, Baptists, Presbyterians, Church of Christ, and Lutherans, but only white churches and no African American congregations (see Shepherd, *Avenues of Faith*).

102. "U.D.C. Denounce Use of Ku Klux Name," *Richmond Planet*, December 11, 1920.

103. Although many white elites opposed the 1920s revival of the KKK in Virginia, reactions varied by state and even localities. For a case study of vigilante activism in Florida, see Ingalls, *Urban Vigilantes in the New South*.

104. Thousands Watch Ku Klux Klan March Richmond Streets," *Richmond Planet*, September 24, 1921.

105. J. Smith, *Managing White Supremacy*, 73.

106. Ibid., 75.

107. Leidholdt, *The Life of Louis I. Jaffe*, 134.

108. Ibid.

109. "Ku Klux Klan," editorial, *Richmond Planet*, November 27, 1920.

110. Leidholdt, *The Life of Louis I. Jaffe*, 183–87; Suggs, "Black Strategy and Ideology," 161–90.

111. "The Ku Klux Klan," *Richmond Planet*, October 30, 1920.

112. "Against the Klan," editorial, *Richmond Planet*, December 11, 1920.

113. Alexander, *Race Man*, 152. This was a persistent rumor at the time, but there is no evidence that Pythian soldiers were indeed used for this purpose.

114. "Against the Klan." editorial, *Richmond Planet*, December 11, 1920.

115. Ibid.

116. Ibid. Black Virginians also fought the KKK through national organizations like the NAACP. For an example of NAACP efforts, see "NAACP Fights Klan," *Richmond Planet*, January 1, 1921. For more on the Richmond branch of the NAACP, see J. Smith, *Managing White Supremacy*, 212–13, 241, 243.

117. "Business Men Make Housing Survey of Richmond. Chamber of Commerce Municipal Affairs Committee Urges Immediate Improvement in Colored Quarters," *Richmond Planet*, April 2, 1921.

118. "Do Justice to the Negroes," *Richmond Times-Dispatch*, March 24, 1921. The reporter is probably referring a denouncement of Richmond by *Nation* magazine in 1914. This article is quoted in *Crisis*, December 1914, 70.

119. Ibid.

120. Randolph (1848–1927) was widely known for her extensive work on behalf of the UDC. In 1910, she created the Mrs. Norman V. Randolph Relief Fund, which is still in existence today.

121. "Do Justice to the Negroes," *Richmond Times-Dispatch*, March 24, 1921.

122. Ibid.

6. Contested Authority

1. "Colored Men and Registration, *Richmond Planet*, June 9, 1917.

2. Morton, "The Negro in Virginia Politics," 75; Bowie, *Sunrise in the South*, 11–15; Dailey, *Before Jim Crow*.

3. For more on Mahoneism, see Morton, "The Negro in Virginia Politics"; Dailey, *Before Jim Crow;* and Rachleff, *Black Labor in the South*.

4. For more on disfranchisement in Virginia and across the South, see Kousser, *The Shaping of Southern Politics;* Perman, *Struggle for Mastery;* and Boggs, "We the 'White' People."

5. Morton, "The Negro in Virginia Politics" 6.

6. Ibid., 135.

7. "The Times and Suffrage," *Richmond Planet*, January 7, 1899.

8. Editorial comment, *Richmond Planet*, June 16, 1906.

9. Walker, *The Honey-Pod Tree*, 125.

10. John Mitchell, editorial comment, *Richmond Planet*, January 13, 1927.

11. For more information on the woman suffrage movement in Virginia and the South in general, see Green, *Southern Strategies;* Wheeler, *New Women of the New South*; and Equal Suffrage League Papers, Library of Virginia (hereafter ESL Papers).

12. Mary Johnston to Lila Valentine, 1915(?), Johnston Papers.

13. Lebsock, "Woman Suffrage and White Supremacy," 62–90.

14. "The Political Situation," *Richmond Planet*, October 4, 1920.

15. Broadfoot, "Interview with Adele Clark," 20.

16. Ibid., 21.

17. Editorial comment, *Richmond Planet*, March 3, 1906.

18. *Richmond Planet*, November 1912. For theories on African American manhood, see Carby, *Race Men*. For theories on African American womanhood, see Brown, "Womanist Consciousness"; and Salem, *To Better Our World*.

19. "Lily-white" was the common, contemporary term for Republicans desiring to push all African Americans out of their organization.

20. "Republicans in Session at Chicago," *Richmond Planet*, June 12, 1920; "Republicans Bar Colored Men from City Mass Meeting," *Richmond Times-Dispatch*, March 14, 1920; "Republican City Bolters Continue Factional Row. Carry 'Lily White' Protest to the District Meeting, but Are Frozen Out," *Richmond Times-Dispatch*, March 16, 1920.

21. "A New Republican Organization," *Richmond Planet*, May 1, 1920.

22. "The Colored Vote Heavily Increased," *Richmond Planet*, November 26, 1921.

23. "What is Truth?," *Richmond Planet,* June 12, 1920. This article quotes various editorials from both the *Richmond Planet* and the *Norfolk Journal and Guide*, showcasing dialogue between John Mitchell Jr. and P. B. Young.

24. "Chairman Pollard and His Party," *Richmond Planet,* June 18, 1921.

25. D. A. Ferguson, "Dr. Ferguson's Criticisms and Observations," letter to the editor, *Richmond Planet*, March 27, 1920; "Didn't Like the Comment," *Richmond Planet*, March 27, 1920.

26. "Denying the Truth," *Richmond Planet,* January 8, 1921.

27. Ibid.

28. Ibid.

29. I. J. Lewis, "Just Wants to Know," *Richmond Planet*, February 21, 1920.

30. Alexander, *Race Man*, 187. For more on these events, see J. Smith, *Managing White Supremacy*, 60–67; and Marlowe, *A Right Worthy Mission*, 184.

31. "Talking Too Much," *Richmond Planet,* July 16, 1921.

32. "Rights Denied," editorial, *Richmond Planet,* July 23, 1921; "Outlawing the Negro," editorial, *Richmond Planet,* July 23, 1921; "Colored Delegates Barred from G.O.P. Convention at Norfolk, VA," *Richmond Planet,* July 23, 1921, reprinted from *Richmond Times-Dispatch*.

33. Annie Schmelz to Janie Porter Barrett, August 17, 1921, Munford Papers.

34. Annie Schmelz to Janie Porter Barrett, August 30, 1921, Munford Papers.

35. Annie Schmelz to Janie Porter Barrett, August 17, 1921, Munford Papers.

36. Ibid.

37. Ibid.

38. Ibid.

39. Ibid.

40. Ibid.

41. Ibid.

42. Ibid., my emphasis.

43. Ibid.

44. Annie Schmelz to Janie Porter Barrett, August 30, 1921, Munford Papers.

45. Ibid.

46. Ibid.

47. Ibid.

48. "Mrs. Annie M. Schmelz Dies in New York," *Richmond Times-Dispatch,* March 15, 1946.

49. "Races Co-operate in Virginia," *Broad Ax* (Chicago), October 15, 1921.

50. "Representative Colored Men Here," *Richmond Planet*, September 10, 1921.

51. "Fellow Negroes," *Richmond Planet*, August 13, 1921.

52. "Representative Colored Men Here." *Richmond Planet*, September 10, 1921.

53. Suggs, "Black Strategy and Ideology in the Segregation Era," 170.

54. Ibid., 161–10.

55. Qtd. in Marlowe, *A Right Worthy Mission*, 184.

56. *Richmond Times-Dispatch*, July–December 1921. Articles mentioning the movement appeared about seventeen times yet were generally only brief mentions of the convention and announcements of the convention.

57. "Negro Would Hold Balance," *Clinch Valley News*, October 28, 1921.

58. "The Political Situation," editorial, *Richmond Planet*, September 17, 1921.

59. Ibid.

60. Suggs, "P. B. Young and the *Norfolk Journal and Guide*," 75–78; J. Smith, *Managing White Supremacy*, 60–68.

61. "Attorney Newsome's Plea," *Richmond Planet*, October 1, 1921.

62. Fred Newman, "An Appeal to Reason," letter to the editor, *Richmond Planet*, November 5, 1921.

63. See Marlowe, *A Right Worthy Mission*, 184; J. Smith, *Managing White Supremacy*, 61; and Alexander, *Race Man*, 188.

64. From the *Crisis*, qtd. in Marlowe, *A Right Worthy Mission*, 184.

65. Alexander, *Race Man*, 188.

66. R. L. C. Barrett, "Mitchell Will Get Big Negro Vote in State," *Richmond News Leader*, reprinted in *Richmond Planet*, November 5, 1921.

67. Ibid.

68. Ibid.

69. Suggs, "Black Strategy and Ideology in the Segregation Era," 172.

70. Ibid., 83; "Colored Republicans Poll 25,000!," *Richmond Planet*, November 12, 1921; "Trinkle Wins by 50,000 Returns Indicate," *Richmond Planet*, November 12, 1921.

71. "Colored Republicans Poll 25,000!," *Richmond Planet*, November 12, 1921.

72. Ibid.

73. "Hon. E. Lee Trinkle Writes Attorney Newsome," *Richmond Planet*, November 26, 1921; see also "Gov.-Elect Trinkle Will Give Negroes a Square Deal," *Richmond Planet*, November 19, 1921.

74. Editorial comment, *Richmond Planet*, November 19, 1921.

75. "A Declaration of Principles," *Richmond Planet*, November 26, 1921.

76. Ortiz, *Emancipation Betrayed*.

77. John Mitchell Jr., "Against the Klan," *Richmond Planet*, December 11, 1920, my emphasis.

7. Rethinking Alliances

1. For more on this national organization first founded in New York in 1911, see W. A. Hall, "Local Urban League Filling Social Needs: Will Emphasize Better Housing and Raise Standards of Living," *St. Luke Herald*, July 13, 1929; and "1930 Annual Report of Richmond Urban League," unpublished typed report, Munford Papers.

2. Jesse O. Thomas to Maggie L. Walker, January 15, 1925, Munford Papers.

3. Maggie L. Walker to Jesse O. Thomas, January 20, 1925, Munford Papers.

4. Jesse O. Thomas to Maggie L. Walker, January 28, 1925, Munford Papers.

5. Branch, "Maggie Lena Walker (1864–1934)"; Branch and Rice, *Pennies to Dollars.*

6. Branch, "Maggie Lena Walker."

7. Oliver, "Maggie Lena Walker," 90–94.

8. Tindall, *The Emergence of the New South,* 177. For more in-depth information on the founding and history of the national Commission of Interracial Cooperation, see Dykeman and Stokely, *Seeds of Southern Change.*

9. "Report of Findings Committee Adopted Annual Meeting Commission on Interracial Cooperation, Asheville, N.C., July 31–August 3rd 1923," unpublished report, Munford Papers.

10. See Hall, *Revolt against Chivalry;* Egerton, *Speak Now against the Day.*

11. Tindall, *The Emergence of the New South,* 180.

12. McDowell, *The Social Gospel in the South.*

13. "Report: Commission on Race Relationship," Woman's Missionary Council, n.d. (early 1920s), Munford Papers.

14. Ibid.; "Action-Women's Missionary Council, Richmond, Virginia, April 1921," unpublished report, Munford Papers.

15. "Report: Commission on Race Relationship," Woman's Missionary Council, n.d. (early 1920s), Munford Papers.

16. Mrs. Luke Johnson to Mary Munford, July 30, 1920, Munford Papers; *Southern Women and Race Cooperation. A Story of the Memphis Conference, October Sixth and Seventh Nineteen Hundred and Twenty,* pamphlet, Munford Papers.

17. "Report: Commission on Race Relationship," Woman's Missionary Council, n.d. (early 1920s), Munford Papers.

18. "Commission on Inter-Racial Cooperation Report, Director of Woman's Work to the General Meeting of the Commission, Atlanta, Georgia, October 1921," Munford Papers.

19. For a study on racial conversion narratives, see Hobson, *But Now I See.*

20. Minutes, Joint Meeting—Women's General Committee Commission on Interracial Cooperation and Interracial Committee—Southeastern Federation Colored Women's Clubs, October 20–21, 1922, Munford Papers.

21. Ibid.

22. Dykeman and Stokely, *Seeds of Southern Change.*

23. "Minutes of a Committee of Ten held Friday evening at 5 P.M. July 11th, 1919," unpublished minutes, Munford Papers.

24. Ibid.

25. For an example of appeals to Munford, see Reverend W. H. Branch to Mary Munford, March 5, 1921; and John P. McConnell to Mary Munford, May 2, 1921, both in Munford Papers.

26. *Southern Women and Race Cooperation.* In this late 1920 pamphlet, the members of the Virginian CIC are listed as the following: Dr. R. E. Blackwell (president, Randolph Mason College) Dr. J. H. Dillard (president, Slater Fund), Jackson Davis (general field agent, General Education Board, Richmond) Homer L. Ferguson (manufacturer,

Newport News), Dr. John M. Gandy (president, Petersburg Normal and Industrial Institute), and Dr. S. C. Mitchell (Richmond College).

27. Mrs. Luke Johnson to Mary Munford, July 30, 1920, Munford Papers; *Southern Women and Race Cooperation*, pamphlet.

28. Minutes, Joint Meeting—Women's General Committee, Commission on Interracial Cooperation and Interracial Committee—Southeastern Federation of Colored Women's Clubs, October 20–21, 1922, Munford Papers.

29. Minutes, Woman's General Committee, Commission on Interracial Cooperation, Tuskegee Institute, Alabama, April 7–8, 1926, Munford Papers.

30. "Action of Members Women's Section Virginia State Inter-Racial Committee, Richmond, Virginia, November 16, 1921," Munford Papers. See also "Action of Women's Section Virginia Interracial Committee," *Richmond Planet*, December 3, 1921.

31. "Action of Members Women's Section Virginia State Inter-Racial Committee, Richmond, Virginia, November 16, 1921," Munford Papers.

32. Of the thirty women present, twenty-one were residents of Richmond. The remaining nine broke down as follows: Lynchburg (2), Bedford (2), Hampton (1), Suffolk (1), Radford (1), Roanoke (1), and Farmville (1) (see "Action of Members Women's Section Virginia State Inter-Racial Committee, Richmond, Virginia, November 16, 1921," Munford Papers).

33. Minutes, Annual Meeting-Woman's Section–Virginia State Committee on Race Relations, Richmond, Virginia, October 9, 1922, Munford Papers.

34. Mary Munford to Mrs. Luke Johnson, November 14, 1922, Munford Papers.

35. Ibid.

36. "Meeting of the Women's Executive Committee State Inter-Racial Committee," Richmond, Virginia, May 24, 1922, Munford Papers.

37. Ibid.

38. R. W. Miles to Mary Munford, December 4, 1923, Munford Papers.

39. Minutes, Annual Meeting–Woman's Section–Virginia State Committee on Race Relations, Richmond, Virginia, October 9, 1922, Munford Papers. See the October 9, 1922, minutes for one list of potential solutions.

40. Minutes of the Committee on Woman's Work of the Virginia State Inter-Racial Commission, November 7, 1924, Munford Papers.

41. R. W. Miles to Mary Munford, December 4, 1923, Munford Papers.

42. Minutes, Annual Meeting of Virginia State Inter-Racial Committee, November 7, 1924, Munford Papers.

43. Ibid. For more examples of the assorted activities of the Virginia CIC, see R. Walton Moore to Mrs. Mumford [*sic*], October 15, 1926: "Review of Ten Year's Work," Commission on Interracial Cooperation, n.d. (1928), unpublished report; and R. W. Carrington to Mary Munford, May 7, 1926, all from Munford Papers.

44. "Law to Provide Better Housing," *Richmond Times-Dispatch*, October 6, 1924.

45. R. W. Carrington to Mary Munford, May 7, 1926, Munford Papers. This letter listed the full membership of the state committees of the CIC. There was no distinc-

tion made between the races, though men and women are listed separately. "Miss" or "Mrs." was still used for white and black women alike, but still none of the men are labeled "Mr." Of the ninety-one individuals, forty-five were from Richmond.

46. "Report on the Tenth Annual Meeting Virginia Commission on Interracial Cooperation, St. Paul's Parish House, Richmond, April 30, 1930," unpublished report, Munford Papers.

47. Mary Munford, Suggestions on Pronouncement (of YWCA statement), undated, but placed in context with other letters probably written around January 1924, Munford Papers.

48. For more on the Interracial Conference of Church Women and YWCA, see Munford Papers.

49. "Social Workers School at Colored Community House," *Richmond Planet*, February 21, 1920.

50. Resolution, Community House for Colored People, Incorporated, January 6, 1921, Munford Papers.

51. For more information on the work of the Community House for Colored People, see "The Community House Holds Second Annual Meeting," *Richmond Planet*, March 19, 1921; L. H. Payne to Mary Munford, April 29, 1921, Munford Papers; L. H. Payne to Committee in Meeting Assembled, December 1, 1920, Munford Papers; and H. H. Hibbs Jr. to Mary Munford, December 23, 1920, Munford Papers.

52. J. Smith, "The Campaign for Racial Purity," 65–77.

53. See L. Dorr, "Arm and Arm"; and G. Dorr, "Segregation's Science."

54. Wallenstein, *Cradle of America*, 310.

55. Holloway, *Sexuality, Politics, and Social Control in Virginia*.

56. Ibid., 2.

57. John Powell, "White America to Become a Negroid Nation," *Richmond Times-Dispatch*, July 22, 1923.

58. Ibid.

59. See Hodes, ed., *Sex, Love, Race;* and Rothman, *Notorious in the Neighborhood*.

60. John Powell, "White America to Become a Negroid Nation," *Richmond Times-Dispatch*, July 22, 1923.

61. Stein, *The World of Marcus Garvey*.

62. Unnamed secretary of John Powell to Marcus Garvey, September 17, 1925, Powell Papers; John Powell to Thomas L. Dabney, September 15, 1925, Powell Papers; Caleb G. Robinson to John Powell, March 26, 1926, Powell Papers.

63. John Powell, "White America to Become a Negroid Nation," *Richmond Times-Dispatch*, July 22, 1923.

64. Ibid.

65. John Powell to Thomas L. Dabney, September 15, 1925, Powell Papers.

66. J. Smith, *Managing White Supremacy*, 76–127.

67. Sherman, "The Last Stand," 72–77.

68. Ibid., 70–71, 77; J. Smith, "The Campaign for Racial Purity," 71–64, 78.

69. John Powell, "White America to Become a Negroid Nation," *Richmond Times-Dispatch*, July 22, 1923.

70. J. Smith, "The Campaign for Racial Purity," 80; Sherman, "The Last Stand," 77–79.

71. J. Smith, "The Campaign for Racial Purity," 93; Sherman, "The Last Stand," 82–83.

72. Sherman, "The Last Stand," 82–84.

73. Ibid.

74. Ibid., 83–84.

75. John Powell to Editor (newspaper unknown), July 11, 1925, Powell Papers.

76. J. Smith, *Managing White Supremacy*, 107–19.

77. John Powell, handwritten note 2, n.d. (content written after handwritten note 1), Powell Papers.

78. J. Smith, *Managing White Supremacy*, 117–55.

79. Jackson Davis to Mary Munford, April 1, 1925, Jackson Davis Papers, Alderman Library, University of Virginia, Charlottesville (hereafter Davis Papers).

80. See Washington, *Up from Slavery*.

81. J. Smith, "The Campaign for Racial Purity," 94.

82. Sherman, "The Last Stand," 84. Chief Justice Taft did provide a private letter taking a stand against the Massenburg bill at the insistence of Mary Munford for Munford to share with Governor Byrd, but he spoke little on the issue publicly (J. Smith, *Managing White Supremacy*, 124–25).

83. J. Smith, *Managing White Supremacy*, 107–29.

84. Ibid., 124, qtd. from a letter from Powell to Walter Copeland.

85. John Powell to Mary Munford, March 5, 1926, Powell Papers.

86. Ibid. John Powell believed that increased interracial cooperation especially signs of support for interracial endeavors from college campuses, such as Virginia Tech, was proof that miscegenation was on the rise in Virginia (see J. Smith, "The Campaign for Racial Purity," 79).

87. John Powell to Mary Munford, March 5, 1926, Powell Papers.

88. Sherman, "The Last Stand," 84. Governor Harry Byrd succeeded Governor E. Lee Trinkle. He was inaugurated in early 1926.

89. J. Smith, "The Campaign for Racial Purity," 95.

90. J. Smith, "Anti-Lynching Law of 1928."

91. See Gavins, *The Perils and Prospects of Southern Black Leadership*.

92. Gordon B. Hancock, "Racial Integrity," letter to the editor, *Richmond News Leader*, March 17, 1926.

93. Ibid.

94. Ibid.

95. T. J. J. Mosby, "Colored Residential District Ruined," *Richmond Planet*, May 29, 1920.

Conclusion

1. Walker, *The Honey-Pod Tree*, 266.
2. Ibid.
3. Ibid., 267.
4. For more information on this later version of interracial cooperation, see Egerton, *Speak Now against the Day;* and Hobson, *But Now I See.*
5. "The Lucy Mason Testimonial," *Richmond Planet,* July 23, 1932.
6. Broadfoot, "Interview with Adele Clark," 39.
7. Annie Schmelz to Janie Porter Barrett, August 17, 1921, Munford Papers.
8. "Mrs. Munford Ends Long Life of Service," *Richmond Times-Dispatch,* July 4, 1938; "Mrs. Munford Leaves Estate of $82,842," *Richmond Times-Dispatch,* July 15, 1938.
9. Although paternalism faltered, the ideology influenced liberal white reformers for many more years. For example, Virginius Dabney, who became editor of the *Richmond Times-Dispatch* in the later 1920s, wrote about whites' paternalistic responsibility to black Virginians in the 1930s and 1940s. Similar to my findings, John T. Kneebone demonstrates how his group of editors wanted reform within the boundaries of segregation (see Kneebone, *Southern Liberal Journalists and the Issue of Race*).
10. "Do Justice to the Negroes," *Richmond Times-Dispatch,* March 24, 1921.
11. Ibid.
12. Ibid.
13. Negro Welfare Survey Committee, *The Negro in Richmond, Virginia,* iii–v, 9.
14. Ibid., 14–15.
15. Ibid., 5.
16. Ibid., 47. Black Richmonders had a birth rate of 24.11/1,000 in comparison with whites at 18.12/1,000.
17. Ibid., 47. The death rate of tuberculosis for blacks was 147.2/100,000 and 49.2/100,000.
18. Ibid., 51.
19. Ibid., 52.
20. Ibid., 75.
21. Ibid., 97. The arrests reported in Richmond for the year 1927 are as follows: 10,162 white men, 8,607 black men, 918 white women, 1,824 black women.
22. Ibid., 89–90.
23. Ibid., 76.
24. Ibid., 77; *Crisis,* September 1915, 220.
25. Gavins, *The Perils and Prospects of Southern Black Leadership.* 79. For a biography of another African American leader in Richmond, see Michael Dennis's *Luther P. Jackson and a Life for Civil Rights.* Dennis argues that Jackson, who died in the early 1950s, was the central black civil rights leader in Virginia. Jackson, a professor at Virginia State College, was an important figure in black Virginians' civil rights struggles in the 1930s

and 1940s, but Dennis downplays other individuals like Gordon Hancock who were also very influential.

26. Gavins, *The Perils and Prospects of Southern Black Leadership*, 116–17, quoting from an article that appeared in the *Norfolk Journal and Guide*, May 10, 1941.

27. "The Time for Mediation," *Richmond Planet,* July 2, 1921.

28. John Mitchell Jr., "A Distinction with a Difference," *Richmond Planet*, November 5, 1921.

29. "Death Announcement. Mitchell," *Richmond Times-Dispatch*, December 4, 1929.

30. "Says Race Well Treated in U.S.," *Richmond Times-Dispatch*, October 29, 1930.

31. Thirteenth Annual Report of the Industrial Home School for Colored Girls Peak's Turnout Hanover County Virginia, 1928.

32. Fifth through Twenty-Third Annual Reports of the Industrial Home School for Colored Girls.

33. Eighteenth Annual Report of the Industrial Home School for Colored Girls Peak's Turnout Hanover County Virginia, 1933, 12.

34. Ibid.

35. Twenty-Third Annual Report of the Industrial Home School for Colored Girls Peak's Turnout Hanover County Virginia, 1938.

36. Ibid., 6.

37. Ibid.

38. James, James, and Boyer, eds., *Notable American Women*, 96–97.

39. "DJJ to Repurpose Juvenile Correctional Center in Hanover," Virginia Department of Juvenile Justice.

40. Logan, ed., *What the Negro Wants*, 226.

41. Leidholdt, *Editor for Justice*, 224–34.

42. Walker, *The Honey-Pod Tree*, 293.

BIBLIOGRAPHY

Archival Sources

Board of Charities and Corrections. Papers. Library of Virginia, Richmond.

Broadfoot, Winston. "Interview with Adele Clark, February 28, 1964. Richmond, Virginia." Virginia Historical Society, Richmond.

Clark, Adele. Papers. James Branch Cabell Library, Virginia Commonwealth University, Richmond.

Davis, Jackson. Papers. Albert and Shirley Small Special Collections Library, University of Virginia, Charlottesville.

"A History of the Y.W.C.A. of Richmond, Virginia, 1887–1937." Mss7:2/R4155:18. Virginia Historical Society, Richmond.

Independent Order of St. Luke. Papers. Virginia Historical Society, Richmond.

Jaffe, Louis I. Papers. Albert and Shirley Small Special Collections Library, University of Virginia, Charlottesville.

Johnston, Mary J. Papers. Albert and Shirley Small Special Collections Library, University of Virginia, Charlottesville.

Mason, Lucy Randolph. Papers. Perkins Library, Duke University, Durham, North Carolina.

Munford, Mary Cooke Branch. Papers. Library of Virginia, Richmond.

Photograph Collection. Hampton History Museum.

Photograph Collection. Maggie L. Walker National Historic Site, National Park Service.

"Piedmont Sanatorium. Burkeville, Virginia." Historical Collections & Services, Claude Moore Health Sciences Library, University of Virginia, Charlottesville.

Powell, John. Papers. Albert and Shirley Small Special Collections Library, University of Virginia, Charlottesville.

Richmond Education Association. Papers. Virginia Historical Society, Richmond.

Saturday Afternoon Club. Papers. Virginia Historical Society, Richmond.

Social Settlements: United States. Virginia. Hampton. Locust Street Settlement: Agencies Promoting the Assimilation of the Negro. Locust Street Settlement, Hampton, Va.: The founder and head worker with her husband and children. The husband is Secretary and Manager of the Building and Loan Society. Photograph. Harvard Art Museums/Fogg Museum, Transfer from the Carpenter Center for the Visual Arts, Social Museum Collection, 3.2002.231.2.

Social Settlements: United States. Virginia. Hampton. Locust Street Settlement: Agencies Promoting the Assimilation of the Negro. Locust Street Settlement, Hampton, Va.: The Sand Box. Photograph. Harvard Art Museums/Fogg Museum, Transfer from the Carpenter Center for the Visual Arts, Social Museum Collection, 3.2002.232.3.

Valentine, Lila Hardaway Meade. Papers. Virginia Historical Society, Richmond.
Virginia Equal Suffrage League. Papers. Library of Virginia, Richmond.
Virginia Republican Party Flyer. Ms2008–058. Special Collections, University Librar-
ies, Virginia Tech, Blacksburg.

Newspapers and Journals

Annual Reports of the Industrial Home School for Colored Girls
Broad Ax
Clinch Valley News
Confederate Veteran
Crisis
New York Times
Norfolk Journal and Guide
Richmond Evening Journal
Richmond News Leader
Richmond Planet
Richmond Times-Dispatch
Southern Workman
Virginian Pilot

Secondary Sources

Alexander, Ann Field. "Black Protest in the New South: John Mitchell Jr. (1863–1929)
and the *Richmond Planet*." Ph.D. diss., Duke University, 1972.
———. *Race Man: The Rise and Fall of the "Fighting Editor" John Mitchell, Jr.* Charlottesville:
University Press of Virginia, 2002.
Anderson, James D. *The Education of Blacks in the South, 1860–1935.* Chapel Hill: Univer-
sity of North Carolina Press, 1988.
Ayers, Edward L. *The Promise of the New South.* New York: Oxford University Press,
1992.
Baker, Ray Stannard. *Following the Color Line: American Negro Citizenship in the Progressive
Era.* 1908. New York: Harper and Row, 1964.
Bartley, Numan V. *The New South: 1945–1980.* Baton Rouge: Louisiana State University
Press and the Littlefield Fund for Southern History, University of Texas, 1995.
Bayor, Ronald H. *Race and the Shaping of Twentieth-Century Atlanta.* Chapel Hill: Univer-
sity of North Carolina Press, 1996.
Beard, Mary. *Women's Work in Municipalities.* New York: D. Appleton, 1915.
Birth of a Nation. Produced and directed by D. W. Griffith. Hollywood, CA: Reliance-
Majestic Studios, 1915.
Blair, Tonya D. "Building Within Our Borders: Black Women Reformers in the South
from 1890–1920." Ph.D. diss., University of Southern Mississippi, 2015.

Blair, William. *Cities of the Dead: Contesting the Memory of the Civil War in the South, 1865–1914*. Chapel Hill: University of North Carolina Press, 2004.

Blee, Kathleen M. *Women of the Klan: Racism and Gender in the 1920s*. Los Angeles: University of California Press, 1991.

Boggs, Jeremy. "We the 'White' People: Race, Culture, and the Virginia Constitution of 1902." Master's thesis, Virginia Polytechnic Institute and State University, 2003.

Boles, John B., and Bethany L. Johnson, eds. *Origins of the New South: Fifty Years Later: The Continuing Influence of a Historical Classic*. Baton Rouge: Louisiana State University Press, 1993.

Bowie, Walter Russell. *Sunrise in the South: The Life of Mary-Cooke Branch Munford*. Richmond, VA: William Byrd, 1942.

Boyle, Sarah Patton. *The Desegregated Heart: A Virginian's Stand in Time of Transition*. Edited by Jennifer Lynn Ritterhouse. Charlottesville: University Press of Virginia, 2001.

Branch, Muriel Miller. "Maggie Lena Walker (1864–1934)." *Encyclopedia Virginia*. Virginia Foundation for the Humanities. Last updates October 27, 2015. www.encyclopediavirginia.org/Maggie_Lena_Walker_1864-1934.

Branch, Muriel Miller, and Dorothy Marie Rice. *Pennies to Dollars: The Story of Maggie Lena Walker*. New Haven, CT: Linnet Books, 1997.

Brawley, Benjamin Griffith. *Doctor Dillard of the Jeanes Fund*. New York: F. Revell, 1930.

Brooks, Clayton McClure. "Dreams of a Brotherhood: Mary Johnston, the Process of Racial Liberalization, and the Roots of Southern White Women's Interracial Activism." Unpublished manuscript. January 2002.

———. "Proper Voices, Radical Words: Mary Johnston, Lucy Randolph Mason, and the Process of Racial Liberalization." Master's thesis, University of Virginia, August 1999.

———. "Unlikely Allies: Southern Women, Interracial Cooperation, and the Making of Segregation in Virginia, 1910–1920." In *Women Shaping the South*, edited by Angela Boswell and Judith N. McArthur. Columbia: University of Missouri Press, 2006.

Brown, Elsa Barkley. "Womanist Consciousness: Maggie Lena Walker and the Independent Order of Saint Luke." *Signs* 14 (Spring 1989): 610–33.

Brundage, W. Fitzhugh, ed. *Booker T. Washington and Black Progress: "Up from Slavery" 100 Years Later*. Gainesville: University Press of Florida, 2003.

———. "Conclusion: Reflections on Lynching Scholarship." *American Nineteenth Century History* 6, no. 3 (September 2005): 401–14.

———. *Lynching in the New South: Georgia and Virginia, 1880–1930*. Urbana: University of Illinois Press, 1993.

———. "Meta Warrick's 1907 'Negro Tableaux' and (Re) Presenting African American Historical Memory." *Journal of American History* 89 (March 2003): 1368–400.

———. *The Southern Past: A Clash of Race and Memory*. Cambridge: Belknap Press of Harvard University Press, 2005.

———. "To Howl Loudly: John Mitchell, Jr. and His Campaign against Lynching in Virginia." *Canadian Review of American Studies* 22, no. 3 (Winter 1991): 325–42.

———. *Under Sentence of Death: Lynching in the South.* Chapel Hill: University of North Carolina Press, 1997.

———. "White Women and the Politics of Historical Memory in the New South, 1880–1920." In *Jumpin' Jim Crow: Southern Politics from Civil War to Civil Rights,* edited by Jane Dailey, Glenda Elizabeth Gilmore, and Bryant Simon. Princeton: Princeton University Press, 2000.

Bullock, Henry Allen. *A History of Negro Education in the South from 1619 to the Present.* Cambridge: Harvard University Press, 1967.

Buni, Andrew. *The Negro in Virginia Politics, 1902–1965.* Charlottesville: University Press of Virginia, 1967.

Caldwell, A. B. *History of the American Negro and His Institutions: Virginia Edition.* Vol. 5. Atlanta: Caldwell, 1921.

Carby, Hazel V. *Race Men.* Cambridge: Harvard University Press, 1998.

Carlton, David. *Mill and Town in South Carolina, 1880–1920.* Baton Rouge: Louisiana State Press University, 1982.

Carter, Dan T. *Scottsboro: A Tragedy of the American South.* Baton Rouge: Louisiana State University Press, 1979.

Cash, W. J. *The Mind of the South.* New York: Vintage, 1991.

Cashin, Edward J., and Glenn T. Eskew, eds. *Paternalism in a Southern City: Race, Religion, and Gender in Augusta, Georgia.* Athens: University of Georgia Press, 2001.

Cell, John Whitson. *The Highest Stage of White Supremacy: The Origins of Segregation in South Africa and the American South.* New York: Cambridge University Press, 1982.

Chesson, Michael B. *Richmond after the War, 1865–1890.* Richmond: Virginia State Library, 1981.

Clapp, Elizabeth J. *Mothers of All Children: Women Reformers and the Rise of Juvenile Courts in Progressive Era America.* University Park: Pennsylvania State University Press, 1998.

Clark, Daniel J. *Like Night & Day: Unionization in a Southern Mill Town.* Chapel Hill: University of North Carolina Press, 1997.

Clark, Kathleen Ann. *Defining Moments: African American Commemoration and Political Culture in the South, 1863–1913.* Chapel Hill: University of North Carolina Press, 2005.

Clinton, Catherine. *Tara Revisited: Women, War, and the Plantation Legend.* New York: Abbeville, 1995.

Cohen, Nancy. *The Reconstruction of American Liberalism, 1865–1914.* Chapel Hill: University of North Carolina Press, 2002.

Cott, Nancy F. *The Grounding of Modern Feminism.* New Haven: Yale University Press, 1987.

Culley, John Joel. "Muted Trumpets: Four Efforts to Better Southern Race Relations, 1900–1919." Ph.D. diss., University of Virginia, 1967.

Dabney, Virginius. *Virginia: The New Dominion, A History from 1607 to the Present.* Garden City, NY: Doubleday, 1971.

Dailey, Jane. *Before Jim Crow: The Politics of Race in Post-Emancipation Virginia.* Chapel Hill: University of North Carolina Press, 2000.

Dailey, Jane, Glenda Elizabeth Gilmore, and Bryant Simon, eds. *Jumpin' Jim Crow: Southern Politics from Civil War to Civil Rights.* Princeton: Princeton University Press, 2000.

Daniel, Pete. *Lost Revolutions: The South in the 1950s.* Chapel Hill: University of North Carolina Press, 2000.

Daniels, Jonathan. *A Southerner Discovers the South.* New York: Macmillan, 1938.

Daniels, Lisa. "National Women's History Month: Mary Gorton Darling." *Daily Press,* March 21, 1991. http://articles.dailypress.com/1991-03-21/news/9103210204_1 _hampton-institute-social-life-trolley-line.

Davis, Arthur Kyle, ed. *Publications of the Virginia War History Commission.* Richmond: Virginia War History Commission, 1923–27.

Davis, J. E. "Fertilizing Barren Souls: The Industrial Home School for Delinquent Colored Girls of Virginia. *Southern Workman* 45 (August 1916): 469.

Dennis, Michael. *Luther P. Jackson and a Life for Civil Rights.* Gainesville: University of Florida Press, 2004.

Dixon, Thomas. 1905. *The Clansman: An Historical Romance of the Ku Klux Klan.* Armonk, NY: M. E. Sharpe, 2001.

"DJJ to Repurpose Juvenile Correctional Center in Hanover." Virginia Department of Juvenile Justice, December 17, 2013. www.djj.virginia.gov/pdf/Admin /HanoverJCC_Press_Release_12172012.pdf.

Dorr, Gregory Michael. "Segregation's Science: The American Eugenics Movement and Virginia, 1900–1980." Ph.D. diss., University of Virginia, 2000.

Dorr, Lisa Lindquist. "Arm in Arm: Gender, Eugenics, and Virginia's Racial Integrity Acts of the 1920s." *Journal of Women's History* 11 (Spring 1999): 143–66.

———. "Black on White Rape and Retribution in Twentieth Century Virginia: 'Men, Even Negroes, Must Have Some Protection.'" *Journal of Southern History* 66 (November 2000): 711–48.

———. *White Women, Rape, and the Power of Race in Virginia, 1900–1960.* Chapel Hill: University of North Carolina Press, 2004.

Du Bois, W. E. B. *The Souls of Black Folk.* New York: Penguin, 1996.

Dunbar, Anthony P. *Against the Grain: Southern Radicals and Prophets 1929–1959.* Charlottesville: University Press of Virginia, 1981.

Dunn, Susan. *Dominion of Memories: Jefferson, Madison, and the Decline of Virginia.* New York: Basic, 2007.

Durr, Virginia Foster. *Outside the Magic Circle: The Autobiography of Virginia Foster Durr.* Edited by Hollinger F. Barnard. Tuscaloosa: University of Alabama Press, 1985.

Dykeman, Wilma, and James Stokely. *Seeds of Southern Change: The Life of Will Alexander.* Chicago: University of Chicago Press, 1962.

Eagles, Charles W. *Jonathan Daniels and Race Relations.* Knoxville: University of Tennessee Press, 1982.

Egerton, John. *Speak Now against the Day: The Generation before the Civil Rights Movement in the South.* Chapel Hill: University of North Carolina Press, 1994.

Ellis, Mark. *Race, War, and Surveillance: African Americans and the United States Government during World War I.* Bloomington: Indiana University Press, 2001.

———. *Race Harmony and Black Progress: Jack Woofter and the Interracial Movement.* Bloomington: Indiana University Press, 2013.

Equal Justice Initiative. *Lynching in America: Confronting the Legacy of Racial Terror.* Online publication. Equal Justice Initiative, 2015. 1–25.

Faulkner, William. *Absalom! Absalom!* 1936. New York: Vintage, 1986.

———. *Sartoris.* 1929. New York: New American Library, 1964.

Finkelman, Paul, ed. *The Age of Jim Crow: Segregation from the End of Reconstruction to the Great Depression.* New York: Garland, 1992.

Flexner, Eleanor. *Century of Struggle: The Woman's Rights Movement in the United States.* Cambridge: Belknap Press of Harvard University Press, 1975.

Foner, Eric. *Reconstruction: America's Unfinished Revolution, 1863–1877.* New York: Harper and Row, 1988.

Fosl, Catherine. *Subversive Southerner: Anne Braden and the Struggle for Racial Justice in the Cold War South.* New York: Palgrave Macmillan, 2002.

Foster, Gaines M. *Ghosts of the Confederacy: Defeat, the Lost Cause, and the Emergence of the New South.* New York: Oxford University Press, 1987.

Fox-Genovese, Elizabeth. *Within the Plantation Household: Black and White Women of the Old South.* Chapel Hill: University of North Carolina Press, 1988.

Frankenberg, Ruth. *The Social Construction of Whiteness: White Women, Race Matters.* Minneapolis: University of Minnesota Press, 1993.

Freeman, Douglas Southall. *R. E. Lee: A Biography.* New York: Scribner, 1934–35.

Gaines, Kevin. *Uplifting the Race: Black Leadership, Politics, and Culture in the Twentieth Century.* Chapel Hill: University of North Carolina Press, 1996.

Gaston, Paul. *The New South Creed: A Study in Southern Mythmaking.* New York: Knopf, 1970.

Gavins, Raymond. "Hancock, Jackson, and Young." *Virginia Magazine of History and Biography* 85, no. 4 (October 1977).

———. *The Perils and Prospects of Southern Black Leadership: Gordon Blaine Hancock, 1884–1970.* Durham, NC: Duke University Press, 1977.

Genovese, Eugene D. *Roll, Jordan, Roll: The World the Slaves Made.* New York: Vintage, 1972.

Giddings, Paula. *When and Where I Enter: The Impact of Black Women on Race and Sex in America.* New York: William Morrow, 1984.

Gilmore, Glenda Elizabeth. *Defying Dixie: The Radical Roots of Civil Rights, 1919–1950.* New York: Norton, 2008.

———. *Gender & Jim Crow: Women and the Politics of White Supremacy in North Carolina, 1896–1920.* Chapel Hill: University of North Carolina, 1996.

———, ed. *Who Were the Progressives?* Boston: Bedford/St. Martins, 2002.

Gladney, Margaret Rose. *How Am I to Be Heard? Letters of Lillian Smith.* Chapel Hill: University of North Carolina Press, 1993.

Glisson, Susan M. "Neither Bedecked nor Bebosomed: Lucy Mason, Ella Baker, and Women's Leadership and Organizing in the Struggle for Freedom." Ph.D. diss., College of William and Mary, 2000.

Goodstein, Anita Shafer. "A Rare Alliance: African American and White Women in the Tennessee Elections of 1919 and 1920." *Journal of Southern History* 64 (May 1998): 219–46.

Gordon, Linda. *Pitied but Not Entitled: Single Mothers and the History of Welfare, 1890–1935.* Cambridge: Harvard University Press, 1994.

Grantham, Dewey W. *Southern Progressivism: The Reconciliation of Progress and Tradition.* Knoxville: University of Tennessee Press, 1983.

Green, Elna C., ed. *Before the New Deal: Social Welfare in the South, 1830–1930.* Athens: University of Georgia Press, 1999.

———. *The New Deal and Beyond: Social Welfare in the South since 1930.* Athens: University of Georgia Press, 2003.

———. *Southern Strategies: Southern Women and the Woman Suffrage Question.* Chapel Hill: University of North Carolina Press, 1997.

———. *This Business of Relief: Confronting Poverty in a Southern City, 1740–1940.* Athens: University of Georgia Press, 2003.

Greenwood, Janette. *Bittersweet Legacy: The Black and White "Better Classes" in Charlotte, 1850–1910.* Chapel Hill: University of North Carolina Press, 1994.

Griffith, Barbara S. *The Crisis of American Labor: Operation Dixie and the Defeat of the CIO.* Philadelphia: Temple University Press, 1988.

Grinnan, Daniel. "Mary Newton Stanard." *Virginia Magazine of History and Biography* 37, no. 3 (July 1929): 217–20.

Hale, Grace Elizabeth. *Making Whiteness: Culture of Segregation in the South, 1890–1940.* New York: Pantheon, 1998.

———. "'Some Women Have Never Been Reconstructed': Mildred L. Rutherford, Lucy M. Stanton, and the Racial Politics of White Southern Womanhood, 1900–1930." In *Georgia in Black and White*, edited by John Inscoe, 173–201. Athens: University of Georgia Press, 1994.

Hall, Jacquelyn Dowd. "Open Secrets: Memory, Imagination, and the Refashioning of Southern Identity." *American Quarterly* 50 (March 1998): 109–24.

———. *Revolt against Chivalry: Jessie Daniel Ames and the Women's Campaign against Lynching.* New York: Columbia University Press, 1979.

———. "'You Must Remember This': Autobiography as Social Change." *Journal of American History* 85 (September 1998): 439–65.

Hall, Winona R. "Janie Porter Barrett, Her Life and Contributions to Social Welfare in Virginia." Master's thesis, Howard University, 1954.

Hammond, Lily. *In Black and White: An Interpretation of the South.* 1914. Edited by Elna Green. Athens: University of Georgia Press, 2008.

———. *In the Vanguard of a Race.* 1922. In *Race and the South: Two Studies, 1914–1922.* New York: Arno, 1972.

Hanchett, Thomas W. *Sorting out the New South City: Race, Class, and Urban Development in Charlotte, 1875–1975.* Chapel Hill: University of North Carolina Press, 1998.

Hanmer, Trudy J. "A Divine Discontent: Mary Johnston and Woman Suffrage in Virginia." Master's thesis, University of Virginia, 1972.

Heinemann, Ronald L. *Depression and New Deal in Virginia: The Enduring Dominion.* Charlottesville: University Press of Virginia, 1983.

Hewitt, Nancy A. *Southern Discomfort: Women's Activism in Tampa, Florida, 1880s–1920s.* Chicago: University of Illinois Press, 2001.

Hewitt, Nancy A., and Suzanne Lebsock, eds. *Visible Women: New Essays on American Activism.* Chicago: University of Illinois Press, 1993.

Hickey, Georgina. *Hope and Danger in the New South City: Working-Class Women and Urban Development in Atlanta, 1890–1940.* Athens: University of Georgia Press, 2003.

Higginbotham, Evelyn Brooks. *Righteous Discontent: The Woman's Movement in the Black Baptist Church, 1880–1920.* Cambridge: Harvard University Press, 1993.

Higham, John. *Strangers in the Land: Patterns of American Nativism, 1860–1925.* New Brunswick, NJ: Rutgers University Press, 1994.

Hine, Darlene Clark. "Black Professionals and Race Consciousness: Origins of the Civil Rights Movement, 1890–1950." *Journal of American History* 89 (March 2003): 1279–94.

———. *Black Women in White: Racial Conflict and Cooperation in the Nursing Profession 1890–1950.* Bloomington: Indiana University Press, 1989.

Hitz, May Buford. *Never Ask Permission: Elizabeth Scott Bocock of Richmond. A Memoir by Mary Buford Hitz.* Charlottesville: University Press of Virginia, 2000.

Hobson, Fred. *But Now I See: The White Southern Racial Conversion Narrative.* Baton Rouge: Louisiana State University Press, 1999.

Hodes, Martha, ed. *Sex, Love, Race: Crossing Boundaries in North American History.* New York: New York University Press, 1999.

Hoffman, Steven J. *Race, Class, and Power in the Building of Richmond, 1870–1920.* Jefferson, NC: McFarland, 2004.

Hofstadter, Richard. *The Progressive Movement, 1900–1915.* Englewood Cliffs, NJ: Prentice-Hall, 1963.

Holloway, Pippa. *Sexuality, Politics, and Social Control in Virginia, 1920–1945.* Chapel Hill: University of North Carolina Press, 2006.

Hughes, William Hardin. *Robert Russa Moton of Hampton and Tuskegee.* Chapel Hill: University of North Carolina Press, 1956.

Hunter, Tera W. *To 'Joy My Freedom: Southern Black Women's Lives and Labors after the Civil War.* Cambridge: Harvard University Press, 1997.

Ingalls, Robert P. *Urban Vigilantes in the New South: Tampa, 1882–1936.* Gainesville: University Press of Florida, 1993.

Jackson, Giles B., and D. Webster Davis. *The Industrial History of the Negro Race of the United States.* Richmond: Virginia Press, 1908.

James, Arthur W. *The Public Function of Government in Virginia: Issued by State Department of*

Public Welfare as a Twenty-Fifth Anniversary Bulletin. Richmond: Division of Purchase and Printing, 1934.

——— . *Virginia's Social Awakening: The Contribution of Dr. Mastin and the Board of Charities and Corrections.* Richmond, VA: Garrett and Massie, 1939.

James, Edward T., Janet Wilson James, and Paul S. Boyer, eds. *Notable American Women, 1607–1950: A Biographical Dictionary.* Cambridge: Harvard University Press, 1971.

Johnson, Charles S. *Into the Main Stream: A Survey of Best Race Practices in Race Relations in the South.* Chapel Hill: University of North Carolina Press, 1947.

Johnson, Joan Marie. *Southern Ladies, New Women: Race, Region, and Clubwomen in South Carolina, 1890–1930.* Gainesville: University Press of Florida, 2004.

Johnston, Mary. "Nemesis." *Century,* May 1923, 2–22.

Jones, Jacquelyn. *Labor of Love, Labor of Sorrow: Black Women, Work and the Family from Slavery to the Present.* New York: Vintage, 1995.

Jones, Plummer F. "The Negro Exposition at Richmond." *American Review of Reviews* 52 (August 1915): 185–88.

Jordan, Elizabeth Cobb. "The Impact of the Negro Organization Society on Public Support for Education in Virginia, 1912–1950." Ph.D. diss., University of Virginia, 1978.

Jordan, Winthrop D. *White over Black: American Attitudes toward the Negro, 1550–1812.* Chapel Hill: University of North Carolina Press, 1968.

Kantrowitz, Stephen. *Ben Tillman and the Reconstruction of White Supremacy.* Chapel Hill: University of North Carolina Press, 2000.

Keith, Jeanette. *Rich Man's War, Poor Man's Fight: Race, Class, and Power in the Rural South during the First World War.* Chapel Hill: University of North Carolina Press, 2003.

Kelley, Robin D. G. *Race Rebels: Culture, Politics, and the Black Working Class.* New York: Free Press, 1994.

Kerber, Linda. *No Constitutional Right to Be Ladies: Women and the Obligations of Citizenship.* New York: Hill and Wang, 1998.

Killian, Lewis M. *The Role of the White Liberals in Changing Patterns of Race Relations in the South.* Houston: Anti-Defamation League of B'nai B'rith, 1962.

Kimball, Gregg D. *American City, Southern Place: A Cultural History of Antebellum Richmond.* Athens: University of Georgia Press, 2000.

Kirby, Jack Temple. *Darkness at the Dawning: Race and Reform in the Progressive South.* Philadelphia: Lippincott, 1972.

Kneebone, John T. *Southern Liberal Journalists and the Issue of Race, 1920–1944.* Chapel Hill: University of North Carolina Press, 1985.

Kollatz, Henry, Jr. "An Artist's Creation," *Richmond Mag,* May 26, 2011. http://richmondmagazine.com/news/an-artists-creation-05-26-2011/.

Kornweibel, Theodore. *"Investigate Everything": Federal Efforts to Ensure Black Loyalty during World War I.* Bloomington: Indiana University Press, 2002.

Kousser, J. Morgan. *The Shaping of Southern Politics: Suffrage Restriction and the Establishment of the One-Party South, 1880–1910.* New Haven: Yale University Press, 1974.

Kraditor, Aileen S. *The Ideas of the Woman Suffrage Movement: 1890–1920.* New York: Norton, 1981.

Kyriakoudes, Louis M. *The Social Origins of the Urban South: Race, Gender, and Migration in Nashville and Middle Tennessee, 1890–1930.* Chapel Hill: University of North Carolina Press, 2003.

Lafferty, John James. *Sketches and Portraits of the Virginia Conference.* Richmond, VA, 1901.

Lebsock, Suzanne. "Woman Suffrage and White Supremacy: A Virginia Case Study." In *Visible Women: New Essays on American Activism,* edited by Nancy A. Hewitt and Lebsock, 62–100. Chicago: University of Illinois Press, 1993.

Lee, Lauranett. "Giles B. Jackson (1853–1924)." *Encyclopedia Virginia.* www.encyclopediavirginia.org/Jackson_Giles_B_1853-1924.

———. "More Than an Image: Black Women Reformers in Richmond, Virginia, 1910–1928." Master's thesis, Virginia Union University, 1993.

Leidholdt, Alexander S. *The Life of Louis I. Jaffe.* Baton Rouge: Louisiana State University Press, 2002.

———. "Louis I. Jaffe (ca. 1888–1950)." *Encyclopedia Virginia.* www.EncyclopediaVirginia.org/Jaffé_Louis_Isaac_ca_1888-1950.

Lewis, David Levering. *W. E. B. Du Bois: Biography of a Race, 1868–1919.* New York: Owl Books, 1993.

Lewis, Earl. *In Their Own Interests: Race Class, and Power in Twentieth-Century Norfolk, Virginia.* Berkeley: University of California Press, 1991.

Link, William A. *The Paradox of Southern Progressivism, 1890–1930.* Chapel Hill: University of North Carolina Press, 1992.

Litwack, Leon F. *Trouble in Mind: Black Southerners in the Age of Jim Crow.* New York: Knopf, 1998.

Logan, Rayford W., ed., *What the Negro Wants.* Chapel Hill: University of North Carolina Press, 1944.

Loveland, Anne C. *Lillian Smith: A Southerner Confronting the South: A Biography.* Baton Rouge: Louisiana State University Press, 1986.

Lumpkin, Katharine Du Pre. *The Making of a Southerner.* Athens: University of Georgia Press, 1991.

MacLean, Nancy. *Behind the Mask of Chivalry: The Making of the Second Ku Klux Klan.* New York: Oxford University Press, 1994.

———. "The Leo Frank Case Reconsidered: Gender and Sexual Politics in the Making of Reactionary Populism." In *Jumpin' Jim Crow: Southern Politics from Civil War to Civil Rights,* edited by Jane Dailey, Glenda Elizabeth Gilmore, and Bryant Simon, 183–218. Princeton: Princeton University Press, 2000.

Marlowe, Gertrude Woodruff. *A Right Worthy Mission: Maggie Lena Walker and the Quest for Black Empowerment.* Washington, D.C.: Howard University Press, 2003.

Mason, Lucy Randolph. *To Win These Rights: A Personal Story of the CIO in the South.* New York: Harper and Brothers, 1952.

Materson, Lisa G. *For the Freedom of Her Race: Black Women and Electoral Politics in Illinois, 1877–1932.* Chapel Hill: University of North Caroline Press, 2009.

McDowell, John Patrick. *The Social Gospel in the South: The Woman's Home Mission Movement in the Methodist Episcopal Church, South, 1886–1939.* Baton Rouge: Louisiana State University Press, 1982.

McGill, Ralph. *The South and the Southerner.* Boston: Little, Brown, 1963.

McNeal, John Edward. "James Hardy Dillard: Southern Humanitarian." Ph.D. diss., University of Virginia, 1970.

McPherson, Tara. *Reconstructing Dixie: Race, Gender, and Nostalgia in the Imagined South.* Durham: Duke University Press, 2003.

Medley, Keith Weldon. *We As Freemen: "Plessy v. Ferguson."* Gretna, LA: Pelican, 2003.

Meier, August, Elliot Rudwick, and Francis L. Broderick. *Black Protest Thought in the Twentieth Century.* 2nd ed. Indianapolis: Bobbs-Merrill, 1971.

Mims, Edwin. *The Advancing South: Stories of Progress and Reaction.* New York: Doubleday, Page, 1926.

Moore, Jacquelyn M. *Booker T. Washington, W. E. B. Du Bois, and the Struggle for Racial Uplift.* New York: Rowman and Littlefield, 2003.

———. *Leading the Race: The Transformation of the Black Elite in the Nation's Capital, 1880–1920.* Charlottesville: University Press of Virginia, 1999.

Morgan, Edmund S. *American Slavery, American Freedom: The Ordeal of Colonial Virginia.* New York: Norton, 1975.

Morgan, Philip D. *Slave Counterpoint: Black Culture in the Eighteenth-Century Chesapeake & Lowcountry.* Chapel Hill: University of North Carolina Press, 1998.

Morton, Richard L. "The Negro in Virginia Politics, 1865–1902." Ph.D. diss., University of Virginia, 1918.

Negro Welfare Survey Committee. *The Negro in Richmond, Virginia.* Richmond: Richmond Council of Social Agencies, 1929.

Neustadt, Margaret Lee. "Miss Lucy of the CIO: Lucy Randolph Mason, 1882–1959." Master's thesis, University of North Carolina, 1969.

Odem, Mary E. *Delinquent Daughters: Protecting and Policing Adolescent Female Sexuality in the United States, 1885–1920.* Chapel Hill: University of North Carolina Press, 1995.

Oliver, Carla P. "Maggie Lena Walker: A Leader of Her Race and Women in the Segregated Community of Richmond, Virginia, 1864–1934." Master's thesis, Virginia Commonwealth University, August 1997.

Ortiz, Paul. *Emancipation Betrayed: The Hidden History of Black Organizing and White Violence in Florida from Reconstruction to the Bloody Election of 1920.* Berkeley: University of California Press, 2006.

Ovington, Mary White. *Portraits in Color.* 1927. Freeport, NY: Books for Libraries Press, 1971.

Owenby, Ted. *Subduing Satan: Religion, Recreation, and Manhood in the Rural South, 1865–1920.* Chapel Hill: University of North Carolina Press, 1990.

Painter, Nell Irvin. *Southern History across the Color Line.* Chapel Hill: University of North Carolina Press, 2002.

Patterson, James T. *America's Struggle against Poverty, 1900–1994.* Rev. ed. Cambridge: Harvard University Press, 2000.

Peebles-Wilkins, Wilma. "Janie Porter Barrett and the Virginia Industrial School for Colored Girls: Community Response to the Needs of African American Children." *Child Welfare* 74, no. 1 (January–February 1995): 143–61.

Perman, Michael. *Struggle for Mastery: Disfranchisement in the South, 1888–1908.* Chapel Hill: University of North Carolina Press, 2001.

Plater, Michael. *African American Entrepreneurship in Richmond, 1890–1940: The Story of R. C. Scott.* New York: Garland, 1996.

Pope, Liston. *Labor's Relation to Church and Community.* New York: Harper and Brothers, 1947.

Rachleff, Peter. *Black Labor in the South: Richmond, Virginia, 1865–1890.* Philadelphia: Temple University Press, 1984.

Randolph, Lewis A., and Gayle T. Tate. *Rights for a Season: The Politics of Race, Class, and Gender in Richmond, Virginia.* Knoxville: University of Tennessee Press, 2003.

Redding, Kent. *Making Race, Making Power: North Carolina's Road to Disfranchisement.* Urbana: University of Illinois Press, 2003.

Reed, Linda. *Simple Decency & Common Sense: The Southern Conference Movement, 1938–1963.* Bloomington: Indiana University Press, 1991.

Rodyhouse, Marion W. "Bridging Chasms: Community and the Southern YWCA." In *Visible Women: New Essays on American Activism,* edited by Nancy A. Hewitt and Suzanne Lebsock, 270–91. Chicago: University of Illinois Press, 1993.

Rothman, Joshua D. *Notorious in the Neighborhood: Sex and Families across the Color Line in Virginia, 1787–1861.* Chapel Hill: University of North Carolina Press, 2003.

Sadowsky, Jonathan. *Imperial Bedlam: Institutions of Madness in Colonial Southwest Nigeria.* Berkeley: University of California Press, 1999.

Salem, Dorothy. *To Better Our World: Black Women in Organized Reform, 1890–1920.* Brooklyn, NY: Carlson, 1990.

Sallee, Shelly. *The Whiteness of Child Labor Reform in the New South.* Athens: University of Georgia Press, 2004.

Salmond, John A. *Miss Lucy of the CIO: The Life and Times of Lucy Randolph Mason, 1882–1959.* Athens: University of Georgia Press, 1988.

Schechter, Patricia A. *Ida B. Wells-Barnett and American Reform, 1880–1930.* Chapel Hill: University of North Carolina Press, 2001.

Scott, Anne Firor. *The Southern Lady: From Pedestal to Politics 1830–1930.* Charlottesville: University Press of Virginia, 1995.

Scott, Daryl Michael. *Contempt and Pity: Social Policy and the Image of the Damaged Black Psyche, 1880–1996.* Chapel Hill: University of North Carolina, 1997.

Shapiro, Henry D. *Appalachia on Our Mind: The Southern Mountains and Mountaineers in the*

American Consciousness, 1870–1920. Chapel Hill: University of North Carolina Press, 1978.

Shaw, Stephanie J. *What a Woman Ought to Be and to Do: Black Professional Women Workers During the Jim Crow Era*. Chicago: University of Chicago Press, 1996.

Shepherd, Samuel C., Jr. *Avenues of Faith: Shaping the Urban Religious Culture of Richmond, Virginia, 1900–1929*. Tuscaloosa: University of Alabama Press, 2001.

Sherman, Richard B. "The Last Stand: The Fight for Racial Integrity in Virginia in the 1920s." *Journal of Southern History* 54 (February 1988): 69–92.

Shockley, Megan Taylor. *"We, Too, Are Americans": African American Women in Detroit and Richmond, 1940–1954*. Urbana: University of Illinois Press, 2004.

Silber, Nina. *The Romance of Reunion: Northerners and the South, 1865–1900*. Chapel Hill: University of North Carolina Press, 1993.

Silver, Christopher. *Twentieth-Century Richmond: Planning, Politics, and Race*. Knoxville: University of Tennessee Press, 1984.

Sims, Anastatia. *The Power of Femininity in the New South: Women's Organizations and Politics in North Carolina, 1880–1930*. Columbia: University of South Carolina Press, 1997.

Singal, Daniel Joseph. *The War Within: From Victorian to Modernist Thought in the South, 1919–1945*. Chapel Hill: University of North Carolina Press, 1982.

Skocpol, Theda. *Protecting Soldiers and Mothers: The Political Origins of Social Policy in the United States*. Cambridge: Belknap Press of Harvard University Press, 1992.

Smith, J. Douglas. "Anti-Lynching Law of 1928." *Encyclopedia Virginia*. Virginia Foundation for the Humanities. www.EncyclopediaVirginia.org/Antilynching_Law_of_1928.

———. "The Campaign for Racial Purity and the Erosion of Paternalism in Virginia, 1922–1930: 'Nominally White, Biologically Mixed, and Legally Negro.'" *Journal of Southern History* 68 (February 2002): 65–106.

———. *Managing White Supremacy: Race, Politics, and Citizenship in Jim Crow Virginia*. Chapel Hill: University of North Carolina Press, 2002.

Smith, Lillian. *Killers of the Dream*. New York: Norton, 1994.

———. *Strange Fruit*. New York: Harcourt Brace, 1944.

Smith, Susan Lynn. *Sick and Tired of Being Sick and Tired: Black Women's Health Activism in America, 1890–1950*. Philadelphia: University of Pennsylvania Press, 1995.

Sosna, Morton. *Southern Liberals and the Race Issue: In Search of the Silent South*. New York: Columbia University Press, 1977.

Southern Cities Social Register. Social Register Association. December 1921.

Stanard, Mary Newton. *Richmond: Its People and Its Story*. Philadelphia: Lippincott, 1923.

Stein, Judith. *The World of Marcus Garvey: Race and Class in Modern Society*. Baton Rouge: Louisiana State University Press, 1991.

Sucre, Richard. "The Great White Plague: The Culture of Death and the Tuberculosis Sanatorium," University of Virginia. www.faculty.virginia.edu/blueridgesanatorium/death.htm.

Suggs, Henry Lewis. "Black Strategy and Ideology in the Segregation Era: P. B. Young and the Norfolk Journal and Guide, 1910–1954." *Virginia Magazine of History and Biography* 91, no. 2 (April 1983): 161–90.

———."P. B. Young and the *Norfolk Journal and Guide*, 1910–1954." Ph.D. diss., University of Virginia, May 1976.

———. "P. B. Young of the *Norfolk Journal and Guide:* A Booker T. Washington Militant, 1904–1928." *Journal of Negro History* 64, no. 4 (Autumn 1979): 365–67.

———. *P. B. Young, Newspaperman: Race, Politics, and Journalism in the New South, 1910–62.* Charlottesville: University Press of Virginia, 1988.

Sundquist, Eric. *To Wake the Nations: Race and the Making of American Literature.* Cambridge: Belknap Press of Harvard University Press, 1993.

Sullivan, Patricia. *Days of Hope: Race and Democracy in the New Deal Era.* Chapel Hill: University of North Carolina Press, 1996.

Tindall, George Brown. *The Emergence of the New South, 1913–1945.* Baton Rouge: Louisiana State University Press, 1967.

———. *Natives & Newcomers: Ethnic Southerners and Southern Ethnics.* Athens: University of Georgia Press, 1995.

Tucker, Susan. *Southern Women: Domestic Workers and Their Employers in the Segregated South.* New York: Schocken, 1988.

Turner, Elizabeth Hayes. *Women, Culture, and Community: Religion and Reform in Galveston, 1880–1920.* New York: Oxford University Press, 1997.

Trattner, Walter I. *From Poor Law to Welfare State: A History of Social Welfare in America.* Edition 6. New York: Simon and Schuster, 1998.

Treadway, Sandra Gioia. *Women of Mark: A History of the Woman's Club of Richmond, Virginia, 1894–1994.* Richmond: Library of Virginia, 1995.

Tyler-McGraw, Marie. *At the Falls: Richmond, Virginia, and Its People.* Chapel Hill: University of North Carolina Press, 1994.

Virginia Industrial School for Colored Girls. *Pictorial Record of the Virginia Industrial School, Peake, Hanover County, Virginia.* Richmond: Division of Purchase and Printing, 1932.

Walker, Thomas Calhoun. *The Honey-Pod Tree: The Life Story of Thomas Calhoun Walker.* New York: John Day, 1958.

Walker, Vanessa Siddle. *Their Highest Potential: An African American School Community in the Segregated South.* Chapel Hill: University of North Carolina Press, 1996.

Wallenstein, Peter. *Blue Laws and Black Codes: Conflict, Courts, and Change in Twentieth-Century Virginia.* Charlottesville: University of Virginia Press, 2004.

———. *Cradle of America: A History of Virginia.* 2nd rev. ed. Lawrence: University Press of Kansas, 2014.

———. *Tell the Court I Love My Wife: Race, Marriage, and Law—An American History.* New York: Palgrave Macmillan, 2002.

Washington, Booker T. *Up from Slavery.* 1900. Boston: Bedford/St. Martin's, 2003.

Whalen, Mark. *The Great War and the Culture of the New Negro.* Gainesville: University Press of Florida, 2008.

Wheeler, Marjorie Spruill. "Mary Johnston, Suffragist." *Virginia Magazine of History Biography* 100, no. 1 (January 1992): 99–118.

———. *New Women of the New South: The Leaders of the Woman Suffrage Movement in the Southern States*. New York: Oxford University Press, 1993.

White, Deborah Gray. *Too Heavy a Load: Black Women in Defense of Themselves, 1894–1994*. New York: Norton, 1999.

Wilkerson-Freeman, Sarah. "The Creation of a Subversive Feminist Dominion: Interracial Social Workers and the Georgia New Deal." *Journal of Women's History* 14, no. 4 (Winter 2002): 132–54.

Williamson, Joel. *The Crucible of Race: Black-White Relations in the American South since Emancipation*. New York: Oxford University Press, 1984.

Witt, Brent. "Toilers in the Sun: Richmond's Wonderful World of Women." *Everywoman's Magazine* 1 (November 1917): 51–71.

Woodward, C. Vann. *Origins of the New South 1877–1913*. 1951. Baton Rouge: Louisiana State University Press and the Littlefield Fund for Southern History, University of Texas, 1971.

———. *The Strange Career of Jim Crow*. 3rd rev. ed. New York: Oxford University Press, 1974.

Woofter, T. J., Jr., and Isaac Fisher. *Cooperation in Southern Communities: Suggested Activities for County and City Inter-Racial Committees*. Atlanta: Commission on Interracial Cooperation, 1921.

Wynes, Charles E., ed. *Forgotten Voices: Dissenting Southerners in an Age of Conformity*. Baton Rouge: Louisiana State University Press, 1967.

———. *Race Relations in Virginia, 1870–1902*. Totowa, NJ: Rowman and Littlefield, 1971.

INDEX

Page numbers in italics refer to illustrations.

THE AMERICAN SOUTH SERIES

Anne Goodwyn Jones and
Susan V. Donaldson, editors
Haunted Bodies:
Gender and Southern Texts

M. M. Manring
Slave in a Box:
The Strange Career of Aunt Jemima

Stephen Cushman
Bloody Promenade:
Reflections on a Civil War Battle

John C. Willis
Forgotten Time:
The Yazoo-Mississippi Delta
after the Civil War

Charlene M. Boyer Lewis
Ladies and Gentlemen on Display:
Planter Society at the Virginia Springs,
1790–1860

Christopher Metress, editor
The Lynching of Emmett Till:
A Documentary Narrative

Dianne Swann-Wright
A Way out of No Way:
Claiming Family and Freedom
in the New South

James David Miller
South by Southwest:
Planter Emigration and Identity
in the Slave South

Richard F. Hamm
Murder, Honor, and Law:
Four Virginia Homicides from
Reconstruction to the Great Depression

Andrew H. Myers
Black, White, and Olive Drab:
Racial Integration at Fort Jackson, South
Carolina, and the Civil Rights Movement

Bruce E. Baker
What Reconstruction Meant:
Historical Memory in the American South

Stephen A. West
From Yeoman to Redneck in the South
Carolina Upcountry, 1850–1915

Randolph Ferguson Scully
Religion and the Making of Nat Turner's
Virginia: Baptist Community and
Conflict, 1740–1840

Deborah Beckel
Radical Reform: Interracial Politics in
Post-Emancipation North Carolina

Terence Finnegan
A Deed So Accursed:
Lynching in Mississippi and
South Carolina, 1881–1940

Reiko Hillyer
Designing Dixie:
Tourism, Memory, and
Urban Space in the New South

Luis-Alejandro Dinnella-Borrego
The Risen Phoenix: Black Politics
in the Post–Civil War South

Clayton McClure Brooks
The Uplift Generation:
Cooperation across the Color Line
in Early Twentieth-Century Virginia